Deep Self Magic

A Step-by-Step Roadmap to Spiritual Authenticity

Bridget Owens

Carnelian Moon
PUBLISHING

To request permissions, contact the author at owensresearch@yahoo.com

Paperback: ISBN 978-1-7376060-0-0
Ebook: ISBN 978-1-7376060-1-7

First paperback edition November 2021.

Edited by The Grammar Goddess, Susan Rooks
Cover art & Illustration by Bridget Owens
Layout by the 2Creative Minds Team

Cover Image a derivitave work from the image "Scenic canyon Antelope" by kavram on Canva from Getty Images Pro.

Carnelian Moon Publishing, Inc.
Ottawa, Ontario, Canada

https://carnelianmoonpublishing.com

Carnelian Moon
PUBLISHING

Dedication

To Bryn. Some people think attention from strangers is an indicator that they have valuable insight to share, but that's nothing compared to having someone who truly knows you - quirks and flaws included - and still wants to hear what you have to say. Thanks for taking me seriously.

Contents

Part I Spirit and Spirituality——————— I

Step One—Authenticity

We each see a different piece of the world, but we all see the same stars — We cannot live each other's lives, but we can learn to speak each other's languages — I am authentic in all my imperfections — If I am not honest with myself, I cannot be honest with anyone else — I am forging my own path; there is no one for me to follow

Part II Shadow Work———— 37

Step Two—Integration

I'm not who I think I am. I am who I demonstrate that I am — I have fashioned my masks from the remnants of my past — It is harder for me to hide from myself if I live where there is light — A fragmented person lives a fragmented life — My actions may speak loudly, but I must open my heart to the message

Step Three —Identity

I am what I have learned to be. I do not grow by forgetting — I am not free to be who I am if I am not free to follow my curiosity — The world may not hear my words, but my inner voice will not be silenced — I am made up of borrowed pieces, but the sum is uniquely me — Understanding myself allows me to understand others

Step Four —Expression

What I have is a reflection of who I am. I cannot change one without changing the other — I never see myself as others see me, I only see my reflection — Home is where I need no disguise — As within, so without — I will shower myself with love and acceptance

Part III Spiritual Detox ——— 131

Step Five —Emergence

To reach my personal truth, I must dig it up from beneath all of my lies — I am the lessons I have learned, but I am not defined by the experiences that taught them — Letting go makes me appreciate what remains — My dreams don't have to make sense to anyone but me — I am called to align my actions with my purpose

Step Six — Agency

I am more than a transmitter. I am an innovator — There is nothing in my own mind or soul I need to be protected from — My truth is mine alone — I can trust myself with my freedom — I will not feel guilty for the things that bring me joy

Step Seven — Creativity

I gain more when I strive to express than when I strive to impress — The assumptions of others do not define me unless I allow them to — Home is where my soul is free — I will not wait for anyone else to grant me space to spread my wings — I do not have to be taught how to be myself

Preface

Writing Deep Self Magic has been less of a project than a battle. It didn't come together easily because it was as much a journey of self-discovery and self-examination as a journey of creation. My hope is that you will get as much out of the end product as I got out of the process of bringing it to life.

This began as a much larger writing project. In 2014, I began work on what I envision as my magnum opus: a deep dive into the history of humanity in search of the fundamental nature and purpose of spirituality. I explain a bit more about the motivations for that project in this book, but essentially I was inspired by a diagram I saw somewhere on the internet that linked the world's religions together into a sort of family tree, which gave rise to the idea that if I went back to the roots, as far back as our anthropological and archaeological knowledge could take me, and examined the development of religion and spiritual tradition over time, I could tease out the reasons why spirituality even existed.

The more I researched, the bigger the project became, and it was over a year before I felt confident in writing the draft of the first chapter. I soon realized that the project wasn't just a book in the making, it was a generator of even more ideas and insights. I still have no idea what conclusion the magnum opus is ultimately headed towards, but I realized right away that the insights gained from researching and writing that first chapter begged to be expanded on and shared.

That's where this book comes from. When I eventually finish and publish the larger project, you'll be able to connect the concepts included in Deep Self Magic back to the things I learned about our Paleolithic ancestors and the preconceived notions modern we've had about where we come from.

But that's also where the struggle to make this book a reality really began.

It began with the idea of a spiritual detox, a sort of temporary exploration of atheism in order to clear the slate and make room for the spiritual elements we choose for our lives. And my first idea was to draw on my spiritual upbringing and create a devotional book. I began creating entries that combined parable-like storytelling, thought provoking exposition, and journal prompts, but it felt forced. The stories weren't real, and it felt distinctly preachy. The last thing I want to be is a preacher.

So I poked at the idea of creating a workbook. A journal. An online class. A coaching program. Outlines were written, strategies mapped out, but nothing felt right.

I periodically set the ideas aside and continued working on the magnum opus. I researched and wrote the second chapter and started on the third. I could see each chapter spawning a shorter, more practical book. I could envision a whole series of books, each spawning side projects like oracle decks and workbooks, ending with the big book that would tie them all together.

More than a few times over the years, I began compiling bits of writing, hoping the ideas would come together into something cohesive. I made it my NaNoWriMo project at least once. Yet no matter how much mental energy and intention I poured in, no book manuscript would emerge.

Even after I met Judith at Carnelian Moon Publishing and committed to finishing the book once and for all with her guidance as a writing coach, the manuscript still fought me every step of the way. I was a full three weeks past deadline when I handed over a very rough, barely proofread draft of Deep Self Magic, and it was the first time in the entire history of the project that I felt I'd adequately conveyed the message in a way that made any coherent sense whatsoever.

Ultimately, the battle wasn't ever about the format or the writing. It was about my own shadow work and my own journey of authentic evolution. This book outright refused to submit to my intentions until I dug down into my own deep self and unearthed my authentic motivations and message.

What Deep Self Magic finally turned out to be is an affirmation that spirituality is real and that it's important, but that nobody can give us any answers. I might have started this journey expecting to find some kind of insight or some chunk of truth to pass on to others travelling the same path, but the manuscript resisted coming together until I realized that my purpose isn't to tell anyone what truth is. I had to understand that my role as author isn't to become a guru or a guide. It's to share my experience of finally settling into a fulfilling spiritual path and practice so that others can do the same.

That's what I hope this book can provide to you: inspiration and a model for how to figure out why you've not found a spiritual path which is truly fulfilling, what you need and want in a spiritual path and practice, and how to find or create it for yourself. Your spiritual practice is not going to look like mine. I don't have that kind of guidance to give. No one does.

Honestly, it's a relief to not have definitive answers or universal truths to share. I've only ever wanted to find my own spiritual direction through this journey, not to possess the sorts of insight or truth that would make me a spiritual leader to anyone else. And I'm glad this book didn't allow itself to be twisted into that kind of guide. As frustrating as the process has been (and as frustrating as shadow work always tends to be), it has truly shown me what people mean when they say, "Everything is as it should be."

So if Deep Self Magic is a difficult journey for you as a reader, it is as it should be. But no matter how long it takes you to read it, no matter how you choose to apply and explore the ideas in it, I hope that the ultimate outcome is that you know yourself more deeply, practice your spirituality in a more fulfilling way, and stop comparing your own path to anyone else's. I hope that my own battle to finally make this project a reality paves the way for you to travel your own path with more ease.

Acknowledgements

Not a single part of my spiritual work would be possible if not for my local pagan Meetup. I am forever grateful to Theresa for founding the community, Beth for making sure it survived over years of changes, and Alice and Simon for helping while I gained confidence as an organizer. There's no way to name all the regulars who have shared their knowledge along the way, but I appreciate every single one of you. If I hadn't found a group which welcomed me when I knew nothing at all and served as a source of inspiration rather than instruction, I don't know where my spiritual path would have led me. And thank you for trusting me to lead the group forward.

My framily has also been a huge support in this endeavor. So to Bryn, Bart, Erin, and John, I want to say thank you for listening to my ideas and encouraging me through the process. With this particular project I ended up asking for more than a pat on the back, though, from some of my framily members. My wife, Kourtnie, deserves a huge thank you for taking on some of the social media burden so I actually had time to write and think. I'm also incredibly grateful to Christine for taking the time to read and critique the manuscript through the eyes of someone who knows a thing or two about magic and paganism.

There's nothing more important to me as a writer and thinker than to be surrounded by other thought leaders who not only inspire me and lead me to new ideas but who challenge my way of thinking. So to Iva and the IPC team as well as all our amazing clients past and present, I want you to know how much I appreciate spending my workdays in such a spiritually powerful environment. Not only that, but Iva, you have been instrumental in convincing me of my own potential. You're a great example of what can happen when we do the shadow work, push through the roadblocks and baggage, and stop questioning whether we're worthy.

My spiritual journey has been especially eventful over the past few years. Michelle, I can't understate how huge it was that you thought I was capable of reading tarot at your shop when I'd never read for strangers before. Thank you for giving me a safe space to grow as a spiritual thinker, author, creator, and member of the community. And thank you to the other readers and local writers and creators who made Alchemist Attic such a spiritually supportive environment.

Speaking of people who have boosted my confidence, I have to thank my oldest and dearest friend, Jenni, for still choosing me for group projects after all these years. I've looked up to you as cooler and more talented than me in so many ways ever since we were science lab partners, shared a table in art class, and wrote English essays together. Any time you ask me to contribute to something you're working on I consider it the highest of compliments, and I can't overstate how much I appreciate your thoughts and ideas.

Finally, I can't thank Judith and Debbie at Carnelian Moon and Susan Rooks with Grammar Goddess Communication enough for their expertise and guidance to bring Deep Self Magic to life. I've never been one to let others into my creative processes very willingly, and I'm so glad my shadow work helped me manifest a chance meeting with Judith at just the right time. I was always skeptical that I could find a publisher who would understand my spiritual point of view and my writing style well enough to help me bring my projects to life in an aligned way, and now I'm looking forward to many future projects knowing my work is in caring hands.

Part I

Spirit and Spirituality

Pause and Reflect

How is your spiritual point of view different or unique?

When you think about having a more authentic spiritual life, what do you imagine that to be like?

Who in your life has the most influence on how you think, act, and feel?

Step One

Authenticity

"We each see a different piece of the world, but we all see the same stars."

I grew up with the assumption that the point of spirituality was finding truth.

Of course, back then for me, spirituality was synonymous with religion because I'm an evangelical preacher's kid. For a very long time, the idea of a spiritual journey as I understood it wasn't an exploration as much as a guided tour. There was a destination we were all supposed to reach, and although we all started out in different places, spiritually all of humanity was intended to converge on the same core truth.

But as I got further and further along in my own journey, swapping out religious labels and drifting from one spiritual tradition to another, I found that the details of that core truth changed every time my direction did. Once I left the religion I was raised in, I struggled to pin down a sense of which take on truth was the right one. I thought maybe I just hadn't figured out yet where we were all headed, or maybe nobody knew for sure (that idea was very attractive for a while), but I kept coming back to the assumption that there had to be a core spiritual truth at the end of all these journeys. After all, the world is filled with spiritual seekers, and there must be a reason.

Looking at my own journey and experience, I could say for sure that human spirituality in all its forms is a quest for those things that lift us up and give us a deeper understanding of who we are and where we fit in the universe. So I decided maybe the only way to find truth was to get analytical and methodical about my own journey. I set out to determine which religious ideas and philosophies were most logical and most likely to be factual. I wanted to find the spiritual ideas that were most likely to be correct.

Spoiler: That's not what I found.

I didn't come away from years of study and research (ongoing, mind you) and spiritual wandering with a spiritual philosophy that qualifies as truth. And the thing is, that's not even ultimately what my spiritual journey and all the searching was really about when I finally got really honest with myself.

It's not unusual these days, especially as more and more of us are pushing formal religion aside, for spirituality and religion to be considered as separate things. Instead of prescriptive traditions, we're reaching for something more personal and internal, something that recognizes that everyone's spiritual needs aren't the same and therefore something as one-size-fits-all as religion isn't enough.

But what exactly is spirituality? Other than being something less rigid, less impersonal than formal religion, the details get fuzzy the more people you talk to. Is it still a pursuit of truth? Is it about nurturing our souls? Is it just the inner, personal element of religion? Or religion in its primitive form? Everyone seems to have a different answer.

I've spent a lot of time pondering on and researching those kinds of questions. In fact, eventually – after growing up Evangelical Protestant, and then becoming Catholic, then Neopagan, then into a laundry list of various theories about life, evolution, aliens, and whether god even exists – my spiritual life became focused on the question of why humans even seem to need spirituality. Why did some of us still find ourselves drawn to and needing spirituality in our lives despite not believing in a deity or higher power who had prescribed such practices? What was the point?

I've tried really hard to come to an answer. And not to be cliché, but it turns out the answer I was looking for wasn't really the answer I was looking for.

There's this thing called the Overview Effect, which is basically a profound change in perspective and shift of consciousness that happens when viewing the earth from orbit. Astronauts seeing the reality of our planet floating in the vastness of space talk about getting a deeper understanding of the fragility of our place in existence, the cosmic insignificance of things like borders and politics, and the visible fact that the earth is alive. It's not a perspective shift the vast majority of us will ever get to experience quite that way.

But part of what I ended up inadvertently doing with all my research, reading, thinking, and attempts to explain spirituality to myself was to step back and get a "view from orbit" of humanity's relationship to spiritual things. We spend an incredible amount of energy searching for truth, fighting each other over it, picking apart this mythology and that dogma, and tossing around theories about what the journey is about and where it's leading us.

When I backed way, way, way up and looked at human history, human behavior, human evolution, human society, even the dynamics of modern humans thrashing around in a sea of spiritual ideas looking for the right floaty thing to grab on to, what I saw was that we're all really just looking to fill the needs of our souls in the moment. Our deepest needs and highest priorities translate into the thoughts and actions we call spirituality.

And that means each one of us is seeking something different.

It's no wonder we have trouble finding a destination.

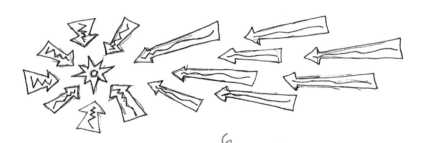

Religion at its best fills a communal, societal need and helps connect us to our social and environmental context, but even within religion each one of us has a different set of needs we're out to fill. Even if we're into religion and we accept the associated dogma and whatever ideal it holds up for us to aim for, our inner spiritual journey is still unique because we bring different stuff with us and start from different places than everyone else. The changes we have to undergo to reach that ideal are unique to us.

There isn't one single spiritual purpose for all of humanity. There can't be.

And when we get that Overview Effect perspective on human spirituality and pull ourselves away until all the different concepts of who or what god is, what the purpose of life is, where we came from, and what is right and wrong and true and false blur together into a big tapestry of human thought, we realize all those things become insignificant details from such a distance. The things that are important to us individually are only important to us because we're so close to them. Our perspective on them is such that they seem huge and overwhelmingly significant. The closer we are to something, the more it dominates our view.

"We cannot live each other's lives, but we can learn to speak each other's languages."

I find there are two main reactions to the idea of the Overview Effect. Some people find it reaffirming and beautiful. This idea that our differences and conflicts are inconsequential in the face of the vastness of the universe reinforces their beliefs about our place in existence. Others find it confronting that their priorities turn out to be irrelevant when seen from a point of view they'll never experience. Those of us who haven't seen the earth from orbit can only imagine the impact of seeing it for ourselves, and one person can't change someone else's perspective simply by imposing their own.

And those who have seen our planet in its fragile spot, floating in the vastness of space, still come back to their lives on earth where there are real consequences attached to every inconsequential boundary and meaningless difference. Their "enlightenment" doesn't fundamentally change anyone else's reality, not even their own. Astronauts don't get to throw out their passports and ignore borders because they couldn't see them from space.

We struggle with this, even when it comes to small shifts in perspective. The things we "discover" about existence become something we want to impose on others. We can call it sharing, but we mean imposing. When we distance ourselves from something and see it in a different context, it becomes something we want to ignore and stop hearing about. This stuff gets translated into spiritual and religious terms as right and wrong, good and bad, do and don't, and that's what a lot of us expect spirituality to be.

So before we leap into this journey together, I need to be clear about what I mean when I talk about spirituality and all the words related to it. There is so much baggage dumped on religion-related words that the baggage is going to get in the way if we don't unpack it. For the sake of clarity, it's time to talk about what words mean, at least when I say them.

Let's start with spirit.

Spirituality (word and practice) is rooted in spirit, which means a lot of things to a lot of people. Even if we were to agree that we're talking about the human spirit in particular, there isn't one consistent understanding of what that means. Is it the part of us that becomes our ghost when we die? Is it our life force? Is it the same thing as a soul?

When my mom and dad talk about spirit, they probably mean The Holy Spirit with all the capital letters, a third and also somehow the whole of who the Christian God is and all the power that comes with that. But they also might mean spirit in the ghostly sense if they're speaking about those who talk to the dead or do witchcraft, in which case they're not speaking of it as something good.

Then there are people who think of spirit as a force larger than our conscious selves. They understand it as a guiding force that is intrinsic to the universe but isn't the energetic remains of a dead person. And if someone who thinks of spirit in this way were to try to have a conversation about spirituality with my mother, that conversation would be a hot mess from the first word onward. I don't want the conversation we're about to have as author and reader to devolve into a similar hot mess of confusion and misunderstanding, so I feel the need to explain my take on spirit.

The thing is, all the definitions out there share some commonalities. There's a general sense of spirit being something intangible, something that isn't physical but is necessary to life, something connected to the concept of life itself in the sense that only alive things have or deal with spirit. Spirituality is a term with a pretty broad definition, too, but it's also rooted in this broad idea of what spirit means.

Part of my struggle to figure out how to label and define my spirituality was figuring out what spirit and spirituality actually meant to me. I did eventually find a helpful and profound concept that has given me personal clarity and also helped me break down and understand all sorts of ideas along my spiritual journey, and I'm going to share this concept to help us speak the same language.

As someone whose beliefs include the unexplained but not the supernatural, having a definition of spirit that isn't related to religious dogma and isn't tied to any traditional concept of an afterlife has been key in developing a workable understanding of spirituality. For a long time I wasn't always sure I knew what I was talking about in conversations with myself. If I didn't even know what I meant when I thought about spirituality, I was never ever going to be able to talk to anyone else about it.

I can't describe how exciting it was to find a definition that actually made sense to me! It's become the framework for my entire understanding of spirituality and how I break down ideas and concepts, so don't skim the next few paragraphs. This is the structural foundation of everything else in this book.

For all the times I've ever heard anyone talk about "body, soul, and spirit" or some variation thereof,

I never really wondered where it came from. It's actually rooted in the ancient art of alchemy. The Three Principles in alchemical terms are Salt, Sulfur, and Mercury. And those who study alchemy, and specifically those who create spagyrics (herbal medicines created through alchemical processes), understand those Three Principles to correspond to body, soul, and spirit. Essentially, everything in the entire universe, literally everything, can be broken down into these three things. Salt or body is the material part of a thing, physical and static. Sulfur or soul is the essence of a thing, what defines and drives its existence. And Mercury or spirit is the life force or animating energy.

Here's the fun part of alchemy: It's all very metaphorical and based on learning by doing. With spagyrics, that means breaking plants down into those three parts, refining each part, and putting them back together into something more refined and elevated. Doing that makes it a lot easier to understand how those three elements look when dealing with things that aren't plants. And I can talk about this stuff forever, but for the sake of maintaining a reasonable word count, I'll just sum it up. When it comes to plant medicine, the body is the leaves, stems, roots, and seeds of a plant. The soul of a plant is the essential oils and other substances that give the plant its functional qualities. And the spirit is the plant alcohols. When a plant is harvested and dried, the soul and body remain, but the spirit evaporates.

But the thing about spirit is that it's not unique to each plant like the body and soul. When we create spagyrics, we use distilled alcohols to draw the essential oils from the physical plant matter, and it doesn't matter that the spirits used are distilled from a different type of plant.

Of course, plants are far simpler than humans. When we talk about spirit in plants, it's alcohols that exist because of the water and nutrients a plant takes in to stay alive, created by the processes of growth, which transforms those things into something the plant can use. In humans, the equivalents are almost infinite: everything from physical stuff like water and nutrients to immaterial stuff like ideas and feelings. But it all boils down to energy: caloric energy, mental energy, emotional energy. Spirit is energy, and it has to be replenished. We have to constantly take more in because we are constantly putting it back out. In a lot of ways, we are always submerged in spirit, swimming in a soup of energy from various sources that circulates through us and is necessary for us to live.

I find this definition of spirit incredibly helpful because, first of all, it encompasses all the other different ideas of what spirit is. It even encompasses a lot of what we often call soul, since in a lot of philosophies spirit and soul are much the same thing or at least overlap to a significant degree. So the concepts of soul that define it as something that exists energetically as a non-physical entity is alchemically part of spirit.

Spirit also includes the knowledge and idea base we swap around and build on.

And that brings us to spirituality. Spirituality in all its definitions is something that only humans out of all the other life forms on earth practice. There is something about our consciousness that requires a more complex form of spirit in order to thrive. We don't just need light and water and food and relationships; we also need ideas and questions and mysteries and challenges.

Once I started thinking of spirit in alchemical terms, it made complete sense as to why humans would crave spirituality. If we stop engaging with spirit, even in the psychological and academic sense, we stop living. We may keep existing, but humans don't thrive if they only exist. It doesn't matter that I don't believe in deities who control aspects of life on earth; I still need to engage with spirit!

Honestly, when I pieced all that together, it was less a moment of blinding enlightenment and more a moment of "Oh, duh. That seems obvious now."

So when I talk about spirit and spirituality, I mean it to be in this alchemical, elemental sense. Spirit is all the forms of energy that flow around us and within us, and spirituality is all the stuff we do to process it. No matter what our own spirituality looks like or how we believe this spirit energy functions in the universe, this basic alchemical way of envisioning spirit is going to be all that's needed to understand the rest of the book.

"I am authentic in all my imperfections."

When we get an Overview Effect perspective on human spirituality, we realize our individual obsessions with defending our versions of truth and fighting to get the entire world to see things from our point of view are ridiculous and pointless in the grand scheme. But as we go through our day-to-day lives, our individual perspective dominates our view of everything else. Spirituality may not be about some kind of global or universal truth, but it is about individual truth.

Spirituality is an activity more than anything else. It's not just philosophy or belief; it's something we participate in and practice. And while spirit may be a universal resource, spirituality is about how we utilize spirit to fulfill the individual needs of our souls. What I seek to gain from my spiritual life is going to be different from what anyone else seeks. There are common threads, for sure, but spirituality is individual in the same way medical treatment has to be individualized. We all go to the doctor for different ailments, but two patients with the same condition may need very different treatment regimens.

Spirituality is the same way. We don't all show up to church (or whatever the equivalent is for us) needing or wanting the same things. That's because we're all different people with different lives and different struggles. Unfortunately, most religions are pretty much one-size-fits-all in their solutions to whatever challenges we're facing, not to mention their standards for how we're supposed to live, think, and behave. There's very little way to adhere to the tenets of an established religion and do so authentically, because when religion determines for us what is right and what is proper, there's very little likelihood those beliefs and behaviors are authentic to us as a unique individual. Religion tells us we are not okay unless we allow it to shape us to fit a specific mold, and that is drastically different from spirituality.

It seems kind of obvious to say, but it's really not how most of us have been taught to think about spirituality. In all of our searching for truth, enlightenment, salvation, or whatever the end goal of spirituality has been in our lives, even if we've been aware we're trying to find the path that resonates most with who we are, most of us have never stopped to consider what that really looks like.

There's a good chance our spiritual paths have consisted largely of trying out different traditions and religions to find one that felt right to us.

I'd be willing to bet a lot of our spiritual experiences have ended with us feeling somehow unwelcome as we are, that we don't fit the mold, or that we're expected to believe things that don't sit right in our souls.

And I think it's safe to say that most humans seeking a spiritual home are really looking for something other than truth. We're looking for a place where we feel encouraged to grow rather than change. We're looking for a spiritual environment where we feel a sense of hope and optimism about our future. We want to be embraced rather than torn down.

The most fulfilling form of spirituality is the one that resonates with our authentic self.

Of course, authenticity is one of those buzzwords that gets tossed around a lot in pop culture. We all want to be more authentic, and we have an instinctual understanding of what that means. We want to be more true to ourselves and do less pretending to be what others want us to be. Spiritually, we want to find a place where we are accepted as who we are and not expected to drastically change ourselves or hide parts of ourselves away. And that's an incredibly important mission.

I can say from firsthand experience as a queer woman in the Bible Belt that there's no spiritual benefit to staying in a religious community that rejects who we are.

The problem with the pursuit of authenticity is that true authenticity demands a lot of us. It demands an extreme amount of self-honesty, which isn't easy. It's far easier and less uncomfortable to point to an ideal of who we wish to be and consider it our "authentic self," rather than embracing the authenticity of who we are in the moment. We often substitute ambition and idealism for authenticity.

We've all dealt with parts of ourselves, aspects of our behavior or thought patterns that we felt were not truly who we are. We do and say things we regret later and feel shame about. I've started taking mental note of when people say things like, "that's not who I am" or "I can't believe I did that, it's so unlike me." Recently a colleague was talking about how she'd realized she had a lot of very judgmental thought patterns towards other people and insisted that part of her "wasn't part of her soul."

But that's where we get authenticity and spiritual authenticity wrong. My colleague may feel bad for those thoughts and want to change that habit, but they're a pattern and part of her authentic self. Our souls are not flawless or free from shadow aspects. Being authentic doesn't mean being perfect. It doesn't mean liking all of who we are. Spiritual authenticity doesn't mean finding a comfortable spiritual environment that makes us feel positive about ourselves.

The challenge of authenticity is finding the courage to embrace who we are in the moment, even if we wish to be something else. Authenticity is radical self-honesty. It's not a choice between whether we need to change or whether we're perfect the way we are; it's really just an acknowledgement and affirmation that we are who we are and we came to be who we are through the experiences we've had in life. We can absolutely desire to be different, and that desire is part of our authenticity, too.

Authenticity in its most simplistic sense is about knowledge of self. It's like with intentions: We have to do some deep digging and self work to figure out what we really mean and why we mean it. We have to uncover the parts of ourselves we don't like and come to terms with those aspects and how we came to have them. We can't practice radical self-acceptance if we don't know ourselves as completely as possible.

We don't tend to be very familiar with our deep selves. Who we really are and what really drives us often include stuff we aren't comfortable acknowledging, especially since so many forces in modern society tell us that we must strive to be better or even perfect. Society compares us to external standards, so we learn to do the same. We look outward to other people to determine if we're good enough or if we still need to be "better," and it leads to a distorted sense of self. Some of us cope by always looking a few steps into the future, claiming to be who we're aspiring to be even if we haven't become that person yet. And some of us turn our attention fully to the aspects we dislike about ourselves, obsessively self-judging. In truth, our deep self isn't good or bad; it just is. Who we are doesn't need to be who we continue to be, but who we are is authentic in the present moment.

Who we are is always changing, and authentic spirituality has to adapt to who we are in the moment to best serve the needs of that authentic identity. We might think of our authentic self as being described best by things like our astrological profiles and other unchanging measures of who we are. I'm a Scorpio with Virgo rising, and I will always be a Scorpio with Virgo rising. I can't change when I was born or move the stars in the sky so I fall under a different sign. But our authentic selves are truly better described by things like the Myers-Briggs Type Indicator and other measures that can return different results over time.

When I was in college, I was given the full MBTI assessment and my results came back ENTJ. Since then I've learned a lot more about the origins of the test and the non-scientific nature of the results, but despite its flaws I still find it to be an interesting window into who we are at the moment when we take the test. When I was tested in college, I remember being blown away by the accuracy of the resulting profile and how I felt like I'd really learned something about myself.

Fast-forward a couple of decades, though, and when I took another assessment, it came back ENFP. I think I've learned to trust my intuitive senses more as I've matured. My 20-year-old self was definitely not in tune with itself enough to be perceptive, and I was in active rejection of my emotionality. It doesn't mean either test was wrong or that either version of myself was less real. There's no value to attach to the change. I'm just a different version of myself now than I was 20 years ago, which is only natural.

The important thing to remember is that my authentic self isn't a future version of myself who I haven't become yet. I'm not in the process of turning into my authentic self. Authenticity is just the act of affirming and embracing our current self, and the essence of spiritual authenticity is creating a spiritual practice where our current self is embraced and encouraged to grow and evolve.

Authenticity isn't something we achieve; it's something we embrace. It's something we own. An authentic self isn't an ideal self. It's not the end of the line of our personal evolution. It's not what we are once we've worked through the things we hide from others. It's not even the process of digging up the self that's deep inside and bringing it unapologetically to the surface. Our authentic self is who we are right now, however we are right now. Authenticity isn't just about what's deep inside us. Being authentic means owning even our masks and facades. Being authentic means owning the stuff we are conflicted about.

The spiritual path we are on (or are looking for) is part of our authentic self. We're on our path for a reason (or many reasons), and those reasons are a window into our soul. What we're looking for is a spiritual life completely centered on authenticity, which helps us know ourselves as we change and then supports the changes we make to be more of who we want to be. And most of all we need a path that guides us toward self-forgiveness, releasing the shame and guilt we feel over the versions of ourselves we have been and the choices we've made that have shaped us.

"If I am not honest with myself, I cannot be honest with anyone else."

Being inauthentic really boils down to not being honest with ourselves about who we are. Becoming more authentic has very little to do with changing anything about ourselves and has everything to do with examining ourselves, asking ourselves the hard questions about our thoughts and motivations, and dealing with what we find rather than trying to be something else.

Of course, inauthenticity manifests in behaviors and choices. It's not a state of being; it's the result of choices we make. When we choose to deny pieces of our identity, not just hide them away from those who might judge them but actually suppress and reject them on an internal level, it causes us to make decisions based not on what we know is best for us but based on what we feel is expected of us. It causes us to act against our own best interests and instead do what will please someone else. It drives us to self-sabotage and makes us resist growth and evolution.

Authenticity is really not about who we are, and it's not totally about how we represent ourselves. Being authentic doesn't mean being willing to tell all our secrets or being totally open about everything in our lives. There's a difference between being private or even closeted and being dishonest about aspects of ourselves. Authenticity is extreme self-honesty, not extreme public honesty. It's mindful action in regard to self. That does NOT mean carefully fabricating a surface image to hide our true selves.

Authenticity is radical self-awareness.

Inauthenticity is disconnection from the soul.

Authenticity means owning the stuff we don't like about ourselves, the stuff we're afraid people will think about us. It doesn't mean we should embrace and become those things. Radical self-awareness and extreme self-honesty mean recognizing there are things we want to transform about ourselves, but also recognizing transformation takes work and time. At any moment there are going to be parts of ourselves we don't like, but we can't pretend they are not part of us. Our vulnerabilities are part of us, and authenticity is acknowledging and affirming that those vulnerable parts exist even if we still want to change them. We can acknowledge in our brains that we keep a horrible mess shut away in a closet somewhere, but it doesn't mean we have to open the closet to everyone. We just have to acknowledge the existence of the closet as part of our reality and take responsibility for whether it ever gets cleaned out.

Many of us tend to imagine that our vulnerabilities and imperfections are temporary and incidental. We like to think they're something we've picked up somewhere or haven't outgrown yet, something we don't have to acknowledge as part of ourselves. We fear having to acknowledge those aspects of ourselves because acknowledging them would open us up to consequences and damage the image we want to build for ourselves. We seem to think if we just hide them long enough, they'll go away. But they're not gone, and that's important. Even if they are going to be gone eventually (which isn't going to happen without some work), they're part of our authentic existence now.

Authenticity means owning the things we are afraid people will judge us for. Inauthenticity is suppressing the parts of ourselves that might give validity to those things we fear people will say, denying they exist, and doing everything we can to prove we are the opposite.

Inauthenticity isn't a state of being; it's the act of lying to and hiding from ourselves.

The thing is, though, we're all inauthentic. There is literally not a single person on the planet who is totally and completely authentic, knows themselves in their entirety, and embraces every aspect of their deep self. Nobody is fully integrated and nobody loves every part of themselves. We all pretend to be someone else at some level, and we all deny parts of ourselves, even to ourselves.

The best we can do is strive for more authenticity and less inauthenticity, constantly working towards an ideal we know we'll never fully reach. There's no end to the process of finding the missing and discarded pieces of our deep selves and working to dust them off, finding where they go, and then deciding whether those pieces need to be released as we go forward.

None of us are incomplete people. All our missing pieces are there inside us; it's just that some of those pieces have been shoved down into our darkest parts and lost to us. They just feel like voids to fill, and we spend our whole lives looking to fill them when they're not actually empty.

The world really is full of spiritual seekers, but it's also full of people who think they know what they're looking for when they really have no idea. But the fact that there are so many people consumed with seeking something significant and profound in their lives, whether it's enlightenment, truth, success, or even love, is evidence for how generally awful humans are at finding what our souls really need. We look outside for what's already inside because we've been lied to about what will bring us wholeness, enlightenment, and happiness.

But without really knowing ourselves at the very deepest level, we don't and can't know what we need. The best we can do is pay attention to the things we feel we lack and then seek them out. We can search for the things we crave or the things others tell us will fill our emptiness, but most of us have been searching this way for our whole lives and still don't feel the sense of completion or fulfillment we hoped for. What we do feel are all the symptoms of inauthenticity that let us know there are still parts of our deep self that we don't know and aren't connected to.

The unsettled feeling most of us have had along whatever path we've taken to our current spiritual state of being is a symptom of knowing that, at some level, the paths we have tried involved some pressure to be spiritually inauthentic. If all we've ever known are traditions that push us to change or to be something and someone we aren't, there's a super high probability we've given in to that pressure along the way, and we continue to carry that baggage around with us. We learn to be inauthentic, we're trained in inauthenticity, and eventually we are so used to those ideas that we take over the job of putting pressure on ourselves to be inauthentic. Nobody else has to continue teaching us we're inferior or wrong; we do it just fine on our own.

Inauthenticity makes us crave validation and acceptance.

Authenticity is about recognizing that we have the authority and ability to set standards for ourselves and consider things to be okay despite them being at odds with the opinions of those around us. Whether we publicly admit to those differences is a whole other thing. We've all been told our whole lives that there are things about us which aren't okay, aren't acceptable, and need to be changed or denied. But we can't just decide one day not to be ourselves and to be someone else. Change and transformation takes time and work. Denial is simple. Denial makes inauthenticity easy. Denial allows us to pretend. It even allows us to lie to ourselves. It lets us believe the opinions and judgments of others over the inner voice of our deep self crying out to be heard and respected.

The more we've internalized those messages that we're not good enough or should be some other way, the more of a temporary relief we can find by accepting rules and limits and the pressure to be inauthentic. It's a relief for a while because we can focus on the illusion of not being "different" or "othered." It soothes the part of our authentic self that wants to be embraced and accepted. The insecurity or need to fit in is part of us, too. It's authentic, it's who we are if we feel it, and we get to decide whether that's a piece of our deep self we want to keep or whether it's something we want to change. But all the inauthentic conformity in the world won't satisfy or soothe that part of us long term.

Inauthenticity makes us defiant. We can't truly conform and still be true to our authentic selves. Either we have to suppress and repress parts of our authentic selves or we have to be selectively defiant within the system we're conforming to. In other words, either we're not entirely conformist so that we can be entirely authentic, or we're not entirely authentic so that we can conform completely. The math doesn't work out otherwise. And selective defiance is cool and potentially fun, but it's not a long-term solution. It almost always leads to wholesale defiance because wholesale defiance is the explosive result of long-term repression.

Just ask the Catholic church. For a while I was

selectively defiant. I disagreed with some of the church's policies and philosophies, but I figured since I agreed (at the time) with the big stuff it didn't matter so much if I disagreed in a few places. But then a few places became more, and pretty soon I began to realize maybe I didn't agree with the big stuff as much as I thought I did. And that was all because I had a cool priest who taught us it was okay to disagree. He gave us permission to reclaim some of our authentic inner voice and be more authentic within the standards of the church.

Nonconformity is hard, though. Defiance takes courage that not everyone has. Courage requires self-trust. But courage is one of the remedies for inauthenticity, so authenticity hinges on developing that trust.

The longer we've repressed and distanced ourselves from aspects of our true self, the more we hate who we are and wish to be different, and the harder it is to become comfortable with our own thoughts and feelings. That leads to distrust of our own inner compass and a need for others to embrace us and lead us. If we don't know our own deeper spiritual self, we are prone to opening ourselves up to whatever spiritual ideas either feel right in the moment or make us feel included in a community in some way. But it becomes a lot like trying to change ourselves to fit in with whatever crowd we thought was cool in high school. It doesn't ever lead to more authenticity or real feelings of connection, just more pressure to be something we're not.

Most of us don't dig deeply enough to understand our core spiritual truth, and then we spend a lifetime bashing up against ideas that contradict that truth without knowing why. We often don't approach spirituality from an internal perspective. We look outward for answers to how we should be within ourselves, rather than looking within for answers as to how we should show up in the world.

For our spiritual path or journey to support our authenticity, it's got to be internal to external rather than the other way around. We first have to connect with and express our own inner spiritual truth before building up a spiritual life and practice. Trying to do it the other way around by fitting ourselves into a tradition or path that already exists and shaping ourselves accordingly isn't unreasonable on the face of it, because we do need community. It's natural to want to fit into a larger spiritual culture or family, but it is incredibly difficult to really dig out space for our own authenticity in a tradition built around something else entirely.

The thing most people get wrong about spirituality (and life in general, for that matter) is thinking it's about finding the belief system that is the most correct and true and then living by it. We tend to completely reshape our lives to fit around a belief system once we're convinced it contains sufficient amounts of truth. Along the way to that truth we either bounce from one belief to another hoping to finally find the one that isn't full of complications and errors, or we embrace a belief

despite its shortcomings and deal with a lifetime of dissonance and conflict around it. Either way, that approach doesn't support our true selves in all our true potential.

Not centering our spirituality around our authentic deep self leads to feelings of purposelessness, restlessness, and doubt. When there's true resonance with what we're doing on a soul-deep level, it produces a sense of purpose and clarity. Inauthenticity and disconnection from our deep self leaves us without a compass for finding purpose and clarity.

It's also exhausting. Authenticity is a way of opening the door to our personal spiritual power. The more inauthentic we are, the less spiritual energy we have access to and the less benefit we get from our spiritual activities. Inauthenticity makes us expend an awful lot of spiritual energy to fill or bridge the gap between who we are and who we're trying to be. It's like being in the closet about part of our identity and spending a lot of emotional energy continuing to hide our true self or smoothing things over to maintain perceived safety.

Authenticity is, on the surface, harder than inauthenticity. We're hard-wired for inauthenticity in a lot of ways. Humans are social creatures, programmed by instinct to seek safety in groups and to therefore do what we must to be accepted and embraced. Tens of thousands of years ago, when our ancient ancestors were nomadic foragers wandering the land in small egalitarian bands, there wasn't the same amount of pressure to suppress individual identity for the sake of the larger group. We know this from looking at nomadic forager societies in more modern times and studying what it takes to even maintain the kind of egalitarian social structure indicated by the archeological evidence. There's a lot of concern in those societies over behavior as it impacts other people, but not the same kind of obsession over belief, identity, and sameness. Those are modern pressures, which have taken the instincts that made us thrive as hunter-gatherers and twisted them into a force for conformity.

But we're hard-wired for authenticity in a lot of ways, too. The symptoms of inauthenticity are all things we're programmed to try to fix. It makes us unhappy and causes distress, which makes us more and more desperate to craft an existence where we don't feel inferior and bad. Humans do have a sense of emotional self-preservation, and it kicks in when we're living inauthentic lives that damage our sense of self and ability to thrive.

We're programmed to want to thrive.

We're programmed to want freedom.

Authenticity is truly a form of spiritual freedom, freedom to intake and output thoughts, ideas, energies, and emotions according to our deep self. It's determining for ourselves what growth, evolution, and enlightenment look like in our own life. It's freedom to be who we are without being forced back into a mold that doesn't fit us. That freedom is spiritual power.

"I am forging my own path; there is no one for me to follow."

The journey we're embarking on in the coming chapters is all about intense self-examination and unraveling some of the things we think we know about ourselves and reality. As much as authenticity is a big deal, it's not something easy to embrace given the way we've all been taught to think of ourselves and our place in the world.

It's worth saying that authenticity cannot really be achieved by modeling it after someone else's authentic self. Especially now that our lives are tied in with social media and we're bombarded with examples of how others supposedly live their lives, it's easy to get our ideas of authenticity and spiritual fulfillment completely twisted. Even if we feel very tied to someone and see ourselves as very similar in lots of ways, their authentic self and our authentic self are not the same. What my authentic spirituality looks like and the path I took to create and build it is going to be very different from anyone else's.

We all crave authenticity, and we're drawn to people who exude authentic energy. Many of us want to exude that same energy so people are drawn to us. It makes it really tempting to try to be that person, to emulate who they are and how they exist in the world, but that's not going to get us to authenticity. Those people can be inspirations for our journey but not models. Their challenges and the ways they've overcome them can be examples for us in the sense that we can look to them for clues to overcome our own similar challenges.

Anytime we compare our own authentic way of being against someone else's, we set ourselves back. Authenticity doesn't always mean being loud and visible about our unique qualities. It doesn't necessarily mean grand courageous gestures or bold uniqueness. There's a difference between safe conformity and being comfortable in our way of being, but for many of us, the braver and more authentic thing is to NOT be pushed into loud rebellion against the norm or put our own differences out on display. So if our authentic spiritual self is reserved and quiet about itself, that's fine.

The most important thing to do before we embark on the rest of this journey is to let go of all preconceived notions of what the process or outcome is going to look like. This isn't about setting goals and achieving them. There's nothing aspirational about this. It takes courage and commitment to honesty, which isn't ever said about undertakings that are easy, simple, and predictable.

Looking for an authentic spirituality probably means our current spiritual life feels dissatisfying and inauthentic in some way. We can try to figure out what's "wrong" with our current spiritual life and practice and then try to "fix" or replace those elements, but that's unlikely to work. In fact, I would bet many of us have been doing exactly that and not ending up with a truly satisfying spirituality.

What we're about to do instead is, first, to get to know and fully acknowledge our authentic selves. It's worth taking stock of how we envision our authentic self to be and how it will feel to fully accept our deep self as it is, not so we can hold up that vision and use it to judge our progress, but so we can release those expectations.

Step One is to prepare for the journey we're about to take by gathering what we need for the road.

It will be very helpful moving forward to have a good method in the toolbox for exploring our own expectations and vision and for releasing things we no longer want to hang on to, so now is the time to explore and practice those skills. The methodologies can range from as simple as writing out thoughts and then ripping up or destroying the paper to as fancy and complex as writing and staging a personal ceremonial ritual about it. Personally, I like burning things I want to release, but that's not always feasible. I've seen people write things down and dissolve them in water or flush them down the toilet. Standing in the shower and envisioning the thoughts and emotions being washed away is a very simple one. Finding a place to scream or cry or otherwise physically feel and release things can be powerful and cathartic. Or it can work to simply speak it out loud and let the wind carry the thought away. Whatever makes sense and feels right is the best way to go.

It's really important at this point to give ourselves permission to do things that feel right to us, no matter what anyone else thinks is "correct."

It's also important to flex our creativity during all of this. The key to building an authentic life in any capacity is to not just acknowledge our authentic identity, but also to tap into our authentic way of being and doing. Most of us are used to having spiritual methodologies taught to us rather than creating and finding our own. It's totally fine to seek out instructions and guidance on how to do things, but that doesn't mean the preconceived and published methods are the only choices or that they are the best fit for us.

I was recently chatting with the local pagan meetup group, and someone asked how to go about blessing something. I know they were hoping a more experienced practitioner would give them the expert answer, so they could be sure to do it the correct way. What actually happened, though, was that we all shared our personal methods for blessing objects, and no two suggestions were the same. One person said they put things like tools or containers of water out under a full moon to bless and charge them. Someone else suggested waving them through incense smoke and saying a blessing incantation. It was even pointed out that the method didn't matter as much as our intention, so we could just point our finger at whatever it is and declare it blessed.

The point is there isn't one right way to do things like explore and release expectations. There are only effective and ineffective ways, and those vary from person to person. So if something works, that's all that matters.

I suggest spending some time experimenting to find the best ways to do deep personal exploration, whether that's meditation, divination, journaling, guided visualizations, going on spirit journeys, whatever. It's crucial to find the ones that make us feel like we're digging up the parts of ourselves we know are true and real but which we prefer to ignore, the ones that force us to be brutally honest with ourselves.

And we need to explore some ways of releasing our most difficult emotions and thoughts. There will be a lot of ideas, memories, and visions that we'll want to let go of as we progress, and that's not something most of us are naturally good at. So whether that means documenting and destroying them, doing cleansing or banishing rituals, symbolic burials, or any of a zillion other potential methodologies, the important thing is to have at least one tried-and-true approach that functions as a catalyst for release rather than suppression.

One caution I have, though, is not to fall back on the spiritual tools we've learned in any of the religions, traditions, or paths that we no longer follow. Unless we're absolutely sure we can separate those old practices from their source (and that they actually work), it's better to find new methods or create our own. However weird or unique to us, it's better to have something new and effective than to rely on something that might anchor us to a tradition we no longer want to be part of.

I recommend establishing a place and method of recording our experiences, thoughts, and observations as we go through this process. Keeping a journal is the obvious suggestion, but do whatever works best. We're going to be

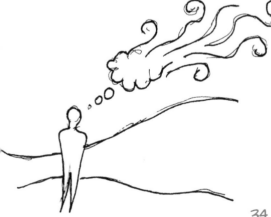

discovering a lot of things about ourselves, poking into our memories, exploring our emotions, brainstorming solutions, and reflecting on the nature of reality, among other things. There's no guide to tell us exactly what our unique, authentic journey will show us, so we have to record that guide for ourselves.

The better we know ourselves, the more powerful we become.

There will be four phases to this roadmap.

The first is the exploration of self. We'll explore the nature of soul, spirit, and body and dig into the deep corners of our authentic identity. This is going to be a process of revealing ourselves not to the world but to our own eyes. It's the process of getting to know ourselves and the ways we judge and limit ourselves because of what we've learned from our past. When we get to the end of the first phase, we'll have a deeper connection to our authentic identity and a deeper understanding of how we got to be who we are.

The second phase is about learning to embody our authentic self. We'll begin to embrace those aspects of self that we've denied and ignored. It's all about finding our voice and learning to use it, shrugging off the baggage that keeps us subservient to the opinions and judgments of other people and entities. It's all about taking responsibility for ourselves.

The third is the process of stepping into our authentic spiritual power. The point of all this isn't to find a religion where we feel comfortable. It's really about learning to guide our own growth and evolution, centering our understanding of spirituality on the practices that truly build us up in alignment with our authentic deep self and use our authentic qualities as sources of power.

And the final phase is putting our new understanding of self and sense of empowerment into a framework and practice that feels like traditional spirituality to whatever extent we authentically need.

There's no way to know exactly how that's going to look and feel until we've gone through the whole process. As with so many things, it's about the journey more than the outcome. Or, at least, it's about the lessons and insights we gain along the way more than the specifics of belief and practice that we end up with.

Once we've let go of all those hopes and expectations for a specific outcome, it's time to move into an exploration of what our deep self really is.

Part II

Shadow Work

Pause and Reflect
———— ———— ————

What habits have you tried and failed to break in the past?

What rules do you think everyone should live by, and where do those rules come from?

Who comes to your mind as an example of authentic living?

———— ———— ————

Step Two
Integration

"I'm not who I think I am. I am who I demonstrate that
I am."

The soul is like an operating system.

The plant metaphor I explained in the passage about
spagyrics is a good way to visualize the relationship
of body to soul to spirit in alchemy, but when it
comes to applying this to ourselves as human beings
specifically, I like using a computer to illustrate it
instead. Body is the hardware and accessories, spirit
is all the data and electricity and other forms of
input and output, and soul is the operating system
or the base programming. It is the part that we take
for granted and tend not to mess around with if we
can help it.

I think this is an appropriate metaphor because,
like our souls, a computer's operating system isn't

unchanging or sacred; it's just complicated and difficult to change if we still want the computer to work as intended. It determines a lot about how the computer functions, but it's not perfect. Regular updates are necessary to adapt to changes in technology and to fix problems that arise, but we can't go in and make wholesale changes to the operating system without wiping a ton of stuff out of memory. At the end of a computer's life cycle, the state of its programming doesn't look like it did when it came out of the factory.

Our souls aren't unchanged or unchanging. They aren't the best of us or more connected to the universe or more divine; they're just the deepest part of us. In fact, if we want to be more connected to the greater powers in existence, we enable those connections by refining and shaping the deepest parts of ourselves. We can't have truly strong connections to anything or anybody if those connections are rooted in poorly functioning base programming.

Our souls are the core of who we are and who we have become over time. As we go through the experience of life and do our best to function, some of what we learn shifts little bits of that base programming, our deepest values and concept of how the world works and our place in it, making little updates and changes over time. Some of those adjustments have improved how we function as people and some are more like bugs and viruses.

This is why instead of calling it a soul, I prefer "deep self." The word "soul" is tied up in all kinds of religious baggage, just like spirit, and probably even more so. What we're dealing with here is the programming that makes us tick, which has evolved through all the experiences we've had in our lives. And the reality is that our soul can't be anything but authentic. It is who we are in the moment, whether that's who we want to be or not.

Most of us aren't as connected to our deep self as we think we are. In fact, the work of connecting to our deep self is something that never ends. But until we really connect with our deep self, it's pretty much impossible to have a relationship with ourselves that embraces authenticity. It's hard work to get to fully know ourselves as we are in the moment. We're constantly changing and growing, either through the parade of life experiences we have or through a more consciously guided process of purposeful personal development, so we can't really stop unearthing our authentic selves and finding all the new things that sneak into our programming that we're not conscious of. It takes a lifetime of close observation and investigation of self to be really connected to our authentic deep selves.

We know we're not connected to our deep selves and not embracing our authenticity when there's a disconnect between what we intend and what we actually do. It's like a glitch in our programming. If I think I am very generous, but I find it difficult to actually share with others because I fear people will take advantage of that generosity, then my deep self isn't entirely programmed for generosity and pretending otherwise doesn't help me be the person I aspire to be. Authenticity means not pretending that I don't have a hang-up about those fears. It means being honest about how I see myself, how I want to be, and the parts of my deep self that stand in the way of that.

My entire life I've struggled with punctuality. I used to say I struggled with time management, but that's not really true. I don't lack awareness of what time it is at any moment, and I'm not as bad at estimating how long it takes to do something or travel someplace as some people in my life would suggest. It's never been that I didn't know how to manage my time better. It's not as though "leaving earlier so we're not late to where we're going" is some huge secret solution I just hadn't thought of. It's also not as though there haven't been negative consequences of my relationship to time. I actually got fired from my first job out of college for being late to work so much.

Now, I could dig into all the reasons why I struggle to get places on time (mostly a factor of not liking to be told to stop doing the things that I care about), and I could beat myself up for not getting control of something that seems to be so simple (like the way I hold myself back from taking on great opportunities sometimes just on the grounds that I'd have to be stricter about my time), but as much as I have wished that I didn't struggle with it, I can't deny that it's part of who I am. In fact, a couple of months ago my wife and I were out shopping, and she pulled me over to a display in a clothing store and thrust a t-shirt into my hand saying I had to buy it.

It said "Always Late" in a lovely script font on the front.

Whatever the reasons behind it and whether I accept or hate that part of myself, it's part of who I am. It's a pattern I've never broken. It's the output that results from a bit of my base programming, which absolutely detests and resents any limits placed on the things I like to do, including the need to pause those things to go to work. That doesn't mean I can't or shouldn't ever change it, and it doesn't mean I have to be happy or proud of it. But it is not something I can claim is not like me. I cannot claim that it's contrary to my character.

It may not be part of who I want to be, but it's absolutely an aspect of my deep self.

How our actions and behaviors portray us is so much more authentic and accurate than our image of ourselves or our idea of who we're trying to be. We can't be someone else by denying parts of ourselves. But the great thing about being human is that, even if we are kind of like a computer, we are blessed with the amazing ability to update and upgrade our own programming. We can trace the events in life that made us who we are and see how those lessons have played out in our life over time.

That's what makes us advanced, evolved beings.

"I have fashioned my masks from the remnants of my past."

Growing up in an evangelical household, there was hardly anything in my life as a kid that wasn't touched by religion. Every rule I had to follow, every decision that was made all traced back to Christian doctrine and morality. Everything from what homecoming dresses were appropriate to what friends I could hang out with to what subjects I should study in school was run through the filter of religion rather than common sense or rational thought. I found it weird at the time. I was very aware that my family was different from most of my friends' families, and I don't just mean that they didn't have the same restrictions. Frankly, I was such a "good girl" growing up that I didn't have a big list of strict rules because my parents knew I could be trusted without them. But I knew that literally our whole life was shaped by religion in ways that other people's lives just weren't.

But it turns out I was wrong in a sense. Everyone has something that is central to their lives and plays into nearly every choice they make. For most people that's not formal religious dogma like it was for me growing up, but no matter what it is, it's a fundamental element of our spirituality because it's a fundamental element of who we are. It doesn't matter if we think of those things as our substitute for religion or not; we all have something that fills those spots in our lives. It's where our moral codes, priorities, and concepts of how we "should be" come from.

We also all have elements of our deep self that are just leftovers from past versions of ourselves and past religious or spiritual paths we've been on.

All this stuff shapes not just who we are authentically, but it also shapes our inauthenticities. In fact, I'd argue that there's no bigger source of inauthenticity than religious rules and concepts about what is acceptable.

We all spend more effort than we probably realize (or want to admit) trying to be a more acceptable version of ourselves to people around us, and what that person looks like has everything to do with whatever functions as spirituality or religion in our lives (or has in the past).

Religious ideas about what and how we should be are the biggest reasons people leave and change spiritual paths over time, and the choices we've made about which paths and traditions and religions to follow tell us a lot about who we are. As we change and grow, we also shift our relationships with the entities in our lives that render judgment on us.

My whole spiritual history directly reflects the things I was learning about myself along the way, and every time I left a church or switched paths it was for reasons that weren't just philosophical. For example, after spending my entire childhood right up through my college years involved in the churches where my dad was the minister, I found myself having to make my own choice about what church to attend. I was newly out on my own, fresh out of college, a nine-hour drive from home, and in a city where I didn't know anyone. I was finding my own way in life, and so I realized I needed to find my own way in my spiritual life as well. I ended up converting to Catholicism because all of my most profoundly spiritual experiences to that point had been in European cathedrals and monasteries.

Fast-forward a few years and I was in a different place as a person. I was in a relationship with the woman who is now my wife. I'd gone through a health scare in which a suspected pregnancy turned out to be a benign tumor, and it had changed my perspective on reproductive rights. I had a fundamental personal issue with the concept of confession because why should I have to go through a priest and confess to things I didn't even think were "sins" to get absolution from a higher power? And while at first I could comfortably sit in those pews as my authentic self and make peace with the few small ways I was out of alignment with what the church told me was important, after a few years I could no longer reconcile my authentic identity with church doctrine.

When we feel that kind of dissonance and pressure to conform, we can respond in a few different ways. We can continue to attempt to conform and fit within the standards set down for us. We can pretend there's no issue, hide our authentic self away and act like there's no conflict at all.

Or we can leave.

I chose to walk away and change directions, but that didn't mean I didn't still carry some of that baggage with me. Those standards about whether I "should" be open about getting into neopagan practices still lingered, making me feel anxiety and guilt. I continued to assume other people would hold me to the

same standards as the church or at least expect me to make an effort to conform. The church's rules and expectations persisted as my default assumption for what the world wanted from me.

Religious traditions are not set up to support our authenticity because that's not the point of them. Religion is cultural and communal, and that means they literally tell us how we "should" be and how to change from who we authentically are to meet this acceptable standard. So it's no coincidence that many of the inauthentic versions of ourselves we pretend to be are rooted in our spiritual and religious past.

We've all been programmed to reject parts of ourselves.

"It is harder for me to hide from myself if I live where there is light."

Shortly after I turned 30, I had a significant shift in my musical interests. And one thing I know for sure about my authentic self is when I get into something, I get really into it, and I want to know everything I can about the things I like. So when I started listening more and more to Nine Inch Nails, I found myself looking up and reading interviews with and articles about Trent Reznor.

Now, I'd lived a life full of repression and denial. I knew that, but I definitely hadn't ever been encouraged to poke at all the things I'd pushed aside. All I knew was I was frustrated with life. I had chased lots of different kinds of success with very limited results. I knew how to find short-term happiness, but not real contentment. And then, in one of those interviews I was reading, I was struck by a statement that felt like someone had gotten into my head and described how I felt about myself and my life. For the life of me I can't remember exactly what he'd said, but I know the interview dealt with Reznor's journey of addiction and self-destruction. And although I've never been a drug addict or rock star myself, his description of the feelings that drove him to destructive behaviors resonated very deeply. I realized even though I turned to self-sabotage rather than cocaine to avoid feelings of failure and judgment, it was fundamentally the same pattern.

It was like tugging a loose thread on a sweater and watching it all come undone. I spent the next few months in deep self-analysis, picking out the patterns that had held me back, the things I was pretending were true when deep down I knew they weren't, all the little things that had happened in my past and resulted in twisted coping mechanisms.

I cried a lot, I listened to a lot of angsty industrial music, and when I got to the point where I didn't really know what to do with all the stuff I'd learned about myself, I got a therapist.

Several years later I realized that those months of intense self-examination and crying to The Fragile in the dark were a form of what is called shadow work.

To be honest, I often hesitate to tell this story to people because it paints shadow work as far more traumatic and messy than it really needs to be. Full disclosure: I had zero idea what I was doing. Also, it's worth saying that doing shadow work can uncover things we're ill-equipped to deal with. It's not fun and games. But I think it's worth starting here because it's a good picture of what shadow work really means.

In the work of Carl Jung, the basic concept of the shadow self is that it's the unconscious part of who we are. Shadow doesn't refer to the "bad" part, and it's important not to confuse our shadow aspects with things we should be ashamed of. It's likely our shadow contains the parts of us that we're already ashamed of or feel necessary to hide from others, but the fact that we DO hide parts of ourselves doesn't always correlate to the value of those parts. Think "dark side" not in the sense that it's evil, but in the sense that, like the dark side of the moon, it remains unilluminated and hidden.

I think for this process it's easiest to explain it like this: Our deep self can be divided into the parts we're aware of and connected to and the parts we aren't aware of or are disconnected from. Our shadow self is the part we're not aware of and are disconnected from. So shadow work is the process of unearthing the shadow self and bringing it into the light, incorporating it into the parts of self we are aware of. The more shadow work we do, the smaller our shadow self becomes, not because we get rid of it but because we embrace and transform it.

Shadow work, like authenticity, requires radical self-honesty. Without doing shadow work, authenticity is pretty well impossible to fully embrace. And the only way to really dig into and get to know ourselves is to look at how our deep self manifests in our actions, choices, and thoughts. The key to the soul is found in the habits we've developed and our reflexive behaviors and choices because all those things are guided by assumptions and expectations we've never taken out and examined. Our deep self shapes how we act and think, so if we act and think in ways we wish we didn't, it means there's stuff in our shadow taking the wheel in our lives.

Back to the computer analogy: The way we find problems with the software or the operating system is by looking for problems in how they function. We start with the error messages that pop up or when apps crash. We take note of when the output isn't correct or doesn't meet expectations. Sometimes it's because of something damaging like a virus, but a lot of times those problems result from unforeseen incompatibilities between different pieces of software.

With everything that's programmed into our deep selves, it shouldn't be a big surprise that some of them are going to conflict with each other and there's going to be a lot we just haven't ever been (or allowed ourselves to be) fully aware of. But no matter what we find there, our deep selves include our shadow selves, even the ugly parts.

We may not like all of our shadow self – that's probably why we have disconnected and repressed a lot of those parts – but it IS part of our authentic being. That doesn't mean our shadow self has to be part of who we eventually become.

We've been programmed to reject parts of ourselves, and that's how we get our shadow self in the first place. Most of our programming has to do with the way we view ourselves, our motivations, and our sense of purpose. It has to do with our place in the world and our responsibility to other people, what we owe people, and what they owe us. And a lot of the beliefs we have about our own value and purpose are shaped by our very early experiences. Most of what sits in our shadow self didn't get to be there because someone sat us down and told us how we should feel about ourselves. We've simply spent a lifetime observing things, experiencing things, and making all kinds of inferences from there. The kind of world we grow up in shapes the very core of our deep selves, and when that world tells us part of who we are isn't acceptable, there's a good chance we're going to shove some of those aspects of self into whatever dark corners we can find.

Those dark corners fill up fast.

It's easier to fill the shadows than to work on changing ourselves, so our shadow selves can become minefields that necessitate having professional help in the wings. Uncovering the things that might have caused us to believe we're worthless might be really traumatic. Trauma teaches us awful things about ourselves and about the world, and it embeds that stuff super deep.

But our shadows also contain things we're just afraid to bring out into the light. Our **deep selves** are the home of our subconscious and our intuition. Our so-called guilty pleasures live there. The sides of ourselves that we only share with our closest and most trusted friends,

51

and the fantasies of worlds where we can be who we want to be without consequences, are all elements of who we are at our deepest level.

I like to think of the process of shadow work as something like cleaning house, and I mean really deeply cleaning house. Of course, when I was going through my intensive shadow work experience, it was more like demolition. I literally envisioned it in my head as me busting down walls with a sledgehammer so there weren't any more dark corners to hide things in. Luckily, I've learned better methods since then, and now it's more like a really deep reorganization project.

My mom is a neat freak, and I'm most certainly not. The result is that when my mom cleans house or rearranges a room, it's just a matter of moving things aside to clean behind and shifting furniture around. When I do it, though, I deal with objects that have never quite found a good place to belong and have been stashed in cabinets or on shelves to get them out of the way. There are boxes of things I've not opened or thought about in years and projects I've forgotten about and never finished. So when I decide things need to be rearranged or deeply cleaned, it becomes this grand project of pulling everything from where it's stored, cleaning the corners, and then sorting through the piles, and trying to bring order to the chaos. And ultimately I'm always left with a pile of stuff that doesn't have a place and things I'm not sure I want to keep.

That's more what shadow work is like.

We drag all the stuff out of the darkness and try to process it, but we're going to find things that don't fit comfortably within us anymore or that we would like to either shove back into a dark place or get rid of altogether. We'll find habits we don't know how to break and judgmental thoughts we have about ourselves we don't know how to stop thinking. There will be things we wish we had the courage to embrace but just don't know how to yet. We'll find reasons why we are who we are, motivations we didn't realize were driving us, and many of them will be things we just don't know how to deal with. And unlike when we clean house, we can't just take all the stuff we don't want to hang on to and chuck it in a dumpster or donate it to charity.

The biggest lesson I learned from my first foray into shadow work is that the uncovering is only the first part. Those months of deep digging into my psyche and history uncovered some really valuable insights about who I was and how I got to be that person. I came away with a much deeper understanding of my authentic self. But I had no idea what to do with it. The image I had in my head of me swinging a metaphorical sledgehammer around my inner self and crushing all the walls I'd built culminated in this sense that I'd created a huge pile of debris I didn't know how to clean up. It was an overwhelming sense that I'd made a mess too large to deal with on my own, and that's why I went to a therapist. As much as I wanted to heal myself on my own, putting my inner self back in order wasn't something I could even convince myself I was capable of without help.

That's why this isn't something that can be done all at once. But the more of our shadow self we illuminate, the more in touch with our authentic self we become. Building a spiritual life and practice that provides what our authentic self needs requires us to really know ourselves as completely as possible and to stop relegating pieces of ourselves to those shadows. If we hide things, we can't heal them. And ultimately, when we build a spiritual life that does support our authentic self, we'll be less likely to feel the need to fill those dark places back up again. An authentic spirituality won't teach us we're unacceptable as we are.

"A fragmented person lives a fragmented life."

Integration is about bringing the shadow parts of ourselves, which we discover through shadow work, together with the deep aspects of ourselves that we were already aware of. We will uncover a lot through our lives as we poke around in the dark corners of our deep selves, and it's logical that we'll have to reacquaint ourselves with those rejected and suppressed pieces. But there's also plenty to be surprised about in our non-shadow aspects of self.

It's really easy to start thinking of our shadow selves and illuminated selves as two separate versions of ourselves, one we've loved and connected with and know inside and out, and the other, which has been metaphorically hidden away in the basement. But it's really not that simple, and those two sides are definitely connected. In fact, they're so strongly linked that we can't just cut away the shadow self and move on. It's not possible any more than it's possible to cut our body in half and try to live without the left side.

The defining aspect of our shadow selves, though, is that they've been unacknowledged. We've lived as though only the illuminated self exists or matters, so the first step in dealing with and embracing our shadow self is to actually exercise and inhabit those aspects of ourselves. There's some healing that needs to happen, a process of being our shadow self and reacquainting ourselves with that side of ourselves without all the internal judgment.

When I reached a natural limit of how much shadow work I could accomplish in one go, I found myself at a loss for what to do next. I had a deep emotional understanding that all the stuff I had uncovered wasn't to be treated like a disease or parasite to be gotten rid of. I had uncovered lots of things about myself I wasn't particularly comfortable with, but I knew they were me. It felt like I'd broken myself into a bunch of tiny pieces, and somehow I had to put them back together into a whole, functioning person.

It's easy to see the shadow aspects of ourselves as antithetical to who we believe we are. One of the things I realized about myself is that I still carry a perception that since I grew up not being able to afford more than hand-me-downs and cheap clothes, whenever I do dress in fashionable or expensive clothes people can tell that I don't belong in them. And that is weird, of course, since at the time I had that little discovery my sense of self was most definitely rooted in not caring about what people considered fashionable or attractive. Of course, that shadow aspect wasn't a thing I wanted to bring out into the light and fit back into my persona, because it didn't belong there.

Except that it was part of me, and it did have an impact on how I presented myself in the world. It was why I had such disregard for pretty, trendy people. It wasn't true at all that I didn't care what people thought about how I looked, and it wasn't true that I thought designer fashion was stupid. It was the impetus for my forays as a kid into designing and reconstructing clothing items into something new. Once I dropped the pretense and acknowledged that I did care about the opinions of others (even if I felt like I shouldn't), that aspect of who I was actually fit very logically into the rest of my deep self. It stopped being an internal tug-of-war between pretending not to care while caring very much inside.

That process of fitting the pieces we unearth back into the whole of ourselves is called integration.

One of the things that I've learned from my own process of coming to a more authentic way of being is that the more deeply in touch I get with my deep self and the driving motivations found there, the more all the pursuits in my life meld and fit together. For a long time, I kept different areas of my life pretty separate. I was one way with my family, another way in my career, another when it came to my hobbies. I put on different personas at different times, and there were parts of my life that I just didn't talk about in other parts of my life. And each of those parts was fundamentally driven by what seemed to be a different goal and purpose. There were things I did for fun, things I did to make a living, things I did because I saw a need in the world, things I did to engage my passions, and somehow all those things were different and compartmentalized.

But as I stopped doing things based on what other people might think and started becoming more comfortable and confident in my own motivations, those compartments began to collapse. Not that everything in my life is just one single activity, but the lines are certainly blurred. My writings and creations are both part of my spiritual life and something of a career/hobby, which comes out in the way I go about my job, something I do because it fits with the same driving purpose and philosophy about what's important in life.

Our deep self values and beliefs will manifest in all parts of our life, even if in slightly different ways. If our deep self is fragmented and our shadow aspects aren't integrated, a lot of those values and beliefs are going to manifest in confused and disparate ways simply because there's so much of our deep self that is unacknowledged and unexamined. The division between our shadow and our illuminated self manifests, too.

Although I think the word is maybe a bit overused, the process of integration really boils down to alignment. It means all the things we do stem from our core beliefs and, therefore, fit together like puzzle pieces. Figuring out how to bring our lives into alignment is difficult. Like working a jigsaw puzzle, the key isn't to try to forcibly fit things together. The key is to live out our core values so all the pieces naturally find their places.

But like a lot of spiritual concepts, it's easier said

than done. And we're not even done talking about the process of shadow work at this point. But as we move forward, it's important to realize that the next step isn't ever going to involve cramming everything in life together under one big umbrella so we can pretend to be integrated and whole. The boundaries between shadow and illuminated and between the various compartments in our lives will begin to break down on their own as we uncover and acknowledge the parts of ourselves that we've rejected and repressed. The more we find the underlying links that connect all our pieces, the more they will naturally draw back together. Those links lead us to our motivations and beliefs.

"My actions may speak loudly, but I must open my heart to the message."

When pressed to say what we believe, we tend to think of either spiritual and religious belief systems or moral and ethical belief systems. We talk about whether we believe in god or how we think humans should ideally behave towards each other, but does that actually mean anything? I would argue that those grand belief concepts are largely meaningless compared to the beliefs that come from lessons we've learned from experience.

Our beliefs are formed the same way our authentic identity is. Things happen to us, and we draw conclusions from those experiences about how the world works. Those conclusions form a belief system and a set of guiding principles for our actions and choices going forward. And it's those beliefs that are fundamental to our authentic way of being.

Of course, the stuff about god and morals can be important, too, but in the interest of thorough shadow work, it's even more important to center our spiritual focus on ourselves rather than on outside deities and powers. Every unexamined or inauthentic belief we cling to holds us back from integrating our shadow and embracing our authenticity.

Beliefs are easy to cling to, but much harder to act on if they aren't rooted in and aligned with our deep self. The only beliefs that really matter are the ones driving our actions and shaping our decisions, and those aren't often the same thing as the ones we claim are important to us.

As we're revealing our authentic selves, the first layer of surface belief to push through is the idea that we are who we decide to be. Not that we can't grow or evolve, even intentionally, but that is a process we'll get to later. We can't just wake up one morning and decide something is important to us and make that our new reality. If it isn't already very much compatible with our core programming, the programming will always win, and our best ideas and intentions about who we want to be become just a disguise we put on.

It's generally easier to figure out what our real beliefs are, the ones that actually determine how we live our lives and how we show up in the world, than it is to integrate and reconcile them in our minds. In fact, that's a big part of why we don't see them. We deny that our real motivations and guiding thoughts have the power they do because we don't want that to be who we are. We don't want to have to confront that bit of our reality. It's not always because they are bad things to believe, either. Often it's just that those things aren't who we are comfortable being or who we believe we should be. But our real beliefs are the ones we act on out of reflex, and they are revealed by the patterns in our choices and behaviors.

We tend to think of beliefs in the same way we think of morals, ethics, and values. They're all tied together, but they're not the same thing. Beliefs are the things we see as true now, not what we think should ideally be true about the world. And that's why big beliefs like a belief in a deity, an afterlife, or a particular concept of how the universe works just aren't as important deep down as the beliefs that drive our actions and choices.

I'm sure we all know someone who professes beliefs they don't act on, especially religious ones. To some extent, we've all been that person. We've all known (and been) the people who are great at telling everyone what they ought to do and are awful at doing it themselves. We get hung up on this stuff, angry at others, and ashamed for ourselves, focused on the hypocrisy and inconsistency rather than the reality.

Functional beliefs aren't about what should be; they're about what is.

So underneath every belief we have or profess to have is a deeper belief that reveals something about our authentic self. Every bit of hypocrisy or inconsistency we find in ourselves points to who we really are at a deep self level. And quite a lot of those underlying beliefs we find this way won't be about the world at large; they'll just be about our place in it.

After my first crazy foray into shadow work, I sought out a therapist. My wife was already seeing one, I got one for myself, and we eventually started seeing one as a couple. It was one of the best decisions I've ever made, and I learned a lot about myself and my ways of reacting to what happens in my life. I've told many, many people over the years how much I think therapy is good for everyone, even if we think our struggles are just small, normal stuff.

That said, though, after a year or so of seeing my therapist (and maybe not even that long), we mutually decided I was in a good place, and we didn't need to continue with weekly appointments. I didn't go to therapy for more than a decade after that. Lots of things happen in a decade, of course, including traumatic things of one flavor or another, but I never got back to a place where I felt like I needed to talk to someone. I could look at the people around me and see how they would benefit from therapy, but I never went for myself. Sure, I had bad weeks at work where I'd end up frustrated, panicky, crying, but it wasn't like I had a diagnosis that necessitated a therapist.

My wife and I started noticing all the commercials for online therapy services, and I eventually suggested that she look into it since she does have a diagnosis that really should be supported by therapy and we didn't have insurance to cover traditional therapy. She very bluntly pointed out I could surely benefit from it as well.

And she was right. I eventually had to admit and sit

with the reality that no matter how much I talked about a belief in the value of therapy for everyone, I didn't include myself. It didn't matter what I said, it just mattered what I did, and I certainly wasn't as open to getting myself back into therapy as my professed beliefs would have suggested. So what was the deal? Was I lying about my belief in the value of therapy? Nope. I could point to every single person I knew and give a list of things they could go to a therapist about.

Did I not think I had issues to work on? I'm self-aware enough to know that if I'm crying and upset on a regular basis, I've got issues to work on. Of course I had problems. I just felt like I had a handle on it.

And that's where it gets to the real, soul-deep truth of it. I believed I was better at working through my own issues than other people because that's how I was supposed to be. I had my spiritual practices, I had learned things from my last stint in therapy, so I was fine, wasn't I? Everyone else had problems worse than mine, and I was supposed to handle myself. It wasn't that I thought I was better than other people or had fewer problems, but I did believe I was expected to not have issues I couldn't handle by myself.

I went back to therapy.

But the point is once I saw it, I could see that belief driving all kinds of other actions and decisions in my life. Whether a belief is backed up by truth is irrelevant to the process of shadow work. It's not a particularly healthy way of going about life, rejecting help when I could use it just because I feel like I shouldn't need it. It feels rooted in a sense of superiority, but I know it's rooted more in insecurity and a learned fear of appearing weak or imperfect in front of other people. That's reality, and acknowledging it is part of shadow work, but working to change it is not. That comes later. But when it comes to understanding and defining who we are, this is the kind of belief that is most relevant and important.

What I do or don't believe about the existence or power of a deity doesn't have a tangible impact on my day-to-day life. It's a conclusion I've come to logically, not one embedded deeply in who I am. It matters a hell of a lot, though, that I believe bad things will happen if I admit I need help or support. That belief is part of who I have grown to be.

All of our actions and patterns point to our beliefs, and it's our struggles that point to the beliefs attached to our shadow aspects. Behaviors that seem out of character to people who know us reveal dissonance between our core beliefs and the way we present ourselves to the world. The things we feel compelled to do but struggle to justify given our professed beliefs reveal things about ourselves, which, for some reason, we don't want to face up to. If we support issues or argue for points of view that contradict the other things people know about us, there's a corresponding disconnect between our deep self beliefs and our professed ideals. We all have those things we either always or never do but can't adequately explain why because we've not examined our deeper motivations. We all have habits we try to adopt or break but fail at.

All our struggles and inconsistencies are windows into who we really are and what makes us tick. They aren't just a sign of the things we need to change and fix, though. It's important to resist the impulse to focus on whether our professed beliefs are more valid or better than what's reflected in our actions. It can go either way. It's not about feeling guilty for not living up to standards and expectations. It's the reasons why our motivations and intentions don't match that reveal our core beliefs.

When we fail to recognize and consider the underlying beliefs that govern our behavior, we set ourselves up for all kinds of spiritual frustration as we try to grow and change and build an authentic spiritual practice. In fact, all the ways we've struggled in the past to make positive change in our lives, to deepen our connections and open our minds to greater understanding, even to just be more successful or happier in our lives, all of those challenges and failures are rooted in the unexamined core beliefs about who we are and our place in the world.

In fact, the larger philosophical or existential beliefs we grasp and hold on to represent the things we want to believe about ourselves more than what we actually believe. They are aspirational ideas, things we want to be true and hold on to as reassurances. We choose these beliefs based on our life experience, and they paint a picture of what we think being a good person means, what our purpose is in life, how society should function, and how we should treat each other. So if there's a difference between what our deep self believes because of the reality we've experienced and the ideal image of how things ought to be (which is inevitable because reality doesn't ever live up to such ideals), that difference points directly at our authentic deep self identity.

As we uncover these aspects of ourselves, our first reflex is going to be to deny and reject some of them and to hide others. We're not going to like all the things we find, and even if we are personally okay with many of them, we'll be reluctant to embrace and embody them all. Whether these parts of us, these deep self beliefs, are good or bad, whether they're something we like or hate about ourselves is all less important than where they come from at this point in the journey towards truly authentic spirituality.

Some of these deep beliefs are remnants of the belief systems we've been deeply involved with in the past, especially those we were raised in. I've been in and left my fair share of spiritual and cultural traditions, and I never fail to be surprised at how deeply some of the associated beliefs can get buried. For a long time after leaving Christianity, I still had surprising twinges of conscience whenever I broke the old rules, regardless of the fact my logical brain didn't believe in the old rules. I got strangely self-conscious anytime I did stuff that was too clearly identifiable as witchcraft, when I talked openly about sex or my sexuality, drank alcohol and smoked, even switched political parties. Sometimes I chalked it up to the excitement of rebellion against the old rules, exploring my freedom and independence by doing things I knew would have been punished for. Sometimes it was more like guilt, shame, or at least fear that I would still be judged.

Some of these deep beliefs come from experiences that were profound and powerful enough to shape our understanding of self and how we relate to the world. This can come from trauma or from something inspiring and uplifting, but if something has been enough to shift our worldview, it's going to manifest as a functional belief. We can't undo the events that taught us those beliefs, but we can put them in perspective.

At one point in my adult life, I finally realized that a lot of my behavior patterns could be traced back to a belief that if I spoke up without being one hundred percent certain I knew everything there was to know about the topic, I'd be ridiculed and dismissed as incompetent. It made me distrust my own thoughts and voice, not trusting my knowledge to be complete enough or my logic to be reliable. It impacted my career path because I didn't speak up in contexts where I actually had valuable input. It made it very difficult for me to network or create connections with people because I believed everyone knew more than I did, so I avoided putting myself in situations where I might be called out for not being an expert.

Searching for the root of that belief took me back to fifth grade. The class had been given an assignment, which, if I remember correctly, had something to do with illustrating an aspiration we had or a job we wanted. I don't remember now what the details were. What I do remember is that I wanted to impress and seem cool to the popular girls and the leader of that clique who was obsessed with designer labels. None of them had any designer goods, but they aspired to, and it was something I was completely unfamiliar with. But I wanted them to think I was cool, so whatever the assignment was, my answer to it had something to do with running or shopping at a Gucci store. What I remember with great clarity is, when it came my turn to share my work with the class, confidently showing and explaining my drawing only to be laughed at and told by the clique leader, in front of the whole class, that there was no such thing as a Gucci store.

I was humiliated, and that experience stuck with me long past the point where I realized she didn't know what she was talking about, either. I may not have actually known anything about designer fashion, but by my logic a brand like that would have stores, and that logic wasn't faulty. Years later, when I lived in Chicago, I remember walking past the Gucci store there. I remember a little voice in my brain reminding me of that day in fifth grade, and I remember feeling extremely smug. But it wasn't until I connected the experience with the belief I'd developed about everyone knowing more than me, then connected that belief with the pattern of silencing myself around others that I was finally able to understand that part of myself and let go of my attachment to the trauma.

Shadow work isn't all about discovery of trauma, though. It's the discovery of self. We are not the things that have happened to us; we're just shaped by them. This is where journaling can help us find and create an authentic spiritual practice and an authentic life, especially when done in a purposeful way. The most valuable methodology to get good at is starting from a pattern or frustrating choice or behavior and peeling back the motivating beliefs until we get down to our core.

My career path has been almost as meandering as my spiritual path, and for a long time I worked in management for a convenience store chain. And like with any large company, there were people and departments dedicated to process improvements to increase profitability and efficiency. So I remember at one point there was a poster distributed to all stores that was supposed to help managers evaluate and troubleshoot processes with their staff. If things weren't getting done correctly or processes weren't being followed, it was meant to get past the surface reasons and excuses and uncover the real reasons why things weren't working.

The process was simple and boiled down to just repeatedly asking why. So, for instance, say the afternoon shift wasn't stocking the cooler. Why didn't they stock the cooler? The staff might say they didn't have time to stock it. Why isn't there time? Because the last part of the shift is the busiest time, and everyone working has to be on the registers rather than stocking the cooler. Why does everyone on duty have to work the register? Because there are only two people scheduled for the afternoon shift.

The idea was that the more we dig down, the closer we get to the real issue. Unfortunately for the company, the core reasons for a lot of issues were things managers didn't have the power to change, but the idea was decent.

It seems like such a simple thing that we shouldn't need to have it explained to us, but humans have two natural tendencies that keep us from digging deeply into our own motivations. First, we prefer explanations for things that place the blame somewhere else, so if the top layer of motivation allows us to feel like we can't change the situation and there's some external force at play, we're going to happily latch on to it. We'll find justifications if we can, because the reality often means taking responsibility for things when we don't want to or acknowledging things about ourselves we don't feel particularly proud of.

And the second tendency is that digging down to our core motivations makes us feel disconnected from our outer reality. Shadow work is never very pretty. I can absolutely say that, while I was slogging through my jump-into-the-deep-end shadow experience, my work goals weren't really top of mind. I wasn't focused on day-to-day priorities any more than I had to be to keep functioning at a base level. It's an uncomfortable place to sit. And we know this instinctually, so human nature is to avoid it.

Step Two on our journey is to dig into our shadow to begin to uncover what makes us tick.

As simple as it is, the process of peeling back the layers of motivation and continuing to ask why (especially as part of a journaling practice or something similar) is a particularly effective way to start our shadow work and uncover our deepest beliefs.

Start with those inconsistencies and disconnects between professed beliefs and behaviors. Why did I resist getting a therapist for myself even as I recommended therapy to all the people around me? Because I didn't feel like I needed it like they did. Why did I feel that way? Because I felt like I had my own issues under control and already knew what I needed to know in order to deal with it.

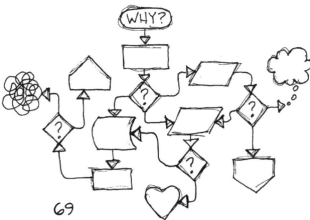

Why did I feel I knew all I needed to know? Because I'd been through therapy once already and had my spiritual practices to use, so I should have learned what I needed already. Because I had always based my sense of self-worth on my intelligence and ability to learn and retain information. Because that was always what I got praised and rewarded for most, whereas when I was emotional and needed support, I was treated like I was doing something wrong. So I have a core belief that I'm expected to know things and solve my own problems because, despite it being absolutely reasonable for other people to need help and support, I'm supposed to not need those things.

The exercise becomes even more revealing if we do it in conjunction with some type of practice, which can help us be more honest with ourselves. This can take the form of guided or structured meditations that work like self-hypnosis and can bring forth the memories and motivations that our logical minds aren't as connected to. If we are particularly good at tracking and interacting with our dreams, doing a pre-bed ritual and asking our dreams to reveal answers to us when we are having a hard time seeing the deeper truths can be a great approach as well.

It's not just a valuable way to uncover the beliefs that drive us; it becomes a way of looking at the world. Learning to look at not just our own behavior but the behaviors of others and see past the surface to what likely lies underneath is how we practice empathy. It's how we gain a fuller understanding of how the world works. But it's worth emphasizing that the things we uncover, the beliefs we find at the center of our authentic selves, aren't problems or flaws to fix; they're simply aspects of self to acknowledge and embrace. The attached experiences and traumas can be healed and put into perspective, but that alone won't change the beliefs we've developed from them, and change isn't on the agenda just yet. This is just the beginning of the process of getting past the way we want to see ourselves, the ways we want others to see us, the things we feel we need to be, and really get down to who we really are.

Step Three

Identity

"I am what I have learned to be. I do not grow by forgetting."

Spirit is universal. It's life force. It's energy. It's thoughts and emotions. In this larger alchemical sense, spirit isn't an inherent part of ourselves. The thing a lot of people call spirit is what we're calling soul or the deep self. What we're talking about here as spirit fits most closely with concepts like the collective consciousness or even the akashic record. Related to the computer analogy, I like to think of it as something like the internet or even the cloud.

After all, no matter what we believe happens to us after we die, the one thing that does persist as our spirit is the memories others have of us, the thoughts and ideas we've left behind, the ripple effect of everything anyone ever learned from us while we were alive. Some people would say that's the energy we put out into the world, and I think that's truer than it might seem on the face of it. All the things that fall under the umbrella of spirit are, in one way or another, energy.

Well, in one way or another, everything in the universe is energy.

But spirit, specifically, consists of the types of energy that we can use and transform and work with as human beings.

Science says energy cannot be created or destroyed, but it can be transferred, converted into other forms of energy, and even stored as mass. We exist in this never-ending, always-changing flow of energy. That's true on a scientific level, and it's true on a spiritual level. Energy flows through exchange. And every exchange of energy is, essentially, a relationship. They are connections. Some are temporary, some are long term, but if we look at the flow of energy and spirit in our life, we'll start to see the web of connections and relationships in which we exist. And I don't just mean interpersonal relationships. Priorities are relationships. Obligations are relationships. All of them are energetic links through which spirit flows.

Of course, there's no way for this flow of universal spirit to be inauthentic. In the same way our deep selves can't be inauthentic because they simply are what they are at any moment, spirit in the universal sense simply is what it is at any moment. So the difference between an authentic spirituality and an inauthentic spirituality comes down to the way we individually interact with, shape, and allow ourselves to be shaped by this flow in relation to our deep self.

There are different ways that we interact with spirit

as individuals. The one that applies to literally every human being is the basic process of human growth and maturity and, well, life itself.

Remember the thing about spagyrics and making plant medicine? That process is a really, really good metaphor or illustration of what I mean here. In the grand sense, spirit to these plants isn't just the alcohol we use to draw out the essential oils in making a tincture; it's also the sunlight and carbon dioxide and water and nutrients they take in and the oxygen they put out while they're alive. Plants take in all of this stuff and transform it into matter, transform it into their essential substances – body and soul. When alchemists do spagyrics, the point is to extract and refine the soul, and that takes a whole different type of spirit than what exists naturally in the plant while it is alive.

The spirit involved in our growth and development to this point in our lives has shaped and been transformed into the authentic self that we are right now. It has shaped our deep self and our physical existence just like the quality of light, water, soil, and air affects and is affected by a plant's essence and the way it physically develops. It takes the right amount of sun, nutrients, and proper temperature for a plant to live and grow. And just as plants take in all that spirit stuff and

use it to get bigger, so do we. We metaphorically bear fruit and seeds, and we bloom if we are in a spiritual environment that supports our growth. Some plants need to be trained, pruned, repotted, and whatnot to make sure that they continue to thrive because their own growth can cause problems for them in the future, and that's true for us, too.

All the knowledge, ideas, and emotional energy that we get from our life experience and the connections around us shape the way we develop as we go through life, but not all change and development is sustainable or good for us. And it doesn't always turn us into a person we end up liking. All that baggage we talked about digging up last chapter? All of that has come to be part of our deep self because of the relationships we've had over time and the resulting flow of spirit.

When we try to grow a plant, we do our best to give the plant the right amount of water and sun and nutrients, the best type to nurture rather than harm. But the plant will take in anything that it can get when it needs it. It can't refuse to take in water from the soil if it's contaminated or move itself to get more optimal sunlight or shade. How the plant grows, what it becomes, has everything to do with where it is planted and what goes on there.

Our development happens the same way if we're not actively engaged in shaping it. Who we are and who we have become have everything to do with the spirit we've been immersed in during our lives. Some of the choices we've made to impact the flow of spirit were probably ones we made purposefully to impact our lives in specific ways, but many were not. Still, all the spirit that has flowed into and out of our lives, filtered in through our soul from all the sources we found ourselves surrounded by, is reflected in who we are.

But that person isn't likely to be the person we envision ourselves to be or the person we want to be in the future. And as long as we convince ourselves that we're a version of ourselves that isn't actually real and doesn't truly exist in the moment, then we aren't living an authentic life or practicing an authentic spirituality.

Inauthenticity is what happens when we try to conform rather than embrace our entire identity. We push our shadow selves back into the darkness rather than integrate them. We learn to hate parts of our authentic selves rather than embrace them. We struggle to grow because the spirit we're immersed in isn't optimal to support the person we are.

Our authentic selves include our shadow selves. We are who we are because of what our life experience and the flow of spirit in our lives have shaped us into. To fully embrace our authenticity, we have to accept that not all of who we are in the moment is who we want to be, and that we can only become who we want to be if we first embrace who we are.

"I am not free to be who I am if I am not free to follow my curiosity."

Spiritually speaking, most of us are probably used to defining who we are in terms of what beliefs we embrace and what religious labels we affiliate ourselves with. Those affiliations tend to be understood as a mirror that reveals things to us about ourselves. We look for a place where we feel like we fit because we think that will reflect who we are.

But spirituality isn't primarily a mirror. Every energetic exchange we have forms a connection, and every connection is essentially a relationship. Our connections to and relationships with people and ideas form a culture around us and anchor us to certain ways of being. I think of it kind of like a net, with all the sources of spirit that influence our life woven together with us at the center. And that net can just as easily be something we're trapped in as it can be a form of safety.

The religious and spiritual affiliations we've claimed over the years have changed and shaped us. When we leave behind a tradition, we invariably carry some remnants with us. We continue to be the person that experience helped to shape, and we continue to see things through those lenses.

After I graduated from college, I moved to Chicago, nine hours away from where I grew up. Ever since I was a kid, I'd gone to church with my family. I'd been the church organist since 7th grade. I hadn't given conscious thought to a change of church tradition. But once I moved and faced the prospect of picking a church and trying it out, I just didn't want to go. It wasn't an anxiety thing about meeting a new congregation or being afraid it wouldn't be a good fit; it was literally me sitting in my apartment on Saturday night thinking I probably needed to make sure I had something to wear the next morning to church and feeling really resentful of waking up that early and going through the trouble. It really felt like, "What's the point of this?"

I never did try to find a church in Chicago like the one I'd grown up with. I didn't go at all for a while, and then I decided to become Catholic.

But the thing is, we don't just participate in religious things when we're formally involved in services. We build up a little microculture in our lives around these things. For me, growing up in a church-centered family, it bled into all aspects of life. It was Sunday dinners. It was starting meals with prayers. It was censoring my language around certain people. It was not feeling free to express interest in certain things in certain contexts. It was the little voice that critiqued things through the eyes and ears of people in the church. It influenced the classes I chose to take in college, how I voted, all kinds of choices I made. And all of those influences persisted for years and years, past the point when I left Protestantism and even after I stopped being Catholic.

When we're part of a culture, even a microculture made up of just a few people, it impacts our worldview. It works its way into all sorts of details of our life like how we dress, who we spend time with, the way we communicate, the media and information we consume. And it doesn't just do this through the rules and teachings.

Religious traditions and spiritual paths function as cultures the same way that family, ethnic groups, and even professions or other identities do. When we form our own family, we don't tend to leave behind everything our family of origin held as traditions, but we do change them. And the closer we stay to our family of origin, the more of a role they continue to play in our life, and the harder it is to let go of those shared traditions even if we, personally, would rather not do them.

It's not different when leaving a spiritual or religious culture behind, even if we left a long time ago. There's a good chance that we're still in contact with people from that circle, even if it's just a general awareness that there are people we interact with day to day who hold those old beliefs. Whatever social pressures were there to keep those traditions and expectations alive persist at least in the form of residual triggers in our deep self, and sometimes in the form of people in our lives who will be upset if we go against what they know to be status quo. The voices that persist in the back of our minds speak up when we do things that used to be frowned upon.

The important aspect of spirituality when it comes to nurturing our authenticity is that we are shaped by the ideas, energies, and information that we take in, and religion is one of the biggest forces in the world when it comes to shaping what forms of spirit we have access to. If we are taught a specific truth, we're being taught to reject everything else. Religion and spiritual traditions shape our judgment of what sources of spirit are trustworthy, what information is fact, and what ideas are acceptable. They even shape our way of communicating with others. Our religious and spiritual pasts inevitably impact how we categorize people, how we determine how to communicate with and treat them, and whether we reflexively look at some people as different from us in potentially negative ways. It is part of how we determine who we listen to.

Religion doesn't just tell us who it's acceptable for us to be; it tells us what it's acceptable for us to think. So whatever formal tradition we belong to can either nurture our authenticity or hinder it, depending on how much it has and continues to dictate what we learn, what we listen to, and how much we're allowed or encouraged to question and think for ourselves.

We pick up and hang on to all kinds of assumptions along our spiritual history, even when we've distanced ourselves from where we learned them. I see this over and over again as someone who leads a group for all sorts of widely varied pagan paths in a very Bible Belt city. It's pretty common for ideas rooted firmly in Judeo-Christian traditions, such as Christianity's specific description of Satan and his agenda in the human world, to still show up in the way a lot of witches approach their craft despite them being very vocal about how much disdain they have for their religious upbringing.

The problem isn't in the ideas, though. The problem is in the limits and filters that religion imposes on what we know and what we think. The single most important part of spirituality isn't picking the right beliefs, but actually engaging in the energetic exchanges and finding our own place and voice in it all.

"The world may not hear my words, but my inner voice will not be silenced."

Storytelling is probably the oldest embodiment of spirituality in human civilization, and part of the immense power of storytelling is that we use it to teach lessons without specifically alienating members of our community. The stories we tell and consume paint a picture of how we see the world and the ways we want it to change.

How many stories do we have in the cultural repertoire about embracing who we are inside and not letting people try to force us to be something different? As a society, we love stories of people finding a miraculous place where they are the same as everyone else after they've been different and ostracized their whole lives, stories of characters who hide parts of themselves to fit in and then find themselves in a situation where that aspect of themselves is the only solution to a problem and they become the hero, and tales of outcasts discovering that what made them different actually turned out to be because they were really special all along. These can be great stories with valuable messages, but they can also muddy the waters when it comes to our quest for authenticity.

I have a lot of conversations with people about authenticity in both a professional and spiritual context, and I've found that what most people expect authenticity to look like is the kind of situation that shows up in those stories. We expect to finally feel authentic when we're embraced and accepted. We'll achieve authenticity when we're in an environment that doesn't make us feel bad for who we are. But authenticity isn't really about how other people treat us. It's not really even about whether we get to be ourselves around other people.

When I first began to explore neopaganism, it wasn't something I felt free to be open about. My wife and I shared a house with my sister at the time, a house we were renting from (and which was next door to) my parents, and the last thing I wanted to do was deal with my strictly Christian family finding out I was dabbling in witchcraft. I had my own business at the time, and I'd borrowed money from my family to get it started, so I was financially dependent on my parents to enough of an extent that I knew I couldn't risk coming out of the "broom closet," as it were.

So I lied about our monthly trips to the bookstore to attend the pagan meetup. We did rituals quietly in the middle of the night when my sister had gone to bed and it was safe to pull the candles and stuff out of our hidden ritual trunk.

I'm sure that seems pretty inauthentic on the face of it, but keeping my pagan bric-a-brac hidden away so I didn't reveal that part of my life was a choice I made with full acceptance of who I was at that moment in my life. My authentic self was simultaneously deeply interested in pagan ideas and practices as well as dependent on the approval of others for my financial security. I didn't agree with their judgment of my path, but I valued my relationship with them enough at that time that I made the choice to keep it to myself.

There have been lots of times that I've grappled with this conflict between my authentic self and my self-expression. After all, I am a queer pagan living in a conservative Christian area of the country, so I've done plenty of coming out as one thing or another to all sorts of people. Looking back on all the times I've lied or concealed aspects of my authentic self out of fear (or sometimes just expediency and convenience) has forced me to sort out my feelings of guilt or shame over those choices and weigh those feelings against the reasons why I felt compelled to hide and conform.

This questioning of our choices and examination of our motivations is part of the process of shadow work. If these were the choices I made, who did that reveal me to be? It's not the choice itself that is indicative of who I am; it's the motivation. Who was the authentic me who made that choice?

What I realized in the end was that it all really did come down to spirit. My family's judgments and beliefs might have been the reasons I chose to hide my sexuality and my spiritual path (among other things) at least for a while, but I wasn't internalizing them. Their opinions didn't change how I felt about myself.

We exist in this vast flow of spirit, and our spirituality is what we take in, what we turn it into, and what we put back out. I think of that flow less like a flow of electricity, and more like the act of breathing. Our lungs take in oxygenated air so our bodies can use that oxygen to keep functioning, and then expel the carbon dioxide from our bodies because we don't need it but other organisms do. We can take in that air and use it to create sounds like whistling, speech, or song. We can blow up balloons or make bubbles with that air. We can put different substances into the air to make it smell different as we're breathing it in. We can inhale helium and make funny voices.

Spirit is the same way. We have access to all this information and energy, whatever we take in gets internalized, and we put it back out in a different form for others to take in. What we take in changes what comes out. Sure, it's all filtered through our programming, our deep self, but it also matters what we choose to breathe in when it comes to ideas, emotions, and experiences. If what we take in doesn't support and strengthen our authentic self, what comes out isn't going to fit our intentions. So while our deep self is always authentic, what we put out in the flow of spirit in our lives might not be. All spirit we take in changes us in some way, so it's crucial that we be mindful of what influences we're inviting in.

Inauthenticity takes root when we allow our own inner voice to be drowned out by the voices of others.

The judgments and opinions of others are spirit, too, so if we allow those voices and those energies to dominate our spiritual intake, it's going to fuel the growth of our shadow and damage our authenticity. The more of ourselves that we shove away and repress, the more inauthentic we become. So while we're doing our shadow work and finding those pieces of ourselves that we've not wanted to reveal or face, it's also important to trace those shadow aspects back to their roots and shut off the flow of spirit that caused them in the first place.

The biggest shadow aspects I found in my own experience had to do with my fear of failure and judgment. All of my big ambitions in life to that point had been attempts to do things my own way rather than take the established path to success. The biggest example was that I'd tried to build a career as an artist without engaging with galleries or exhibitions. I'd started my own art gallery and gift shop despite not having experience, connections, or the money to promote the business, imagining that I could come up with enough creative solutions to make up for all that. I came up with my own far-fetched, optimistic plans for doing things without needing anyone's help or approval, and then as soon as things looked like they might not work out, I made what felt like desperate attempts to make things work but were really bad decisions and self-sabotaging behaviors. But in the end I could lie to myself and say that I'd given it my all, but outside forces had gotten in the way of success. It was a reassuring lie, one I did a decent job of convincing myself was truth.

As I began doing my deep shadow work, I quickly realized that my authentic self was scared of criticism from others. I avoided asking for help or approval because I was afraid to be told that I wasn't good enough. I could pinpoint the times when I had thought I was excelling, thought I was on the path to success only to be derailed by someone with the power to tell me I wasn't good enough or that I wasn't doing things the way they wanted, and those voices were the ones I had been listening to ever since.

I'd internalized those experiences and kept feeding them back to myself. I'd pushed away the parts of myself that wanted to succeed, wanted to be accepted, because those were the parts that had been rejected by those voices. My self-destructive patterns of make-believe effort and self-sabotage were really my attempts to be something different, to conform to the world that I believed wasn't ever going to let me succeed on its terms.

Authenticity is extreme self-honesty, remember? Sometimes the path to authenticity hurts, but that's because it's a form of growth. And the truth is that the struggle to embrace our authenticity never hurts as much in the long run as a lifetime of inauthenticity does.

Growth feels like a stretch, like stepping outside of a comfort zone, and the pain and vulnerability are accompanied by feelings of hope and optimism. What hurts most is the uncovering of those wounds and scars that we've learned to avoid touching or seeing. Shadow work comes with a lot of emotions: grief, regret, anger. But emotions are spirit, too, and when we're engaged in this process of self-discovery and self-honesty, we're using that emotional energy to fuel the process. It's a spiritual experience in itself, pain included.

Inauthenticity, on the other hand, feels like hiding or constantly being on the run from those forces that threaten to uncover what's in the shadows. It often feels like being out of options or out of control, of being resigned to an outcome we didn't choose. Inauthenticity hurts because it is suffocating and restricting, and even though it's always a choice, it can feel like an incredibly heavy burden. The dominant emotions are fear and insecurity.

In the end, what we want to uncover in our shadow work is the voice that comes from our deep self, not the one that parrots back the voices that pushed pieces of us into the shadows in the first place. This is where it becomes a spiritual matter, because even if we can't distance ourselves from the sources of those opinions, judgments, and damaging energies, we can stop consuming and internalizing them. Identifying those messages and shutting them out of our internal spiritual space has to happen, so we can actually listen to our authentic inner voice and hear what it has to say. How else can we truly get to know our deep self?

"I am made up of borrowed pieces, but the sum is uniquely me."

As we get older, we start recognizing the influence of other people in us. I always hated the idea that someday I would turn into my mother, and I hated that people talked about it like it was inevitable. Sure, I might look more and more like her as I age, but surely given how much we disagree on, I wouldn't end up morphing to be like her.

Of course, more and more I find myself saying and doing things that I have totally picked up from my mom.

It's not so much that I've become her, but I've got lots of her mannerisms, and I do find myself thinking and acting in ways that echo her enough that I know it's something I've learned. Every time I get frustrated about something not being the way I want it to be in my house, I hear myself speaking in her voice. When I'm networking or meeting new people, especially when I feel intimidated or that I need to impress people, I can feel myself emulating her. Not to mention all the bits of baggage from our mother-daughter relationship that I've worked through with therapists.

But the bottom line is that I'm not my mom. I can't (easily) control how much I look like her, but I can unlearn a lot of the behaviors and reactions I've learned from her. I can take some of the pieces of her influence and embrace and claim them as my own if I choose, and in choosing them I make them part of my authentic self.

The biggest challenge in connecting with our authentic selves is figuring out who we really are. We're all unique, but we're also the product of our experiences, so it can be hard to figure out where our authentic, unique self ends and the voices and thoughts of others begin. We know we've lived our entire lives buried in the judgments and expectations of other people, and we know we're going to keep being bombarded with those things. Digging out our own identity from all that and claiming a strong sense of self can be hard.

But there is no version of ourselves that is entirely disconnected from the influence of others. A lot of who we are is going to come from other people. That's just how it works. Our inner voice is sometimes going to sound a lot like the voices of others. The web of spiritual relationships and connections in which we exist is important because those sources of spirit keep us alive. Spirit is life. Babies are a genetic combination of their parents, and our spiritual identity is a patchwork of influences that have made us who we are.

There is no version of us that isn't formed from pieces of others, but it's worth considering who we are when nobody is around. If we shut ourselves off from the flow of opinions, guidance, judgments, and ideas from everyone else and sat with ourselves, what would we hear in that silence? Some of what we would hear is our own inner voice, the one that maybe doesn't get heard clearly if we've never learned to value it. Some would be voices and thoughts that seem unlike who we imagine ourselves to be, and that's our shadow self. It is an integral part of who we are, even if we don't like it. But what's truly important is what we wouldn't hear anymore: the voices we've become accustomed to hearing but which don't come from and aren't echoed within us.

If we want to get an authentic understanding of self, we have to be able to insulate ourselves now and then from the pressures and spiritual influences in our lives, so that we can listen for our own inner voice away from all the noise. If outside voices get to chime in while we're trying to learn who we are deep down, no matter how well-meaning and spiritually enlightened the source of those voices are, our relationship with our deep self won't be built on a foundation of authenticity. We'll hide, suppress, and repress things because of what those voices might have to say about us.

I think one reason people have such a hard time with shadow work is that no one can do it for or even with us. Others can support us through it, certainly. It's important to have people around us who care about our mental and emotional wellbeing. But at the end of the day, the work is internal. We have to do it alone. Only we know what we are finding and what to do with it. So in order to do shadow work, we have to set up some boundaries and establish a safe zone where only we are allowed to work while we do all this deep diving.

The safest zone for doing shadow work and processing what you find is in a deeply meditative state. Meditation and other similar practices facilitate deep engagement with the inner landscape apart from the interference of the external. It allows us to build a mental and spiritual space of our own where we can process what's going on inside us. Even just sitting in silence with our thoughts is a window into who we are, shadow aspects included.

Pretty much anything we do that gives us the opportunity to give ourselves a bit of reprieve from the constant input from others is a step towards deeper understanding of self. It allows us the chance to shake off inauthenticity and sit with what's been hidden underneath. Sometimes the biggest step forward in our shadow work is gaining the ability to be alone with ourselves. And for many, this can be challenging. The more we don't like ourselves, the harder it is to spend time alone without distractions.

A popular and sometimes contentious topic in our household is extroversion vs. introversion. Neither my wife nor I am particularly extroverted in the sense that we just love going to social events and being around people. And although my wife claims otherwise, neither of us are particularly introverted hermits, either.

The thing about introverts and extroverts is that the distinction (besides not being a particularly clinical or precise description of a person) is related to but different from a lot of other things. Sometimes people who seem like introverts actually crave connection but suffer from anxiety around social interactions. Some people who seem like extroverts don't really love being socially active but feel compelled to make and nurture all the connections they can to succeed at their goals. What looks like introversion could be depression and exhaustion. And what looks like extroversion can be a fear of being alone.

I've never had a particularly difficult time being alone. In fact, I would almost kill for solitude most of the time. I would much rather spend time in my head than spend time listening to everyone else. But I know that's not true for everyone. I've had quite a few friends over the years who were always in motion, always doing something, and rarely doing it alone. As a kid, they were the girls who hosted the sleepovers and led the activity on the playground. In college they were the ones always at parties, always in other people's dorm rooms, always headed off with a group of besties to get coffee or go shopping.

For a very long time, I envied those people. I wanted to be just like the girls who seemed socially successful and well-liked because it seemed like no matter what they did, others wanted to be around them. I felt rejected because very few people seemed at all interested in doing the things I wanted to do. It took me a very long time to realize how many of those social butterflies literally engineered their social lives, dragging people out with them all the time because they couldn't stand being alone. They weren't popular because others had made them popular. They sought out people who would be there for their non-stop social activity for the same reason some people end up in addiction and other forms of self-destruction: it numbs and drowns out the unpleasant reality lurking in their thoughts and feelings.

It's not always comfortable to listen to our own voice and sit with what it has to say. Shadow work isn't ever rainbows and puppies. But drowning out that voice is never a sustainable solution. Inauthenticity is a misguided form of self-defense. If we're not willing to sit with ourselves and really own our authentic inner voice, we will never be able to truly embrace our authenticity.

"Understanding myself allows me to understand others."

Our identity is so closely related to our personality that it's hard to talk about one without sometimes meaning the other. I've been talking about finding and getting to know our authentic identity, which ties into the unchanging roots of who we are. When a caterpillar turns into a butterfly, it's the same organism, even though almost everything about it has changed. We can alter our appearance all we want, but our DNA will still reveal who we are. And our spiritual identity is the same way. Our personality can change over time, but there are elements of our deep self that will remain constant.

But that's not the entirety of our identity. Those changeable things like our thoughts, feelings, and habits that make up our personality are arguably the biggest part of our identity and probably the most important. They are definitely most important when it comes to shadow work. Our shadow aspects are almost exclusively changeable bits.

Our personality is also distinguishable from our identity in that it has to do with how we convey our identity to other people. At some level, most of what we talk about when we talk about spirit and spirituality is communication in some form or another. Other people perceive our authentic identity through our inauthentic interactions the same way our first language comes through as an accent when we're speaking other languages.

When I was in college, I traveled to France as part of a study trip for a summer. I was a French minor, so I wasn't exactly fluent, but I could speak French well enough to function. We were assigned a book to read that outlined some of the major cultural differences that generally trip up Americans trying to get around in France, little things like the differences in how they interact with strangers in public and customs around things like shopping or asking for assistance. We were told about the big differences in how the French dressed in public; this was the late '90s, and they did have to specifically say things like "nobody wears biker shorts in public." Some of us tried very hard to fit in and not stick out like American tourists, but even when we thought we were blending in well, it was pretty easy for the locals to spot the differences. We felt pretty good if they guessed we were Canadian or even British.

That's how we try to bend or conceal our identity when we've got a lot of shadow aspects to deal with. On that trip we assumed that if French people discovered we were American, we'd have a much more difficult time navigating and enjoying our time there. Similarly, a lot of our shadow aspects come from assumptions we make about what will happen if we reveal our authentic selves, and the subsequent efforts to pass ourselves off as someone less objectionable. But ultimately, our personality is one of the most important things to embrace about ourselves.

Of course, most of us really only know how to define or describe our personality in relation to other people's personalities. When we talk about our personality, we pick out the ways we're different from other people and the ways we're the same. I honestly find it funny how many of us like to define ourselves by all the ways we're unique and different from other people, but at the same time struggle to embrace and accept our authentic selves because we're afraid of the ways we're unique and different from other people.

But there really isn't a better way of defining ourselves. Our personality communicates who we are to others, and all communication requires a common language foundation. I can say a lot of words to someone, but it doesn't guarantee that they understand anything. So to communicate our identity to someone else, we end up comparing and contrasting each other as a base code of personality communication. We watch and interact with other people and internally compare their behavior and way of being to everyone else we know. We put it into context and paint an internal picture of who this person is based on their personality.

Humanity has come up with all sorts of ways of defining personality on various scales. I imagine the longest-used language of describing a person's personality boiled down to cultural or racial patterns and early stereotypes. These days we have all sorts of personality assessments to use to communicate who we are, everything from Buzzfeed quizzes to astrological charts to the Myers-Briggs assessment. All those things categorize us by groups, place us alongside those we share traits with, and separate from those who are different. I believe this desire to group and compare is part of our core human nature. It's how we understand the world in general, and we do it because we find it useful. Knowing someone's personality gives us insight into their motivations, that insight makes them easier to predict, and being able to predict what others will do is an important survival instinct.

One of my siblings is an astrologer and numerologist, and their main fascination with those fields is how they help us get to know our strengths and weaknesses and how they fit together. The more information we gather on how we are alike and different from others around us, the more we start to understand how our deep self operates. Knowing more about us lets us predict our own self better, and when it comes to personal evolution, that kind of insight into self is priceless.

Step Three on our journey to spiritual authenticity is to describe ourselves as we are in the present moment as completely and in as much detail as we can.

The biggest rule about uncovering and acquainting ourselves with our personality is to remove all our internal judgment about it. Nothing about a personality is inherently good or inherently bad. It's a lot like extroversion and introversion, actually. My wife calls herself an introvert and complains about how the world considers extroverts good and introverts abnormal. But it's not supposed to be about which is better. They are two ends of a spectrum, both valued in the same in the grand scheme of existence (even if not in a particular society).

If we take a lot of personality tests or know a lot of detail about our astrological chart, we'll notice very quickly that these assessments don't quantify aspects as good or bad. Sometimes they deal in binaries like thinking/feeling or masculine/feminine, but they are just opposites, not values. The really important thing to note when it comes to these assessments is that when we get to reading the results, every aspect and every value on every scale has ways it can be positive and ways it can be negative.

There is nothing in a person's personality that is universally good or bad. As much as my wife has been made to feel otherwise, introversion isn't universally considered bad. The world needs introverts. The only reason there's so much pressure on people to be more outgoing is because most of us live in a very dense society where social interactions and relationships are key to survival. In places where a social life is hard to come by, the ability to enjoy our own company is incredibly valuable. There are situations where an extrovert must endure feelings of loneliness, boredom, or the discomfort of solitude to achieve something important. Likewise, there are times when an introvert must work past their shyness, anxiety, or overstimulation because of an important end goal. Understanding where our personality traits are advantageous, and where we might be challenged is important shadow work.

The next important step to revealing and embracing our authentic personality is to open ourselves to uncomfortable truths. Authenticity is radical self-honesty, and we'll only understand ourselves to the extent that we can be honest with ourselves.

Like millions and millions of others around the world, at one point in my life I got really into Harry Potter. One of the very first things anyone does first when they enter that fandom is to figure out what Hogwarts house they would be placed in. It's absolutely genius marketing because, really, humans cannot resist comparing themselves to everyone else and trying to categorize all of existence. For those who aren't familiar, in that particular fictional world, children are grouped into four "houses" at a magical boarding school, grouped by personality traits. Theoretically, each group would be equally desirable because these are children we're talking about, and it doesn't seem reasonable for a school to label 25% of 11-year-old children as evil before they've even finished their first meal in the dining hall. Even so, there's one house that the vast majority of the villains in the story belong to. The students in that house have their dormitory in the dungeons and even have a snake for a mascot. The heroes in the book mostly belong to another of the houses, the one whose rooms are in a tower and has a lion as a mascot. It's hard for most people not to categorize one as evil and one as good, regardless of how many

Slytherins do heroic things or how many Gryffindors betray the heroes along the way.

The amusing and important thing, though, is that not everyone has the same idea of good and evil. Lots of people are happy to identify with the wrongly villainized or to embrace the dark aesthetics, to dig beneath the surface trappings of evil and danger. Likewise, lots of people don't want to be lumped in with the privileged and praised in the favored, popular house because they know many heroic victories come at high cost to those who often pay the price and never see the accolades. Despite how clearly the story codes the groups as "good" and "bad," humanity as a whole doesn't honor those labels.

I will absolutely admit to taking the official assessment, ending up in Gryffindor, and immediately starting over with a different email to get the result I felt was more correct. But it's that kind of thing that also tells us a lot about who we are. Getting to the bottom of why we want and don't want things to be true about our personality is also important shadow work.

Ultimately, there is no one good or right way to assess and describe a person's personality. If there's one guiding principle to follow, though, it's that we are all very complex people and no one test or profile will paint a complete picture. It's not about getting a result; it's about the evaluation and understanding. We all change over time and personality isn't static. So whether we turn to

astrology and numerology or to psychological evaluation and personality profiling, the more information and descriptors we can use, the more complete and accurate our understanding of self is going to be. All of it has to be taken in context.

When I worked in management, the company I worked for gave all applicants a personality assessment. I hated that we did them because I knew that I had, at one point in my life, failed one of them and not gotten a job at a different company because of it. No one at that company had ever talked to me or made their own assessment of my potential; they'd just trusted this test to tell them who was a good hire and who wasn't. I always wondered how those tests worked and how I could fail at one company but pass at another.

As a manager, then, I got to participate in a "recalibration" of the test for the whole company because they'd started to see the test being less and less effective at predicting performance. The process showed exactly how the tests worked and what the results really meant. Essentially, the way the test was calibrated was that a large sample of employees was tested, and then their supervisors rated their real-world job performance. In other words, they profiled a bunch of employees and management told the system which of those people we regretted hiring and which ones we'd hire again. Those results were used to create a profile of what an ideal employee would be like.

I was floored, but suddenly a lot of things made sense. We weren't hiring the applicants statistically most likely to have the skills to do the job. We were hiring the applicants who were most like the employees that managers already liked. Once I understood that, I stopped using the test to help choose applicants, because those results had nothing to do with what I wanted for my staff. I knew a lot of other managers tended to promote and fire for reasons I didn't agree with, so why should I hire based on what they thought?

It's crucial that we think just as critically about the standards and scales we use to describe ourselves. A big deal has been made of how unscientific and meaningless personality assessments are, and I think it's good to acknowledge that. This isn't science we're dealing with, but it doesn't matter. These assessments give us a language to use to define and describe ourselves and the ways we change over time. They give us a starting point from which to build our self-image. And they help us begin to understand our strengths and challenges, so we can embrace and embody them.

Step Four
Expression

"What I have is a reflection of who I am. I cannot change one without changing the other."

Science doesn't just tell us that energy is never destroyed; it also tells us that energy can be converted into matter. Body is the physical, material form created from spirit, which is shaped by soul.

Of the three essences, body is the physical manifestation of the deep self.

Of course, we're dealing in spiritual terms, so this isn't our literal human bodies. Here's where it becomes really important to clearly define what we mean when we talk about spirituality. There's the physical aspect of deep self, which stems from stuff like genetics and our health history, and there's the physical aspect of spirit, which includes the things we consume to keep physically living, and so the physical manifestation of those things is what shapes our human bodies. That's not what we're talking about here, and I want to be really clear about that. If we don't make that distinction, it becomes very easy to latch on to really harmful ideas like blaming congenital health conditions on spiritual shortcomings or judging one's level of enlightenment or consciousness against how visibly "healthy" they appear to be.

What we're dealing with here is the spiritual aspect of deep self and the spiritual aspect of our material existence, so the physical body we're talking about includes the way we live and behave, the way we present ourselves, what we possess, and the things and people we surround ourselves with. It's about our physical way of being, our belongings, and our environment.

Yes, people are part of our material existence. In fact, in many ways they're the most important element in our physical environment. They are sources of spirit in ways that some other elements of our environment are not, but just like our belongings and the places we spend time, we can choose which ones to spend time with or listen to and how much we allow them to impact our lives. We choose who we listen to and how seriously we take what we hear from them.

We manifest what's in our soul by creating, building, and collecting stuff (and people). What's in our deep self shows up in our physical environment. We convert our beliefs into action and action into "stuff." It shows up in how we present ourselves to the world, how we dress and treat our bodies, and how we communicate and interact. Our deepest core values are reflected in how we treat our material possessions and the people around us and the value we place on them.

Body is the part of the triad that can be the most challenging to wrap our head around in a spiritual context because so much of modern spirituality strives or at least aspires to be pretty well disconnected from the physical. We largely consider spirituality to be internal and not involved with material things. We can't take it with us to an afterlife (according to modern traditions, at least – the ancient Egyptians might argue the point), so any spiritual paths focused on what happens after this life tend to frame physical reality as irrelevant at best and a dangerous, addictive distraction at worst. It's mundane rather than sacred, so paths built around ideas of transcendence and divine connection tend to encourage distance from the trappings that tie us to the material world. Nearly every spiritual tradition has something to say about how much or how little we're supposed to care about the kinds of material concerns non-believers might focus on.

This is especially true with things like money, which can somehow simultaneously be the root of all evil and a sign of great spiritual attainment within a single religious tradition, depending on who is doing the teaching. But it's also true in other ways. Being part of the pagan community, I know there are strong opinions about how modern humans have ruined nature and those ideas sometimes result in strong judgment against urban witches, those who embrace technology as part of their pagan practices, and anyone who buys supplies from mainstream retailers.

But as all alchemists know, nothing in all of existence is disconnected from material reality, not even within esoteric spirituality. Without exception, everything in existence consists of all three essences, so everything has a body. Besides, even if we tend to think of our physical reality as separate from our spirituality, if we draw up distinctions between the two realms and prioritize the spiritual over the material, our material environment still reflects our spirituality. We are physical beings in a physical universe, and we experience all of life in physical ways. Our thoughts and emotions are even real, observable electrical and chemical reactions in our brain tissue. Nothing is truly not physical, no matter how invisible or intangible it is to our senses.

And just like everything else in the universe, the physical form that our deep self manifests into through spirit is a part of our being, not just incidental to it. It's simply the external part of the more complex whole. Our deep self is entirely internal. We process spirit internally, even though it comes from external sources, but body is definitively external. It's what is created when we transform spirit and put it back into the larger spiritual context. It's what is created when we take in spirit and use it to grow and develop. Thoughts, ideas, and feelings may be internal and have no persistent form, but they become physical when they are expressed as sounds, words, symbols, and actions.

There are a lot of challenging aspects to the relationships we have with our own material existence. Everything we are, shadow self especially included, manifests and is reflected in the way we are and the way we live, so the things we hate most about our lives and ourselves are often tied right into those pieces we don't want to acknowledge or integrate. Our physical selves and lives are also what other people see and judge us by, so it's where we make all of our attempts to mask and cover up whatever parts of our authentic selves are most uncomfortable or vulnerable. Plus, our material existence also includes people and relationships, which adds a whole other layer of challenge to sorting out the dynamic between soul, spirit, and body.

That's why we shy away from a deep dive into the physical in most spiritual pursuits. It feels so much easier and so much more like enlightenment if we give ourselves permission to ignore the tough issues like what we acquire with our time, money, and energy, and what we surround ourselves with in our lives. I think we all instinctively know that if we start digging into our collection of "stuff" that we'll be thrown head first into some serious shadow work. But that's precisely why it's so important to include it in our spiritual exploration. When it comes to our spirituality, we actually do ourselves a disservice by trying to separate from and ignore the material and physical part of our lives. The things we have, the way we show up in the world, the relationships we're in, the way we use our resources, the environments we exist in – all of those things are both manifestations of who we are and influences on who we will become. There's no way to truly embrace our authenticity and support our evolution without embracing the ways our authentic self manifests and shows itself.

"I never see myself as others see me, I only see my reflection."

The single biggest obstacle in our mission to embracing our authenticity and letting it manifest in our physical environment is that we know other people expect our environment and our appearance to be a certain way. We can have our own private internal space for our authentic self, our authentic way of thinking, but the authentic manifestation of who we are isn't as easy to keep to ourselves. It's everything from what we have and what we do with what we have to how we present ourselves to others. And our religious or spiritual paths, whatever they've been, have inevitably included very specific judgments about what is acceptable and what is not.

Because of that, most of us are carrying around emotional baggage because we've been judged, criticized, or even punished or shunned for what we have or don't have and how we look or don't look. And nearly all of us have things we do or avoid doing because we associate certain ways of being with groups we don't want to associate ourselves with.

Even after I left Christianity, I still had Bibles in my library and a collection of cross necklaces in my jewelry box. Those things weren't me anymore, but there were all sorts of reasons why it took me a very long time to get rid of them. In a lot of ways, those things were anchors to a past version of me, but I didn't get rid of them because some were gifts from people in my life who I knew wouldn't be accepting of my authentic self. There were people I knew would notice a lack of Bibles on my shelves and ask questions. And, to be honest, there were remnants of my religious upbringing still lodged so deep in my psyche that it felt wrong to just throw away a Bible, even if my logical brain knew it was just paper and cardboard.

And it's not just what we keep; it's what we hide. Our authentic self wants to manifest itself in our material existence, and too many of us end up hiding important parts of ourselves to try to keep from being judged. We talked before about how religions and spiritual traditions form cultures to which we belong, and those cultures define themselves via physical manifestations, too. So if we have things that speak strongly to our deep self but don't fit within our cultural environment, we're going to either hide or deny them.

The issue of being "in the closet" is the obvious example here. But it's smaller things, too, like concealing our affinity for or curiosity about certain things that others might look down on.

It's logical to assume that it's the more orthodox, more dogmatic religions that are hardest to exist authentically within, and that if we're not following those types of paths or traditions, authenticity is less of a spiritual issue. But plenty of less-formally-restrictive paths also have a culture of narrow expectations. It doesn't matter what circle we run in. There are still assumptions about what we should or shouldn't be like.

I'm an urban witch. I'm happiest and most energized in a big city environment. I find nature to be beautiful, but I don't particularly enjoy being out in it. I'm not a fan of camping. I don't do well in sunlight. I hate being touched by bugs. But I find an amazing amount of beauty in the built environment. I love unique architecture and the diversity of expression and energy found in places with large populations. I love technology and cutting-edge ideas more than I'm drawn to the old ways.

That means I'm often the odd one out in witchy groups. And yes, there is judgment. I've been frequently cornered into conversations with other pagans who are convinced that if they take me to their favorite place, I'll fall in love with nature. I've been in many conversations about the presumed evils of modern technology and how "real" pagans and witches reject it to embrace nature and old-fashioned ways of living.

Of course, that's not everyone, and there are plenty of other urban witches out there like me. But my point is that it's not just strict Christian traditions that make their followers feel bad for not conforming to expectations. Every tradition has its share of pressure to conform.

No matter what any of the traditions we've been part of had to say about our authentic self or how we should express it, the core issue isn't how wrong they are. The core issue is the extent to which we've internalized those expectations. When we're participating in a tradition, the judgment comes from outside of us. But what we carry with us after we've parted ways with the tradition or when we're existing outside that circle becomes our own baggage. We learn to self-enforce and self-police. We hold ourselves to those standards before anyone else gets the chance to.

For instance, I go into pagan gatherings expecting to be the odd one out. I expect to not be fully embraced. As much as I embrace my authenticity and validate myself, I never expect others to affirm and embrace me. I've internalized the idea that being an urban-inclined, tech-dependent magical practitioner is unusual and generally looked down upon, and I often struggle not to act accordingly. I've had to work on overcoming reluctance to engage with other pagans because I instinctively expect to be treated as an outsider.

But the bottom line here is how this conformity affects our authenticity. Our physical environment and outward appearance aren't just manifestations of our authentic self; they're also part of what shapes our growth. The more we're surrounded by reminders of what we're "supposed" to be, the more we're feeding those ideas back to ourselves. The less supportive our environment is to our authenticity, the harder we make it to be ourselves. The less comfortable we are in our skin day to day, the less able we are to really embrace who we are.

As we've already talked about, religions are not generally supportive environments for authenticity by virtue of their structure and purpose. And while it's likely that we've all dealt with things we've been taught about who we should be and how we should think and feel, it's the stuff we still hear in our heads about what our lives and our identities should

look like to others that's both hardest to shake and most harmful to our growth.

"Home is where I need no disguise."

I've never been a tidy person. During my teenage years, my mother and I were constantly in conflict over the state of my bedroom and why I couldn't do simple things like put my shoes in the closet when I took them off or why I always had half-finished projects strewn about. I couldn't understand the point of putting away shoes that I would just be putting back on the next day or making a bed nobody would even see before I would be sleeping in it again. She was concerned about appearances and felt that if it looked like she couldn't keep house, it would reflect badly on her skills as a wife and mother. I, on the other hand, developed a significant amount of resentment over having my interests and projects considered less important than where my shoes were and if my bed was made.

Sometimes it's the little things in our manifested physical environment that reveal big things about our authentic selves.

The thing is, I've never gotten any less messy. It's not because I don't know how to clean or because I don't like being in a clean house; it's just that it's never going to be a high enough priority for me to spend time and effort on. Every moment I spend cleaning house feels like a sacrifice because that time is so valuable. I'd rather devote myself to creative and spiritual pursuits, to the search for amazing and enlightening experiences, and die with a messy house than spend all my time picking up after myself to satisfy other people.

Yes, there's judgment because of it.

Because I'm not a consistently neat person, though, I am very familiar with the phenomenon of hiding away the messes we don't want others to see so that we put our best foot forward. It's a good analogy for shadow work, but it's time to talk about how it's not even just a metaphor. Our environment literally reflects who we are and it's the first place our inauthenticities turn up.

My untidy house is where my authentic self feels most at ease. I don't worry about someone making me put away a project before it's done. I can collect all the weird books I want and use the fireplace for alchemical operations and not have to explain myself to anyone. I can (and do) fill the front yard with festive lawn flamingos during the holiday season simply because it amuses me. I can control who comes into my home and how much of it they get to see.

I think most of us want to live and spend time in places where we feel completely at home, completely free to be ourselves without worrying about what everyone thinks about us. We want to dress the way we want, eat what we want, surround ourselves with the belongings that we enjoy the most, collect stuff we like, entertain ourselves with the stuff we enjoy most, and not have to make ourselves uncomfortable for the benefit of anyone else. We want to be in control of who comes into our spaces and how much time they get to spend there.

Our physical, material reality is what we're most often referring to when we talk about things like "lifestyle." When we talk about the life we want to build for ourselves, we talk in terms of our material existence. Even if we're talking about what we do with our time and how we make a living, we're nearly always thinking about the experiential reality of it, not the philosophical.

So the key question here is this: Is the life we have the one we thought we wanted, and are either of those the life our authentic self truly needs? Are we pursuing a life we think will please or impress others, or are we building one that truly supports who we are?

This process is still about becoming self-aware, including becoming aware of how we feel moment to moment and situation to situation. We've all been places, done things, and been versions of ourselves that felt supremely right. Situations where we felt fully in control, fully realized, comfortable in our skin, comfortable in the space we were in. They may have been somewhat fleeting experiences depending on the path our life has taken, but we've all experienced a range of such situations.

And that means we also know what it feels like to feel unwelcome in our own life, restricted, othered, excluded, pushed into a mold we don't naturally fit into.

It's pretty common when we're younger to be told how we should be, to have our choices and self-expression questioned at every turn. Unfortunately, we tend to keep doing that to ourselves as we get older. We assess what the world seems to expect and want from us, and instead of letting that pressure just come from outside, we put that pressure on ourselves.

So in doing this shadow work, we're looking for the places in our environment that exert the most pressure on us and make us feel most uncomfortable. Does the portrait of our uber-religious great aunt look down on us from the wall as we go about our daily life, making us feel silently judged about our spiritual choices? Does the space we set aside for meditation but never use make us feel guilty for not upholding some kind of daily spiritual practice that never really felt authentic? How much of the way we fill our environment and present ourself to the world is left over from past versions of ourself?

I used to be a very sentimental person. I kept keepsakes of literally every little thing that happened in my life. The bottle cap from the first drink I consumed legally right after midnight on the day I turned 21 (it was a Zima, unfortunately). Wrappers from beverages I drank when I traveled in France in college. I bought souvenirs from every place I traveled. I kept gifts I was given even if I didn't like or use them, just because they came from people I cared about. I had tons of stuff. I held on to all of it because it was a tie to my past. It reminded me of people and experiences I wanted to remember and honor.

But then I had to move from one apartment to another, while living alone in Chicago without a vehicle and without family or friends around to help. And I was suddenly faced with this pile of trinkets, slips of paper, and nostalgic objects that I was going to have to literally drag from one place to another on a luggage cart because I could only afford a small moving truck long enough to get the big pieces of furniture moved.

Suddenly, nostalgia wasn't enough reason to hold on to a lot of it. I even had my family's holiday nutcracker set with a basket – it was so old I didn't ever remember us NOT having it full of walnuts at holiday time – and I ended up calling my parents and asking if it was so important that I should keep it. Lots of stuff ended up thrown away. After all, it only had worth to me, and suddenly I realized that my life was changing in ways that also changed the value I put on those items.

It's not that an inauthentic version of me collected all that stuff or that there was a sudden change; it just became clear at that point that it didn't make sense to keep attaching the same significance and value to those items as I had in the beginning. Plus, getting rid of some of that stuff helped facilitate a shift from living in a space that was filled with reminders of a previous phase of my life and into a space filled with more currently significant things. It opened up space in my life that I filled with stuff that was less nostalgic and more relevant to the moment I was in.

When we make big changes in our lives, or when our lives change in big ways around us, those changes tend to send ripples out across the various aspects of how we live. We rearrange our existence to

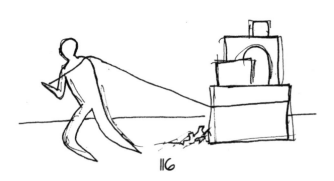

accommodate the change (or if we're being particularly resistant, we might tend to reinforce things to try and keep things from changing). A new relationship means making space for new activities, bringing new people into our social circle, and maybe eventually sharing a home. A new job comes with new clothes, a reorganized office space, and different meal routines. But when the change happens more slowly or in an area of life that doesn't require big accommodations, those ripples might not happen at all. The internal changes don't end up reflecting on the outside. We lose sight of the changes because they've been small and cumulative. It's not until something calls our attention to how far we've shifted that we start to realize how much baggage we're still dragging along.

And sometimes even when the change is big and sudden, we end up fortifying our physical existence to resist the ripple effects of irreversible changes. There may also be a bit of mourning going on when we leave behind parts of our spiritual past. Maybe we don't believe in the religion we grew up in, but there are lots of other aspects that came with it that are deeply meaningful to us. Maybe our grandmother's orthodox traditions aren't something we believe in, but we have deeply emotional memories of her teaching us the rituals that were part of that tradition. Or maybe we no longer celebrate the religious holidays we grew up with, but still love to attend the family gatherings anyway. So even if our authentic spiritual self isn't at all connected to those beliefs, the reluctance we may feel when it comes to letting go of the core tradition may really be an attachment to the memories and associations. The connection isn't to the old ways; it's to the people and relationships. And those things can absolutely be separated. We live in a postmodern world where everything can be broken into pieces and rearranged and compartmentalized at will. Is there a downside to that? Sure. But the advantage is that our history doesn't have to be an anchor. We can let things change and fade away from our lives and still hold on to the pieces that truly are important.

And that's the real kicker. These things can become anchors that hold us back from authenticity and growth, especially when they're ever-present in our life, seen and touched daily. Their constant presence reinforces, even if we don't mean for it to, the old thoughts and ideas and ways of being that we might think we've successfully left behind.

Our environments reflect back to us who we're trying to be, and the more inauthenticity we're surrounded with, the harder it is to really connect with and inhabit our authentic self.

"As within, so without."

One of the best ways to think about our material reality is in the anthropological sense. Material existence is one of the ways human evolution is measured, because without written language, all we have left to study from our ancient ancestors are their belongings, constructions, and human remains. We mark ages of human history by the materials of which they made the tools they used – stone, bronze, iron – because the course of human development and history has been shaped by the advancement of our technologies. Big inventions like writing or combustion engines or computing have had a huge impact on how we live, how we think, and how we interact. The advancement from one type of technology to the next is really the story of how each generation of humans built on what came before to become what we are today. And while I think we tend to read far too much meaning into ancient objects, we also definitely tend to undervalue our own modern belongings when it comes to meaning and significance in our lives.

That's not to say that every single thing we own is a reflection of some deep personal truth, but it's not exactly untrue, either. My wife has set up a few beloved action figures on a side table in our living room. They have a lovely little doll furniture set complete with a TV. It's silly and it's frivolous, but it's also adorable.

If humanity were to be largely wiped out at this moment and an alien archaeologist dug up our living room sometime in the future, the assumptions they'd make would probably be pretty far off the mark. She doesn't worship comic book characters, I promise. But when it comes to her own journey to embrace and connect to her deep self, they're most certainly a window into aspects of who she authentically is.

But there are also things in our home that are an indicator of not just who she is right now, but the changes she's undergone over the course of her personal evolution. There are lots of objects that mark prior phases of her life and various milestones reached over the years. And it's not just true of her, of course. Most of us surround ourselves (or want to surround ourselves) with things to remind us of our life journey. It all paints a bigger picture of growth and evolution and development over time.

All of this is true of our physical appearance, too. Our physical bodies aren't, themselves, manifestations of our spiritual self per se. Our subconscious minds may be capable of some remarkable things, but they can't override our DNA, protect us from aging or disease, or always heal us. But we are more than our bodies when it comes to expressing ourselves to others.

Going back to this idea of archaeologists and anthropologists trying to understand our ancient ancestors, the only way to even begin to piece together the identity of a set of remains from early human history is to look at the remains of what else they were buried with. The tools or other objects they had with them and what is left of their clothing and jewelry give clues to who they were. If all we're left with are bones, all of that information is gone as well. As limited as the insight may be, even just a few pieces of body decoration or a personal object or two are enough to give us a window into the identity and experience of someone who is separated from modern humanity by many thousands of years.

And we're no different. The way we choose to dress and groom ourselves, the objects we surround ourselves with, the places we frequent, even the people we choose to spend time with are a means of expressing ourselves to the people around us. We've all learned to read these things and make judgments about other people, even if those judgments aren't always very accurate. And because we've learned to visually read the material existence of other people and come to conclusions about who they are, we shape our own physical appearance and presentation based on the conclusions we hope others will draw about us.

When I was in college, a sorority sister of mine was assigned a sociology project about exploring social norms and taboos. She was supposed to intentionally challenge a norm and make note of strangers' reactions. Being the late 1990s, it wasn't an everyday occurrence to see people with wildly colored hair in the heart of the Midwest, especially multiple colors at once and especially in professional or conservative contexts. So she put temporary streaks of rainbow colors in her hair and went walking around the campus of a local Bible college.

She was quickly asked to leave because her presence was disruptive.

It seems so silly now, but while we all thought it was ridiculous that just having unusually colored hair would be enough to make a person unacceptable to the staff of this uptight religious school, we also made kind of a big deal about how crazy it was that she did that to her hair at all. We talked about it as a noteworthy memory for far longer than a bit of temporary hair color really warranted in hindsight. But we knew that, even just out and about in the world, lots of people would make assumptions and judgments about her that we knew would be wrong. We may have thought it was dumb, but we all knew that rainbow hair wasn't going to be seen as the mark of a very intelligent, very professional woman.

There are very few things in life we have a more complicated relationship with than our own bodies. There's a whole ton of expectations and external judgments placed on what we should look like and be able to do, and we internalize these things in a profoundly different way than most other external standards and opinions, probably because those things get tightly tied in with our fundamental identity.

Our physical existence is one of the most important bits of our entire spiritual life. It's where our inauthenticities manifest and become part of how others know us. It's easier in a lot of cases to do the internal work necessary to embrace authenticity than it is to express our authenticity in the face of all the judgements and pressure from others. We can change our minds and change our hearts, but when we change the way we show up in the world, others will notice.

But there's a direct connection between our shadow self and our material life. The things we're hiding in the "real world" have a lot to do with the shadow aspects we've buried in our deep selves. In fact, looking at the things we keep secret or concealed, whether out of shame or out of a desire for privacy, reveals quite a lot about who we are and what's important to us. The things we write only in a diary, our deepest thoughts and secrets, are a core part of who we are. But so are the objects we cram in the back of the closet out of fear that someone will discover we have them. The reactions we fear, the reasons we believe we shouldn't be seen with them are signs of our shadow self clashing with what people think we ought to be.

And it's not just the stuff we hide; sometimes it's the stuff we hide behind. The more insecure we feel about the judgments of others, the less confident we are in our authenticity, the more we might use our belongings and our physical expression to put distance between us and those whose attention we want to avoid. Rather than try to impress or fool them, we wall ourselves off and create barriers to any type of interaction or intimacy.

Like I mentioned before, I'm a notoriously messy person. At some points in my life, the places I lived were downright overwhelming to everyone but me. I've never quite been a hoarder, but some of my apartments wouldn't have looked entirely out of place on that kind of reality show. People in my past have offered all sorts of ideas for why I didn't keep a tidy house, usually centering around accusations of laziness or defiance. But the truth is that when my spaces were at their worst, especially to the point where they couldn't be cleaned up quickly enough to accommodate guests on short notice, the real issue was that I didn't want anyone in my space. I didn't want people coming in to see how I lived and make judgments about it even when the space was clean, so if it was messy I had a reason to keep everyone out. It might seem ironic to keep a messy home that people judge because I didn't want people to judge my home, but our shadow selves don't always express themselves in ways that make a lot of sense.

So what would we change about the way we look and the spaces we inhabit if we knew that nobody would judge us for our choices? If there was nobody in our life

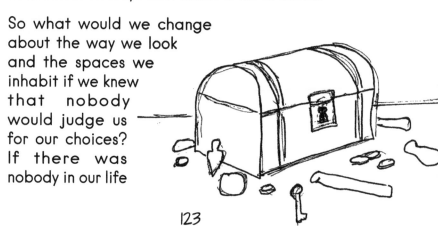

to render judgment based on how they interpret our appearance and lifestyle, would we feel relieved that we could relax and stop trying to impress or avoid people? Would we finally feel free to spread our wings and step into our full personality?

"I will shower myself with love and acceptance."

I'm not a big fan, personally, of the minimalist tidying trend for a lot of reasons. There's a pile of lovely cardboard boxes in my house that would universally be considered clutter but bring me a significant amount of joy because they're just so nice. I do think, though, that the idea of actually considering our physical possessions based on whether we feel connected to them is a powerful bit of shadow work. I imagine there are lots of people out there who start trying to go minimal and tidy their spaces and struggle to let go of things that they own because they feel obligated or expected to keep them.

The challenging nature of our relationships with the material is one of the reasons I didn't want to start this exploration with the physical and work back to the deep self. It's not just a difficult relationship; it's one that's not easy to understand at face value. It's almost impossible to figure out who we are just based on what we manifest. How do we know what's a mask and what's a manifestation of a repressed part of ourselves? What's just a remnant of an old version of ourselves, and what's an anchor to some hard-to-release baggage? Are we hiding parts of our lives from others because they stem from an unintegrated shadow aspect or because we're afraid of the larger response to our authenticity? It's too hard to know any of that without first having some insight into what lies at our core.

How many of us hang on to clothes even if we can't fit into them anymore or don't ever wear them, just out of hope that we'll get back to that size or out of the fear that we'll need them for a specific occasion? Maybe they were special-occasion things – wedding dresses, for example – and we hold on to them because they're tied to important memories we don't want to lose or because we hope what was important to us will be important to the next generation.

Whatever the reason we keep them, they're remnants of people we aren't anymore or only think we could or should be. And for whatever reason, most of are reluctant to admit even to ourselves that we're not the size we used to be, that our memories and hopes are bigger than a dress or an outfit. It takes more courage than seems logical if there's a lot of unresolved crap shoved into the literal dark corners of our lives. So much of what we surround ourselves with is rooted in aspects we struggle to release and move on from.

The result is that our environment reflects some blend of authentic and inauthentic. Separating the two is far too hard a task to undertake, especially while we're still in the process of doing shadow work. Our existing environment is full of things that are out of alignment with our deep self, and we can use elements of our material existence as a jumping off point for digging into the dark corners and unearthing our shadow aspects. But to get the full picture, it's important to also figure out what sort of environment feels authentic and safe to us. We may not be able to build it, but most of us have developed some ability to find it, at least from time to time.

Step Four is to find our safe and sacred spaces where we can explore and embody our authentic self.

What we can do to help cut through all the baggage and inauthenticity and get a sense of what sort of environment and expression is most authentic to us is seek out places where we feel the most comfortable, the most embraced, the most free to be authentic. Even if these places and circumstances are ones we don't share with others, they're important to have and to allow ourselves.

I know that the local pagan meetup I've been attending for well over a decade now is such a place for a lot of people in my area. This part of the country is not an easy place to be anything but Christian, and many local pagans have no other place where they can freely discuss and explore with other like-minded people and feel safe doing so. Some of the people who attend the meetup use an alias so their names can't be recognized on the RSVP list. But what matters most is that when they are there, they are free to be themselves in a way they aren't able to in other areas of their lives.

It doesn't matter if we can only indulge this freedom in secret. These are the places we feel safe and unburdened. They're our comfort zones.

Now, a lot of people think of the comfort zone as a place we're not supposed to be. Every life coach and motivational speaker who has ever tried to guide people to attain goals and develop as individuals has taught some philosophy about how we have to leave our comfort zone to grow. I'm not going to say it isn't true. Growth and evolution don't happen if we exist only in the places where we feel protected and comfortable. Our safe spaces can very easily become isolation bubbles. But the problem isn't within the comfort zone itself. The problem is how afraid we can be of stepping outside it.

We'll deal with the fear later, though. For now, we're not yet seeking growth and evolution. We're just trying to understand who we are.

We're all likely to have different comfort zones and safe spaces for different areas of our lives and different aspects of ourselves. For many of us, one of those places will be our home. That depends a lot on who else we share the space with and how much control we exert over the space, but at the very least our home tends to be where we can physically take off our masks and other inauthentic forms of self-expression. When I've been at a social event or at a friend's house, I'm going to be mindful of the expectations of others. I'm going to probably be dressed a certain way, and I'll be more careful about everything I do. Even if I'm with someone who is a good friend and with whom I'm very comfortable, there's going to be a difference in how I behave.

But once I'm home, the shoes come off. The pants may even come off. I won't be as careful about my manners or how tidy I am. Home is a zone free of most of the expectations I feel when I'm outside of it. My favorite thing is going somewhere on vacation to enjoy the freedom of not worrying about all the little day-to-day obligations that exist at home. And then, after a few days of being mindful of our volume so we don't disturb others in the hotel or making sure we properly clean up after ourselves in whatever vacation rental we're using, I love the freedom of going home to where I can make whatever mess I want.

The one thing all of my comfort zone spaces have in common is that they are places where I can be alone. There was even a time in my life when every night and morning I walked between my two jobs because it gave me time alone with my music and my thoughts. Otherwise, at the time, nearly my entire day was spent at work, dealing with coworkers and customers.

But not everyone is going to find the most comfort in solitude or at home. For some of us, our comfort zone isn't a specific place as much as a specific group of people. Maybe it's when we're doing a particular activity. It can even just be a particular set of circumstances. The important thing is to find those environments in our life and accept what that reflects about who we are and what we need. If we don't know the freedom of embodying and expressing our authenticity even in small doses and limited circumstances, we're going to have a really hard time nurturing and embracing ourselves.

Plus, it's just not healthy to not have any opportunity to set down the stress of inauthenticity and be free of that burden for a while.

In a lot of ways, finding these comfort zone spaces is a crucial form of self-care. Inauthenticity takes a huge toll on a person, and creating a life that's supportive of our authenticity is the best gift we can give ourselves, even if we have to give it to ourselves in small doses. This is an excellent place to start building personal rituals for ourselves as we move into the next phase of our journey.

Embrace the concept of retreat. This doesn't necessarily mean running off to an expensive luxury enclave for mud baths and healing rituals. It doesn't necessarily mean physically going anywhere at all. A true retreat simply means cutting ourselves loose from the obligations, expectations, and pressures that push us toward inauthenticity and spending quality time in a place that allows us to be authentic on our own terms. It's not just an escape, it's an opportunity to fully experience and explore a state of authentic freedom so we know what we're trying to nurture as we move forward.

Part III

Spiritual Detox

Pause and Reflect

——— ——— ———

If you think about retreating and taking time for solitude and self-reflection, do you like the idea or dread it and why?

What things do you keep secret from people around you?

What do you love most about yourself, and do you show that aspect of yourself to others?

——— ——— ———

Step Five
Emergence

"To reach my personal truth, I must dig it up from beneath all of my lies."

Growing up in a religious household, I didn't really understand what life looked like without religion. The entire premise of Christianity is that God is necessary in our lives, full stop. In fact, of all the ways my life took a different path than my parents envisioned and hoped for me, their finding out that I was an atheist was the one that got the worst reaction.

Yes, even worse than when I came out as gay.

But at the beginning of my spiritual journey, it never occurred to me that a life without formal spirituality was possible. In fact, we were specifically taught that people who lived without faith were miserable, awful people who were probably one bad day from committing mass murder. Not in those exact words, of course, but that was the idea. People who didn't believe in god would be left without a sense of morality, so what would keep them from just doing what they wanted without concern for anyone else? What would keep their relationships and families together? How would they cope with life?

It wasn't until I first got to know people who didn't have those beliefs ruling their lives and then actually experienced a life without a religious or spiritual framework that I really gave much thought to the why of it all. What is it that makes us spiritual beings? Is it an inherent part of human nature or is it something we've learned?

Eventually that became the driving question at the center of my spiritual life. I started studying ancient human history to search for insight into the origins of human spirituality, and that project became the core focus of my practice. And the weird thing is that I did find what I was looking for, just in a different way than I expected.

It doesn't take a whole lot of picking apart the

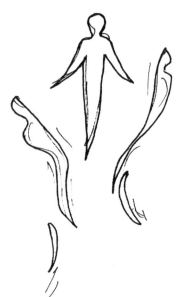

anthropological research and archaeological evidence of early humans to realize that we really don't (and can't, honestly) know what our most ancient ancestors believed. Despite everything I'd ever been taught in both religious and academic contexts, ideas like paleolithic animism are only guesses. And an awful lot of what we thought we knew is based on some really biased and skewed "research" done by missionaries and colonizers.

Stripping away all the guesses and only looking at what we know from evidence and data painted a much different picture of early human spirituality. Putting aside any conclusions based on unsubstantiated assumptions and really questioning why early researchers had come to those conclusions changed my entire understanding of humanity's place in the universe. We know for sure that our ancient ancestors were artistic, creative, and expressive, but that doesn't mean they worshipped anything.

In fact, we know that they were good at figuring out how the world around them functioned. Humans created trade routes, cultivated plants, domesticated animals, manufactured special pigments, engineered monumental constructions, and even did dental work before they invented written language. Most of the guesses we've made about the origins of human spiritual thought don't even make sense when we look at the evidence and consider what their relationship with their environment actually looked like. When you realize how masterful ancient humanity was at using, shaping, and thriving in their environment, it's hard to reconcile the idea that they were so baffled and threatened by the quirks of nature that they imagined everything to be inhabited by terrifying spirits.

The earliest researchers had a distinct worldview shaped by colonialism and Christianity, which has left a distinct fingerprint on a lot of the things we've been taught about early human society.

Looking at the history of spirituality through a more critical lens made me realize that maybe the best way to figure out my own spiritual motivations was to do the same with my own understanding of myself. Strip away the things I'd thought had to be true, the old beliefs I hadn't let go of, the baggage I still dragged around left over from the various paths I'd followed in the past, and what would be left?

It seems obvious to me now, but if we strip away all the old baggage and programming and habits left from the spiritual and religious traditions and practices we've had before, all the "shoulds" we've lived by but don't believe in, what's left is our authentic self.

When we take away the spiritual crutches, we find abilities we might not have known we had. If we step back from the rules we've been taught and the assumptions about how the world works, we're left with our own perspective on life and our own deeper values and priorities and boundaries.

Our authentic self is what remains after we take away all the "stuff" we're carrying around that doesn't belong to us.

"I am the lessons I have learned, but I am not defined by the experiences that taught them."

Despite all the ways that our spiritual history can be the source of our inauthenticities and the reasons we suppress parts of our authentic selves, there are definitely elements of that history that have shaped our deep selves in positive ways. We are the result of our experiences, and there few, if any, experiences that are entirely detrimental.

Within every religious tradition there is an element of spirituality. If we ever identified strongly with a religion or tradition, that strong connection stemmed from that spiritual element. But spirituality and religion are wrapped so tightly together in our culture that most of us aren't used to separating them, and even those of us who do consider ourselves more spiritual than religious still have a hard time shaking off the religious aspects of spiritual life.

Religion usually leads to some kind of idealized end goal. Religion is a group thing, so even if we fit comfortably within the ideal mold set by that religion's beliefs, it's a one-size-fits-all situation.

Spirituality is the opposite. Spirituality is NOT one-size-fits-all. It's tied in with our deep self. Our spiritual lives don't serve the same purpose as our religious lives. They're tied together, absolutely, but even within a religious framework, our spirituality is individual and serves a different purpose than religion. Within a more formal tradition, the spiritual elements are about bridging the gap between our authentic self and the self the tradition needs us to be in order to fit the expectations of the religion.

Religion is for a group. Spirituality is for us as an individual.

Or, more simply, spirituality within a religion includes all the mental and emotional work necessary to align with the teachings of the religion. It's the process of learning lessons from the experience of participating in that religion.

When I was in high school, I spent a lot of time in the city library. It was across the street from school and so every afternoon that's where I waited for my parents to get off work and come pick me up in the years before I could drive. And I spent that time reading all kinds of books, chasing all sorts of curiosities. I didn't usually check any books out; I just read them while I was at the library, so nobody was there to question what I was looking up.

I read a lot of books and researched a lot of topics that my parents would have thrown a fit about.

That's where I first read about things like psychic abilities and metaphysics. I read romance novels. I studied ancient civilizations and things my parents didn't think existed, like dinosaurs. But I was also still very much an honest believer in what the church taught. I shared my parents' faith. So the whole time I was reading books that I knew were outside of what was acceptable in our household, I was also devoting thought to reconciling my curiosity with what I was being taught. Ultimately I decided that curiosity is a good thing and that there's no harm in challenging one's beliefs. To the contrary, if we never challenge our beliefs, how can we be sure that our beliefs sit on a strong foundation of truth?

I actually find it pretty amusing that my parents to this day are so bewildered by the fact that I've wandered so far from the spiritual beliefs they tried to instill in me, and that I'm not the only kid in the family to do so. For all their concern about the influences of worldly society, all their objections to ideas like evolution or global warming, and their distrust of the "liberal elite," they still encouraged us to excel at school and go to college. I understood being a good student as a way of being obedient and "acceptable." It wasn't just a matter of getting scholarships and a good job; being a good student was part of our moral code. My parents' belief runs so deep that I'm sure they were confident that the more we learned, the more we would agree with their worldview, or at the very least that our religious upbringing would ensure that we would reject ideas that stood in opposition to doctrine.

What really happened was that we all learned to do research and think for ourselves, which predictably led me and most of my siblings in our own spiritual directions. I don't say that to make the point that my religious upbringing was wrong. But curiosity is authentic, and when we give ourselves freedom to explore, our spiritual selves will find their own way forward.

The thing is, I know a lot of people would argue that I learned to embrace curiosity and to value learning and knowledge despite what I was taught rather than because of it, but I can honestly say that my religious upbringing helped me establish those personal values. I didn't realize it at the time, and I know my parents didn't realize that they were reinforcing this lesson, but being encouraged to value knowledge and academic success linked the ideas of faith and logic together in my own spiritual way of thinking. My love of learning was a product of my spirituality as it existed within the religious context as I understood it, even if that wasn't the intended outcome.

139

To be authentically ourselves, we have to develop a strong sense of self. And religion often takes that away from us or supersedes it. But even within those contexts, we end up discovering and developing parts of our deep self. The important thing is to separate those parts of ourselves from the religious context that either shaped or revealed them.

We can thank our past religious experiences for teaching us things about ourselves, retain the lessons, and release the religious ties. The knowledge we gain about ourselves is always ours no matter what the circumstances are that revealed that knowledge. The ways we develop and grow as people are inherently part of us, and those who were part of the experiences that enabled that growth don't get to claim credit.

So it's important to reframe those lessons we still embrace and cherish from our time in paths we no longer follow and not allow them to become anchors to old sources of inauthenticity. They are now natural parts of who we are, and even though it's good to be aware of how we became the people we are today, it's even more important to see ourselves as whole beings whose parts and pieces are all inherently, authentically us.

"Letting go makes me appreciate what remains."

Years ago, an article about fasting caught my

attention. I'd been doing this paganism thing for a while and for all the secret circle casting I'd been doing in the middle of the night, I hadn't really experienced the kind of energetic awakening I imagined might be possible. I'd been doing some research on techniques and rituals that were supposed to cause shifts in personal energy, alignment of spirit, that sort of thing, and some marketing algorithm led me to the idea of fasting.

I was skeptical but also curious, so after some research, I decided I wanted to find out for myself how it would make me feel. Not only was it supposed to be a profound experience, it was also something of a challenge. And for someone who really, really loves food, I was interested to see if I could actually do it. So after some preparation I did my first liquid fast, weaning myself from my regular diet to fresh fruits and veggies, then to juices and broths, and finally to water only for about a day. Then back through all the stages until I was eating regular food again.

Now, I don't know that I experienced anything truly profound, life-altering, or mind-expanding, but it was much less difficult than I expected it to be. It was, certainly, an exercise in cleaning out my system, and once I adjusted to the liquid-only portion of the experience I did attain a state of mental clarity where the distraction of hunger fell away, and I could focus on all the things that didn't have to do with food. Plus, it reset my energies and gave me time and space to rethink my relationship with food.

For the most part since then, I've not done fasting as a way of trying to induce a spiritual experience as much as to reset my energies on a more physical level, but I have continued to do them when I feel they might be beneficial. I do them as a way of clearing my system when I feel weighed down and tired. The idea isn't to lose weight or permanently change how I eat; I don't come back from a fast craving kale and hating ice cream. The whole idea is to step back from whatever habits I've been engaging in and wipe the slate clean, so when I do go back to eating regular food I'm more mindful about it.

In a physical sense, the food we eat is a form of spirit. It's energy locked up in matter that we consume to fuel the activity of our bodies. So food often makes a really great metaphor for spirit in more metaphysical and philosophical contexts. And I don't know of anyone who doesn't need to spiritually clean the slate now and then; we just don't generally have a method for doing it. It's not part of our spiritual repertoire. In fact, most formal spiritual or religious paths actively discourage any reduction in engagement with rituals and practices.

When I was a kid, when people didn't show up to church, my dad would go check on them. And sure, that sounds totally reasonable if we think of church as a strongly connected community of people who all know and care about each other, but it's a little different when we look at religion as one of those things people often engage in out of obligation. I'm glad when I left the church it was because I moved nine hours away so I didn't have a preacher show up at my door investigating my attendance issues.

In the pursuit of spiritual authenticity, it's in our best interest to step back and take an opportunity to breathe and reset now and then. Spirit is like food in that we can absolutely consume junk rather than the nutritious stuff, and after a while all that junk will make us feel bad.

Our authentic self is what's left after we clear away all the "stuff" and "junk" in our spiritual system. So yes, I'm recommending a spiritual fast or detox in the interest of spiritual authenticity.

This is something I did pretty much by accident in my own spiritual life.

When I first started exploring neopaganism and magical practices, I dove straight in. I did a lot of experimenting and exploratory workings early on. I switched directly from lazy Catholicism to active magical practice without any pause in between. But as time went on and I started getting a bit paralyzed by the task of sorting through countless schools of thought on the nature of magic and the purpose of spirituality, I started spending less and less time engaged in my practice.

It wasn't purposeful, and I think it would have been infinitely more valuable an experience if it had been, but for probably a whole year I just stopped doing spiritual things. I missed sabbats and moon phases, my journals and grimoires sat untouched, my crystals gathered dust, and I stopped going to any events I wasn't obligated to be at. The only thing I kept doing was going to the meetup gatherings, but even then I wasn't actively participating as much as just doing what I had to do to keep the group running.

I started a blog and planned writing projects, but a lot of my active practice ground to a halt because I was too engaged in trying to philosophize my way to uncovering the meaning of life and the secrets of existence. Eventually I found myself missing even non-pagan holidays, which is crazy because I love holidays.

One day I realized that I had essentially disconnected from spirituality altogether. I wrote about it in an academic sense, but I didn't actively engage with it anymore. I realized this because there were parts of my life that were stagnating and suffering because of the loss of that spiritual connection. I'd stopped marking the solstices and equinoxes with self-care days, and that meant I didn't do enough self-care. I stopped experimenting and reflecting on my magical endeavors, and that meant I wasn't really trying to manifest change in my life.

After all that time spent looking for the reason why I even needed spirituality as someone who didn't believe in a deity anymore, it turned out that there were benefits of an active spiritual life that I didn't get from other activities. It was something of an Overview Effect moment. It took separating and distancing myself from my spiritual practice (even if it was unintentional) to find the perspective that I'd been looking for and see its value.

On the other hand, once I started reviving the important elements of my spiritual life I also learned that there wasn't anything particularly necessary about having a consistent daily routine practice. My life isn't measurably better, spiritually or otherwise, if I hold myself to a strict regimen. That was an important thing to reinforce in my own thinking because it had been a source of guilt and shame in the past.

A spiritual detox can help reframe our relationship to spirituality. The point is to really get to know our authentic deep self so when it's time to build up an authentic spiritual life, we know what our authentic self needs to grow and thrive. All we have to do is stop engaging in spiritual activities for a while, as broadly as we can reasonably define that in our life. Maybe it's mostly religious activities if that's where we're at in our spiritual path, but it can also include anything that performs a similar function for us. We need to take time out from all the engagements and obligations in our life that impact the way we see ourselves and the world so that we're able to focus on integrating and embracing our shadow self without the voices of others getting in the way, even our most trusted sources of guidance. This isn't just not consuming the stuff we think might be contributing to our inauthenticities; it's cutting our consumption of all of it.

If we only gave up the stuff we thought was bad for us, it would just be a diet. But this is a detox. It all goes.

We can't forget that our spirituality also happens outside of the parts of our life that feel spiritual. We need to take a step away from all the thought- or emotion-altering messages and opinions we can for a while. Turn off the news and the reality TV and skip the social engagements with people who bring the drama and gossip. Fill those spaces with neutral input instead, things which make us think and reflect inwardly, more than respond and react to what's around us.

What we've been trying to do with all this shadow work is to find all the pieces of our authentic self and assemble them into a whole inner person. But no matter how complete and whole our integrated deep self is, our spiritual existence as it stands won't meet all the needs of our authentic soul. After all, the self that chose the spiritual path we're on was the self we were before all this shadow work, and that self had no interest in the work we're doing now so we can't really trust its choices.

The baggage we carry from our past doesn't just include the messages we've gotten from our past spiritual history. It also includes the reasons we've been told we need religion and spirituality in the first place. We all have preconceived ideas about the place spirituality is supposed to occupy in our lives, the purpose it's supposed to fill, and what our place in it should look like.

We've learned to turn to various spiritual and religious entities and practices for comfort and solutions during hard times in exactly the same way we've learned to eat carbs when we're upset. We've internalized messages about what to expect from life, why there's so much suffering in the world, and whether there's a purpose to the hardships we face.

The hardest part of a fast from food is that we're forced to confront our cravings and consumption habits without the things we usually use to satisfy those appetites. If I have an upsetting day during a detox, I can't turn to ice cream for comfort. I have to find some other way of dealing with those feelings.

That's the purpose of a spiritual detox. It brings us face to face with the ways we've used and potentially abused spiritual and religious practices as a way to avoid facing our emotions, dealing with our challenges, or pushing our limits.

Sometimes when things happen that take away things we previously thought were important, we come to realize we can live without them after all. Doing a short spiritual detox is not the same as a natural disaster wiping away our belongings and making us start over. But it is true that when we lose access to the things we're accustomed to having, it forces us to either adjust to the absence or replace what's missing. Of course, when we have things taken from us and face a sense of sudden absence, we are much more likely to get reactionary. Grief and loss make us less likely to adjust. That's the difference between starvation and fasting. When it's done to us, we focus on what's been lost. When we choose it, we focus on adjusting to the change and valuing what remains.

The thing about a detox is that we don't just stop consuming. It's not starvation. The idea is to carefully choose what we consume and when. It's a process of gradually eliminating all but what we absolutely require.

During the middle portion of the juice-fast process, I only consume water, clear juices, and clear broths. But leading up to and away from that middle part I drink other kinds of juices, sometimes even smoothies. I'll eat raw fruits or vegetables as I'm transitioning away from and back to solid food, sometimes things like yogurt that are soft but not really liquid.

And the same kind of thing goes here, too. There are types of spirit that are benign and gentle and supportive of the process rather than something we have to "digest." Stuff that impacts our emotional energetic state but doesn't add more stuff for us to process, like certain types of music or the comfort of a natural and mindless activity.

The first things to get rid of are opinions and big viewpoints, the stuff that gets us engaging with how other people see the world and especially how other people want us to see the world. This is a huge chunk of what we most often consume, especially in a spiritual sense. The more of this we take in, the less our spiritual life is ours, and the less authentic it becomes because it's really just an amalgam of outside influences.

But even once we have a spirituality that we consider ours, we're still left with the stuff that we consume because it reinforces the stuff we want to be and think. It's all those indirect sources of other worldviews. It's what we take in because of all the baggage we still carry in the form of the things we think we "should" value or are afraid to not hold as important. Other people we want to please and emulate and impress, standards we choose to try and live up to not because that's our authentic desire but because that's what we've internalized over time. So that's where the fasting process starts. When we disconnect from all the rest of the sources of spirit that usually play a role in our lives, the stuff we turn to because we think it's good for us, we're left to confront the core ideas. We're left to either confront the feelings that come up because we're not actively reinforcing and moving towards our ambitions and changing into who we want to be, or we're left to realize that our drive to do and be those things isn't as strong as we thought.

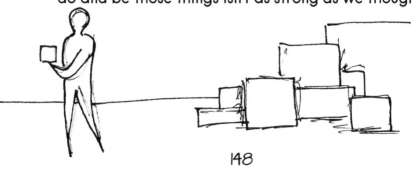

After we strip that away, we're left with the messages we take in that tell us whether we're doing well or not, whether we're making other people happy. It's spirit in the form of judgment and encouragement. And yes, we need to disengage for a while from the encouragement part, too, to find out what happens when we're left to make our own self-judgments and encourage ourselves. It will bring up all kinds of stuff about our relationship with the approval and disapproval of others that will have to be flushed out.

Next is the stuff that we think is just entertainment, just for enjoyment, totally inconsequential forms of spirit. Fun time we spend with our spiritual community just for kicks. That stuff may not seem very relevant, but it can be a very effective distraction and escape mechanism, so we can avoid dealing with other things. Not to mention that our spiritual community is a source of spirit because that's what the community culture is defined by.

Then we're down to the more benign forms of spirit. Functional spirit. The things we need to learn and engage in for the day-to-day responsibilities of our lives to be met. Spending time looking up how to repair the leaking kitchen faucet. The conversations and interactions we have to have for work. The decisions we have to make with our spouses and families.

And when we're alone with our thoughts and our ideas and our own way of being, the processing of what's in there does lend itself well to creativity and art, both as intake and output. The spirit we put out into the world during this time doesn't need to be in the form of opinions and assertions for the reasons I already stated. But it is important to purge and to get some of the stuff out of us. That output doesn't have to be received by anyone, at least not in the short term. This is the best time in the world to be artistically creative, whether we think we're artistic or not. The stuff we bring up and want to get rid of in the detox has to go somewhere. We can't continue to bottle it up.

And as those who have ever done a physical fast or a detox know, during the process our body does purge stuff. It's not pleasant. And the stuff we create may not be pleasant, either. It may not be anything we want to keep. It's perfectly fine to throw away or ritually destroy the results of this creative purge, but it's important to let it out.

"My dreams don't have to make sense to anyone but me."

This entire spiritual endeavor of mine, the journey that has led to me to dig into the nature of spirituality, all started with wondering why humans seemed to need religion or religion-like things so much. Part of the answer to that is that, as restrictive and prescriptive as religion can be, having someone tell us what we should be saves us from having to figure out who we are. For some of us (or maybe all of us to varying degrees), it's a relief to think we are shaped, directed, and guided by something or someone who knows and understands more than we do. Otherwise we're entirely responsible for figuring it out ourselves, and that can be more responsibility than we want to accept.

So when we take a step back from traditional religion

and spirituality, we're likely to find there are aspects of ourselves that we've always defined externally through those ideas and cultures more than through our individual understanding. Specifically, a lot of us turn to spiritual philosophies and ideas to help define the purpose of our existence, the core of our identity. The idea that humans in general and ourselves as individuals were placed on the planet to accomplish a larger purpose is so pervasive that very few people question it. And I think a lot of us are comforted by this idea that we have been assigned a reason to be here, a purpose to find and fulfill in life, because it means we're important to a higher power in some way. I suspect that we like this idea so much mostly because it lessens our sense that our life lacks direction. Without a preset answer, we struggle to pin down a sense of self and purpose. We feel inconsequential or powerless in the world.

As kids, we're all asked over and over again what we want to be when we grow up. I thought I had my life figured out at the age of 13. I knew that I really loved art and writing. I wanted to be an artist more than anything, but what I heard from the adults around me was that artists didn't make a sustainable living, so if I didn't want to be sad and destitute all the time, I needed a "real job." I also knew I was good at math and science, but the idea of working in an office or a lab all the time sounded awful to teenage me. And I hands down did not want to be a teacher under any circumstances whatsoever. So in a stroke of what I still think is pretty impressive logic for a 13-year-old, I decided that the perfect solution was to become an architect. It would combine art and math and physics, and I'd get to go to building sites and not just be cooped up in an office all day.

So I poured myself into that dream. I took drafting in high school and worked to get scholarships to the architecture school I wanted to go to. I graduated with my Bachelor of Architecture, cum laude, and moved to Chicago to work in a firm.

And that's how I discovered that it's a dumb idea to expect teenagers (or even adults, really) to know what they want to do with the rest of their lives.

I had no idea at 13 what my life would be like, what the world and the field of architecture would be like, or how I would change over time. That last one is the biggest key, of course. I wasn't the same person at 23 as I was at 13, and the things that were important to me had changed because of all the things that had happened over the ten intervening years. My life experience and all the spiritual flow I'd been subject to all that time had reshaped my deep self and shaped my growth.

That's how life works, right?

I left architecture behind after three years because I realized it wasn't the career path I wanted anymore. It wasn't the life I wanted to live. It didn't fit my feeling of purpose, and by that I don't mean purpose given to me by anyone or anything else; I just mean my own sense of place in the world. My priorities had shifted and I was a different person with different desires. My beliefs about what life is about and what makes it worthwhile had changed.

We explored, already, the idea that our choices and actions reveal our beliefs. And while beliefs aren't the core of our spirituality the way we have probably learned in the past, they drive us to do what we do and make the decisions we make. Beliefs don't mean anything at all if they don't drive action, but when they do drive action, they help define and express our authentic identity. It helps us pinpoint our purpose.

Purpose is part of authenticity because it's tied to our individuality. If we were just like everyone else and our motivations were just like everyone else's, our authentic selves would all look alike. Our purpose would be defined at species level. But here we are, individuals in a sea of humanity that thrives on endless individuation. Each of us is unique, each of us forges our own path, and each of us is driven to follow a different purpose. That purpose isn't assigned to us; we find it. We all find it in different ways, and that's valid, too.

What is important, though, is that this process of finding our purpose is really about emergence. Discovering, integrating, and embracing our authentic selves is one thing, but to truly live and grow authentically we have to be that authentic self out in the world. We have to fully embody our identity and not just keep it to ourselves, hidden away in the dark. That's what we've done to our shadow aspects for so long, and it should be obvious now where that gets us.

Fully embodying our authentic identity means living our purpose. It means shaking off all the things that stand between our deep self and the world, all the masks and crutches and things we've let the world impose on us, and learn what it feels like to expose our uniqueness to those around us. Left without the guiding expectations of others to give us a mission to accomplish or an ideal to chase, we have to choose our own goals and dreams.

In some ways, this might sound like coming out to the world as ourselves, but this is more like the much earlier process of exploring and understanding ourselves in context. Here's some insight into personal discovery from a queer woman who has done her share of coming out: The exploration and contextual understanding of self has to happen before the coming-out bit. There might have been a moment when I first realized I felt attraction towards someone who wasn't a straight, cisgender dude, but that wasn't the moment I fully understood myself as a queer woman. I had to figure out how that changed the way I thought of myself, how that changed the choices I made in my life. Only after all that was I ready to embrace myself and embody my full identity out in the world. And the coming out big came even later.

In this journey we're taking together, we've done the spiritual self-discovery thing already, and now we're stepping into this new understanding of who we are and figuring out what it's like to live honestly and how  that changes the dynamic of our lives.

The more inauthentically we've been living, the more clear the rules of how we are supposed to act and live have probably been in our heads. It can be so simple to take a culturally accepted standard for living and try to map ourselves to it because then we don't have to question what is and isn't okay or what reactions we can expect from people as we go through our days. It's an exploration not just of ourselves but of our relationship with the world around us when we begin to emerge in authenticity. We go into this exploration still burdened by all the messages we've internalized over the years about how our authentic selves aren't acceptable, so we begin under an expectation of rejection and judgment.

We have to train ourselves to keep a proper perspective on the rejection and judgment of our authentic selves, to recognize that the voices of dissent and opposition aren't the only voices to hear, and that they don't change who we are. No amount of disapproval changes the nature of who we are, and the process of emergence is all about embracing and accepting our nature and prioritizing it over the opinions of others.

Stripping away all the things we've used to define ourselves in the past, especially in a spiritual sense, leaves us with our own current definition of self. Once we really step into our authenticity and act on our deep motivational beliefs rather than whatever has driven our inauthenticities in the past, we begin putting down deeper roots and really feeding our soul so it can emerge and bloom.

"I am called to align my actions with my purpose."

When we release the expectations of others, we have to step into that void and set our own expectations for ourselves or we'll soon find some other set of external ideas in that space. Someone has to hold the reins in our lives as we move forward, and it's crucial to the pursuit of authenticity for that someone to be us.

Step Five on our journey is to begin a spiritual detox.

The ultimate goal of this spiritual fast is to settle into a life free from the spiritual crutches we've relied on in the past. In a fast from food, the point is to reach a stage where we feel good without consuming food, where our energy is high, and we feel like we've detoxed and wiped the slate clean. The point is to get to a state where we can enjoy the feeling of being lighter and cleaner the way we usually enjoy the feeling of eating food.

In this detox, there will be a point where we find a sense of freedom and greater control over what happens in our day-to-day lives. There will be a stage where we find a lightness because we let go of the burdens we didn't realize we were carrying (and a few that we actually were aware of). We will end up feeling like we've got a clean slate.

When we've reached that state of feeling comfortable, light, and free without our masks, crutches, and other inauthenticities, we will have successfully developed a strong sense of self, but that sense of self will only really persist for as long as we retain control of our path going forward. As soon as we revert to giving ourselves over to the expectations and demands of others, we begin to lose ourselves again.

That doesn't mean we never again do what others think is good for us. We can absolutely agree with those around us and still be authentic. Contrary to what we may have thought as pre-teens, pushing all the boundaries and breaking all the rules doesn't make us unique or individual. It just makes us reactionary and difficult. In fact, constantly doing the opposite of what we feel expected to do is still living according to those expectations. The only way to be authentic and to be true to our sense of self is to have a deep understanding of our own guiding values.

This detox gives us an opportunity to settle into a sense of personal values and ethics aside from those provided by whatever has guided us before. That doesn't necessarily mean that there's any difference between what we've been taught and what we authentically feel is our own personal code and system. They may be one and the same. But there's a difference between holding beliefs because we've been taught they're right and holding beliefs because they resonate deeply within us. There's a difference between making a choice based on what it says to other people about us and making a choice based on what we know to be true about ourselves.

To nurture and support the full expression of our authentic sense of self, we have to find our personal North Star in terms of our values and ethics. The things we value most as individuals become the standards, behaviors, and guiding principles as we live by our values. Everyone has different guiding values, so an important thing about this process is letting go of our need to impose our own guiding values on others. We've just discovered how deeply the expectations and values of others have impacted our spiritual growth and development. Let's not do that to anyone else.

Along the process of finding and getting to know our deep self, there has undoubtedly been some shifting of viewpoints and solidifying of what's deeply important to us. These new priorities and guiding values could have to do with culture, family, ideas, personal challenges, even personal likes and dislikes. But all those shifts will have shifted the foundations of our spiritual understanding and worldview. Even if we end up with a life that looks, on the surface, much as it did before we started our shadow work, the underpinnings and connections to that life on a spiritual level will end up deeper and more aligned with our authenticity. And it makes all the difference in the world to engage in spiritual activities for authentic reasons, even if the activities themselves aren't different.

The spiritual detox process should reveal a lot of these core values by illuminating patterns and getting us to ask ourselves questions about our motivations. In giving up some habits and activities and forcing ourselves to assess whether those things were necessary, whether we could fill those voids with other more authentic things, and why they were or were not important, we should be able to reveal quite a lot about what drives us.

Let's start with the motivations and values that stem from our own personal histories. There are things that become important to us because of what we've gone through in our lives and the experiences we've had, from the deepest traumas to the warmest good memories. Maybe one of our deep beliefs is that the forms of help and support we've gotten from people in our life is something we think should be paid forward. Or maybe we went through something difficult, and it's important to us to make sure others don't have to endure like we did. Maybe it's really important to share knowledge and teach others what we know because that's what we value most from our past. Maybe extreme independence is a deep self value because something in our life taught us that it's crucial to be self-sufficient.

This is another point in the process where it's important not to attach judgments to motivations. Our values are our values. We can change them, but not simply by changing our minds or making ourselves feel bad for them. We have to accept them and embrace them now so that we can transform and release them later if necessary. We can't release what we don't recognize as belonging to us.

The next layer of soul or deep self beliefs to explore are the ones connected to culture and family. We know there are aspects of spiritual and cultural tradition that we have held on to in the past because of the collective values of the people who form our most important communities. There are things that have been part of our life because of an expectation of participation. There are things that have been part of our life because that was the dominant belief in our social environment, and maybe we weren't even aware of other possibilities until much later in life. There are things that have been part of our spiritual life because they felt important to our culture, our origins, or the context from which we came, and even if the actual beliefs didn't run very deep for us, the reverence for our origins did, and it can feel almost impossible to separate the two.

This is where we differentiate things like obligations from priorities, relationships from identities, cultural truths from universal truths. We all have beliefs that lead to deeper core values, and we all have connections that shape our actions superficially but don't actually constitute a root-deep relationship.

For instance, there are obligations I feel towards various people in my life because of practical considerations, a general concern for holding up my end of agreements or maintaining beneficial relationships. Being cordial with someone we don't like because their spouse is a dear friend, and we don't want to cause trouble is very different than reaching out to someone because our deep beliefs call us to connect with them. If there are things we feel we owe to those who share our family identity or cultural roots, the reason we hold those ideas is because of some core value. Perhaps we find it important to preserve cultural traditions because so much has been lost over the long history of cultural suppression by colonizers. Maybe our personal values enshrine the importance of keeping close ties with our families.

There are no right answers here. Our values and how we define them are never universal. Despite what we've potentially been taught, if we gather together the people whose experiences closely mirror ours, it will always be a minority. There are no universal or widely held beliefs to follow.

We always have to figure ours out for ourselves.

This is important because we're back to the issue of our spiritual life needing to be rooted in our personal authentic self and not in what others expect of us, even if there's a point where those things overlap. It's all about being brutally honest with ourselves about the why because at some level we have to bring our core values into action. To be truly authentic, we must live our values in our everyday life. The things we believe often paint us a picture of how the world should be, at least our small part of it. There's something in those motivating beliefs about how to make things better, and if our spiritual lives don't involve us acting on those visions, then what good are our core beliefs? What do they even mean?

So what stands in the way of us acting on and working towards those things we're called to do by our core values?

One of the things I realized that my core beliefs called me to do was to work towards social justice causes, especially during the times when those issues were at the forefront of larger cultural concerns. And while not everyone who undertakes the same activities for the same causes does so out of spiritual reasons, it's that kind of embodiment of core priorities that both has the deepest impact and is the purest manifestation of those beliefs. But I also know that acting on that call to change the world wasn't always something I felt able to do or comfortable with. For a very long time, I felt like there was a great risk to me doing so, and even though I recognized my agency in the situation, I didn't feel empowered to change anything. I didn't feel empowered to push back against the limits I felt.

Of course, not all the things our core values call us to do are difficult or require us to work on our sense of empowerment. They can take all kinds of forms. It can look like focused devotion to family. It can look like a dedication to self-development and discipline. It can manifest in support of the activities of others. It can be as simple as focusing on spending more time with friends and family.

What is important in the short term is choosing to regularly engage in values-based activities, to express those things we believe by choosing to devote time, energy, and resources to what those beliefs enshrine as most important. This may be a huge shift from what our lives looked like before, but the change doesn't have to be drastic and all-encompassing. We don't have to spend every waking moment and every bit of energy devoted to changing the world. It's not all or nothing.

One of the biggest criticisms that gets leveled at publicly religious people is a disconnect between their actions and their faith, and I can't think of any bigger indicator of a disconnect between authentic self and professed belief. Frankly, what we do is a bigger indicator of our authentic beliefs than anything we claim out loud. So if we look at what our beliefs ask us to do, the role they ask us to play, and we find it hard to even consider manifesting them in action, either the core beliefs we're dealing with aren't truly our authentic beliefs or our authentic beliefs include some contradictory ideas about our own abilities and the value of our actions.

For instance, if our core beliefs mean it's vital for humans to help those less fortunate, yet we have a hard time actually committing ourselves to contributing or volunteering to do so, then it's time to figure out why. Do we have a hard time getting past the feeling that those less fortunate aren't doing enough to help themselves? In that case, there are some core beliefs about human value that we haven't fully come to terms with. Or if we have a hard time feeling that our contributions are worthwhile, there's probably some deep belief about our own ability to change the way things are, maybe even about the ability of humans in general to change reality.

But when it comes down to it, usually the things that stand in the way of us living out our values come down not to our very core beliefs but our more superficial issues. We don't have to be heroes about this stuff. We don't have to be perfect. In a lot of cases, it just means being more mindful about the stuff we already do. But I do think most of us would benefit from spending some dedicated time on the stuff rooted deeply in our core values. Picking one thing to do for ourselves, for our loved ones, or for the community based on our core values and doing it in a dedicated spiritual manner is a good way to start building an intentional, authentic life.

Step Six
Agency

"I am more than a transmitter. I am an innovator."

One theory about the origins of humanity says that what separates humans from the rest of the animal kingdom is that we have the unique ability to build on the developments that came before. It's called Cumulative Cultural Evolution.

Other animals, especially primates, learn from each other much like we do. Young animals learn skills from their parents, and lots of primates have the ability to watch others doing something and pick up knowledge that way. And each generation passes those skills on to the next. This is different from the instinctual, genetic method by which a lot of other organisms learn various behaviors. Humans and primates don't come into the world with all the skills and bits of knowledge they need to survive. Those things have to be learned, which means they have to be taught.

It's not just primates, either. I've seen enough adorable videos on the internet of kittens mimicking their mothers to know that lots of animal babies learn the basic skills they need for survival by watching and imitating.

Humans, though, are different. Part of that difference is that we have spoken and written language, so we can convey ideas across space and time without having to sit down next to someone and show them what we know. Part of it is also that we can easily transmit not just facts and skills, but ideas and philosophical musings and our deepest feelings and desires.

But the biggest difference is that we learn things from each other, and then we gather all that knowledge and combine it to form new stuff that we then teach to others. That's why our technology has continued to advance from stone tools to metallurgy to creating writing systems and building machines and so on. Each generation doesn't just learn what the previous one taught it. Each generation takes what it's given and makes more out of it. We innovate rather than simply imitate.

The weird thing, though, is that when it comes to our spirituality, a lot of traditions and philosophies keep us stuck very firmly in the imitation mode rather than the innovation mode. We take in spiritual knowledge, but very few of us do a lot of spiritual thinking outside of the box that already exists. We share spiritual ideas as if they are history rather than philosophy, something to be preserved rather than something to be explored.

I thought about this a lot as I began studying alchemy. This may come as a surprise, but alchemy isn't just a historic hobby pursued by weird old guys hanging out centuries ago in crazy dungeon labs full of toxic stuff, trying to make gold and achieve immortality. It's still alive and well as a modern pursuit and a lot more philosophical than most people expect. Modern alchemy is a lot less cooking strange substances in dark cellars and a lot more talking about the finer points of home distillation with people on the internet.

What drew me to alchemy is that it's not about learning a specific truth; it's about the exploratory work. It's a discipline, not a doctrine. It's not a religion; it's just a field of study. My authentic self loves few things more than learning interesting things and spending time crafting and creating, so alchemy really flipped all my switches.

As I began my studies, though, what I was most struck by was the cumulative evolution of the field itself. Key figures in history have brought forth revolutionary and original ideas to push the work forward, often creating completely new takes on the core ideas. That's one of the key differences between a religion and a field of study: Religion purports to confer absolute truth and resists change, but a field of study is ever-changing because there's always more to discover.

But clearly not everyone studying alchemy saw it the same way. When I sought out other alchemists on the internet, the weirdest thing to me was the way some of them cling to old ideas like sacred tradition and look down on the ways new alchemists have incorporated modern spiritual philosophies. It struck me as exactly the opposite of what alchemy is about. Did all the notable alchemists of the past turn their nose up at the "new" ideas that we now consider "old"? Clearly not, or we wouldn't know about them now. They wouldn't have been published and discussed and circulated.

Especially in a discipline centered around experimentation, the idea that we should just keep repeating what our forefathers did is absurd.

Humans are spiritual beings, and that means our brains work at a higher level. We have that cumulative cultural evolution thing going for us precisely because we have the ability to look at all the bits of knowledge, thought, and inspiration around us and build new things out of them. It's like buying LEGO® kits designed with instructions for building whatever is shown on the package. Even if we follow the directions the first time, most people eventually dump the pieces into one big collection and build whatever they want with them.

So why don't we do that in our spiritual lives?

If there's one thing I've found sorely lacking in spirituality it's space for our own thoughts and ideas. One of the most harmful spiritual or religious bits of baggage that we drag around with us, the one that holds us back the most, is the idea that we are unqualified or somehow going against truth to think for ourselves spiritually.

Authenticity isn't just a lack of agency in our spirituality. It's not just about not making our own choices in our spiritual life, because the ability to choose doesn't mean much if our choices are limited by someone else. Truly creating an authentic spiritual life means tossing out the limits and rules and exploring the spiritual dynamic in our own deep self, the ideas that resonate with our deep self and the way we create our own ideas from them.

When I was in high school, one of my art classes included a section on ceramics. We were taught how to work with the clay, all the things we could and could not do if we didn't want our pieces to have air bubbles and explode in the kiln. One of the things we were warned against was slamming the clay down on the table as we were kneading it. We were told again and again that doing so would introduce bubbles, and we'd end up with ruined pieces.

And then we watched a video about a ceramics artist who made really cool sculptures, and in the footage of her at work in her studio there were repeated shots of her throwing lumps of clay at a table with great force, specifically to achieve a certain texture.

I have a feeling the teacher hadn't watched the video before she showed it to us.

Of course, we all latched on to the discrepancy, and she offered some theories for why that artist could make it work. The force was probably so great that it pushed out the air bubbles, and we couldn't throw it that hard in the classroom. And we didn't know how many pieces of hers exploded in the kiln.

That whole thing stuck with me, though. Did anyone tell that artist not to throw her clay down like that? Or did she just do it because no one had ever told her she couldn't? Did my teacher just tell us that because she tried it and had something explode when it was fired, so instead of figuring out how to prevent disaster she assumed it was a sign she'd done something wrong? If she was sharing a lesson she had learned from experience, there was still a chance it had nothing to do with the way the clay had been handled and was just an unpredictable accident.

What would that artist's career have been like if she hadn't tried throwing her clay like that, if she hadn't broken this "rule" that we'd been taught was so important to follow?

It's just like the spiritual rules we've learned to follow, especially the ones that discourage us from actively participating in shaping the flow of spirit in our own lives. How much of our inauthenticity comes from following these arbitrary rules?

Well, most of it, to be frank.

The stuff that ends up being our shadow aspects all comes from being told what we're not supposed to think, say, feel, believe, like, or question. Just like our authentic souls are what's left when we toss out the spiritual baggage we've been toting around with us, our authentic spiritual dynamic is what's left when we toss out all the limits that make us silence our own voice.

"There is nothing in my own mind or soul I need to be protected from."

I think any of us who have grown up in a family who actually practiced and cared about religion have the residual voice in our heads that speaks up when we do things that were once against the rules. This is particularly true when it comes to the rules we used to have to follow about what is acceptable to say, learn, read, think, etc.

The easiest way to twist someone's sense of self is to demonize and undermine their relationship with their own thoughts and feelings. I really don't think it's the point of religion overall to do that to us, but it's pretty obvious that religions and cultural traditions are entirely group-focused rather than centered on the individual. Cultural identity is great if it leaves room for individuality and authenticity, but that's not usually true of any group that wields a great deal of power in a society. Once we prioritize being part of a group and define what it means to belong, people who feel they fall outside those standards will feel a great deal of pressure, not just to conform but to agree and defend. If the group is the priority, individuality that undermines the group identity can easily be perceived as a threat.

We've all been part of a group where we were on the fringes. For me, it's being the urban atheist alchemist in the pagan bunch. The good thing is that the pagan community doesn't have much they agree on beyond not being part of mainstream organized religion and maybe a few other extremely broad commonalities. But the more power a group has to set its expectations and hold people to them, the more spiritually damaging it is to the individual.

The point here isn't to focus on the harm that might have been done by whatever religions we were part of in the past. We all know that plenty of religious traditions make a practice of coercing people to do and pretend to be things they are not until they're very literally damaged by the experience, and even worse punish them for what they think and feel. Most of us have lived through it to some level, which explains how some of our inauthenticities have come to be, but doesn't tell us what to do about them.

The important thing to do is to recognize that we still carry bits of those experiences with us and to see the impact of those remnants. We may still feel either irrational guilt or irrational excitement over breaking rules we no longer consciously adhere to. We may

have anxiety over the kinds of thoughts and feelings we have but can't control. We might be consumed with the desire to flaunt the things we weren't able to say or talk about just to feel the power of being able to do so.

There are a lot of things I've done over

the years that don't meet the standards of my very religious family of origin, but what surprises some people is that I can confidently say my parents are more disappointed and upset over my atheism than my queerness. Belief is more important than anything else in the culture I was raised in. Being gay is bad, but the problem wasn't really the being; it was the acting on it. But atheism is unforgivable because unlike pretending to be straight, pretending to believe isn't ever good enough.

I'm really surprised that my parents were so encouraging of our education. Ideas were dangerous to faith, and faith was everything. It mattered what kind of things we listened to and read and watched because the most dangerous things in terms of the state of our souls were ideas that would lead us away from the things we were supposed to believe.

Trying to narrow down a story that best illustrates the ways our particular brand of Christianity restricted free thought and drew hard boundaries around certain types and sources of thought and information is actually pretty hard. There's the time I chose to do a report on a book about people with psychic and telekinetic abilities, and when my mom found the book in my room, I had to lie and tell her the teacher assigned that specific book in order to keep from getting in trouble. Or the shocked reaction from finding nude figure drawings in my portfolio from my college drawing class. Or the time I read Silent Spring for a science project and got lectured on how environmentalism went against God, and the teacher shouldn't be allowed to teach such things.

All that stuff is more than censorship and being too

173

conservative. It's really about limiting certain types and sources of spirit. It's about only allowing and welcoming the sources of information and thought that reinforce the chosen version of truth. The fact that I was okay drawing naked people, fascinated by the possibility of psychic ability, or open to science even if it contradicted the Biblical narrative was evidence that I was vulnerable to being led astray, so in the minds of my parents I needed to be protected from those influences.

The single most defiant thing I ever did was to break all those boundaries and study the things I wanted to, explore fascinating ideas, and embrace the experiences that I felt drawn to out of curiosity. But that definitely doesn't mean that there wasn't the voice in the back of my head piping up to remind me that I was doing something some people thought was wrong.

I absolutely still felt a weird pang of something akin to guilt the first time I picked up a book on witchcraft.

I also know that I've always been defiant like that, picking out books from the library on topics I knew weren't "acceptable" and bringing them home anyway, or taking classes to explore the things I wanted to explore rather than following all the rules.

But not everyone feels comfortable pushing those boundaries, even once we've left behind the spiritual authorities that put the boundaries in place. We have an innate sense of self-protection and self-preservation that naturally wants to keep us from the threat of consequences, and it takes a long time to learn that those consequences aren't anything to fear anymore.

The thing is, though, to allow our authentic self to emerge from beneath the rubble and baggage left from our religious path, we have to clear away those things that hold us back. That definitely includes those boundaries and rules about what is okay to think, consume, and explore and what's not okay. It means not just giving ourselves permission to break those rules but making a deliberate choice to break them. Every one of those rules and boundaries is really a restraint on our authentic connection to spirit. Certainly not all information or ideas are beneficial, factual, or even worth engaging with, but those limits are not for anyone else to place on us. They're ours to choose for ourselves.

It means learning to ignore the voice that tells us we're doing something wrong when we're thinking for ourselves, following our curiosity, or having experiences that we weren't previously allowed to have. And it comes down to learning to trust our own judgment as much as or more than we used to trust religious and spiritual authorities on matters of what is spiritually good for us and what is not.

"My truth is mine alone."

So while we're giving things up for this whole spiritual detox, one thing we need to flush out of our systems is this idea that our own spiritual worldview has anything at all to do with what everyone else thinks. And I don't mean that the opinions of other people about our spiritual ideas should be ignored and we should push those ideas out on everyone anyway. I actually mean that our spiritual ideas aren't meant for anyone else.

Spirituality isn't about truth.

It may feel weird to question that. Why would we willingly believe things that aren't true? But the obvious elephant in the room is that not everything we all believe can possibly be objectively true because every one of our truths contradicts someone else's truth. We all embrace certain things as truth that cannot be proven, things we consider truth but that are not fact and therefore are open to being questioned by others. And then there's the immeasurable amount of knowledge, facts, and understanding that we simply don't possess as a species.

So as much as we may like to think that our spiritual beliefs are rooted in some level of truth, what does truth even mean?

There's a difference between fact and truth. There's a difference between what my life experience shows me to be true and what your life experience shows you to be true. There are small truths that point to certain logical conclusions, but those conclusions are completely transformed when our perspective opens to reveal a much larger, broader truth.

Truth changes based on context. Truth changes based on our level of knowledge. Truth changes based on perspective. Truth is an interpretation of fact. It's a conclusion, shaped by perspective, following some personal sense of logic, jumping off from what is perceived to be fact. There are different types of truth because there are different interpretations based on different perspectives rooted in selective sets of facts. Truth is far more fluid and far less real than we like to think it is, which I know is triggering for people. "Truth isn't real" sounds like an argument that invalidates belief in general. But our need to justify our spiritual beliefs as truth actually undermines our relationship to our beliefs. I know that might sound illogical, but we usually only have two kinds of approaches to spirituality: Either it's about a truth we possess that needs to be shared with others or it's about seeking a truth that others can share with us. Either way, it becomes a matter of suppressing our own experience and perspective (or ignoring the experiences and perspectives of others), so that the dissonance can be ignored.

Dissonance should never be ignored. It's the incubator of personal growth.

It's important to acknowledge and work with the doubts, questions, and contradictions we encounter in our thoughts, beliefs, and feelings. It's important to question and examine the things we hold as fact, truth, or even just personal conviction so we understand where these things come from and what they're based on. Especially in our modern, diverse, connected world, we'd have to work very, very hard to avoid encountering ideas that contradict our worldview. Not to mention the internal contradictions already in our heads that no amount of escapist solitude will get rid of.

My big internal contradiction for many years was my spiritual path itself. My beliefs were a strange enigma to many, and I wasn't always able to explain them. Being an atheist who believes in magic is one of those oddball things that tends to throw people for a loop, where on the one hand, there's this question of how in the world someone who doesn't believe in a supernatural being is going to believe in supernatural powers, and on the other hand, there's the question of how someone who practices magic can do so while rejecting a lot of the underpinning beliefs about how magic works. I struggled internally for a really long time to reconcile it all for myself. I do believe in science, that everything in the universe is subject to the laws of science, but I also believe that we don't understand the laws of science as well as we like to think we do. And a belief in magic doesn't necessitate a belief in powers that exist outside of science in a larger sense, even if it does mean belief in a phenomenon without any reasonable explanation for its existence. It was important to me for a long time to find a nice little pocket of possibility alongside some more factual, logical sense of universal truth in which to nestle that belief.

So that's the first and biggest kind of truth: universal truth, which ideally would be based on logically sound, universally accepted facts from an elevated perspective rather than our own. But that's not something that's within our grasp. This goes straight back to that bit about us just not understanding as much of reality as we like to think we do.

But we don't have an abundance of that kind of factual knowledge, and our perspective is much narrower than necessary for this kind of higher-level logic, so the bottom line is that universal truth is just simply not something we can possess. Even if we consider truths being somehow given to us by something or someone higher, that would be a truth based on the perspective of whatever or whoever that is, and the validity of that is subject to our perception... It's a bit of a house of cards.

Sure, it's totally worthwhile to include in our spiritual practices some amount of effort towards advancing our understanding, moving us closer to universal truth, but on an individual level we functionally undermine our spiritual pursuits by focusing on truth. Everything we understand comes from our unique perspective and therefore isn't universal. We may share some of that unique perspective with a larger group, which means some of what we've believed to be universal truth is really cultural truth. The facts and interpretations at work come from some kind of group authority, longstanding tradition, or even official dogma. Cultural truth represents a shared perspective and it exists because of a group agreement about what is important fact and what is important perspective. Those priorities are taught, shared, and passed on, even if in an informal way. But no one group represents all of humanity, much less all of existence. Cultural truth isn't universal truth.

While we're detoxing, even our cultural truths need to go because the only thing that's really important is personal truth, which rests more than anything on what our unique experience teaches us individually about the nature of reality. Our experiences shape our perspective, shape our perception of what is fact, and therefore result in truths we build that are individual to us.

It's so easy to get caught up in this debate and conflict over whether our individual experiences can be objective or definitive in a factual sense, but the conclusion isn't helpful or relevant to our spirituality. If we've experienced something that has been profound to us, that shows us what seems to be the factual nature of reality, but that experience is profoundly different from someone else's, both people's experiences are actually a type of truth: They both experienced what they experienced, and it's one hundred percent certain that we all have contradictory experiences within the same overall reality. Pitting one against the other is never going to lead to a resolution, much less enlightenment, no matter how much we want our own personal truth to be accepted as universal truth. It just isn't.

And this is where we get in trouble mistaking our truth as fact. I know I'm not alone in having had these discussions with people where my own experience and understanding is different from theirs, and it leads to us both trying to defend our truth against each other.

If I had a nickel, right?

For me, it usually comes down to other people experiencing a connection with a deity, with ancestor spirits, with the spirit world in general. People seem to have this need to convince me to not only internalize their experiences as my own without having experienced them for myself, but also to then draw the same conclusions from them, to adopt and validate their truth.

What if, instead of needing our personal or cultural truth to be universal truth, instead of treating those disconnects as a call to establish a collective truth, we simply embrace the personal and non-factual nature of truth? That means we understand that our own experiences don't define everyone else's lives, and it also means that the truths others try to sell to us are not definitive. What would it feel like if we were all able to share our truth without anyone feeling threatened or contradicted by someone else's truth? Of course, we can't just snap our fingers and make other people stop trying to push their truth on us, but we can work on our own reactions to the personal truths of other people. and we can refrain from trying to convert people to our own truths.

Remember the Overview Effect? At some distance from our immediate life experiences a larger context exists that includes and encompasses all of our truths and reveals them to be details that have very little impact in the larger picture. It means that in a cosmic sense, our personal truths are inconsequential. Pushing our own truth on others is pointless and counterproductive, both to them and to us. But that personal truth is relevant to us because it helps define who we are. It is a manifestation of our spiritual existence. It's inconsequential to others but our personal truths have a huge impact on and are shaped by the flow of spirit in our lives.

The foundations of our spirituality are really simple and basic. It's all about our relationship to our world as we experience it. Spirituality is like feeding our deep self, and most of what we feed it is external ideas, information, and opinions. Everything from the media we consume to the conversations we have with friends and family, the fiction we love to read because it's escapist or the news channels we watch because they reinforce our worldview and get us all riled up on adrenaline – all of it gets fed straight into our deep selves to be digested. Some of it we consume in large quantities because we're never quite satisfied with how much we have. Some of it we consume in secret and in shame. Some of it we consume around others because we want to be seen consuming the "right" forms of spirit.

The stuff we give attention to and choose to consume has a huge role in shaping our spirituality and, in turn, changing our deep selves. If we're not mindful about it, those changes might not be ones we want to make. And since this whole process is about being more authentic, getting more in touch with our authentic deep selves, it's time to turn our attention away from all the external stuff for a while no matter how much we enjoy it and turn that attention toward our inner selves.

Attention is energy, and that means it's spirit, too.

The thing about a detox is that we have to stop the input so we can process and filter the stuff that's already inside us. All of our own experiences and our worldview have to sometimes be processed in something of a closed environment. Just like when we fast and our body starts processing and fueling itself with what's already stored in our fat cells and such, if we cut off our intake of opinions, ideas, and judgments, we have no choice but to start leaning on our own unique understanding to drive us forward. That's where we discover our personal truth.

It means making decisions based on what we've experienced to be true and what we already know without trying to measure against some external standard. And yes, that means turning off the voice in our head that tells us what we're "supposed" to believe and think and leaning instead on our own thoughts and beliefs.

But the point of all this isn't to ignore everyone and everything and just stick by our own opinions. That sounds like fun, but that's not growth. The point is to shut off the intake, so we can assess what's going on without it. It means actually investigating what's already in our deep self, what our inner voice is already saying, and actually examining the ideas that come up. We have to block out the noise around us so we can listen to ourselves, not because our own thoughts are better or more right, but because that's the only way to be sure about what we're hearing.

We can't believe everything we think any more than we can believe everything we hear.

When it comes to authenticity, we learn more from paying attention to our own feelings, reactions, and opinions than we do when we prioritize other people's input. This experience of sitting in silence with our own inner monologues and our own memories puts the focus squarely on who we are and who we have been rather than on who we think we want to be.

Mentally disengaging from the information and energy coming at us from outside isn't a tenable long-term way of life any more than living without food is, but it's a good skill to have in the toolbox to use as needed. It gives us spiritual space to get in touch with ourselves and assess what we need to heal, grow, and evolve. There is healing in silence. Integration happens in silence. So it's imperative to turn off the flow of spirit often enough to support our spiritual health.

And then when it comes to actually nurturing our growth and expanding in our authenticity, we have to be able to turn that flow of spirit back on. But not just any form of spirit, either. Anyone who's done a cleanse or a fast knows that if we don't gradually transition from our usual diet to our fasting regimen and back again, our body will have some unpleasant things to say. And the diet we do transition back to after a fast can't be exactly the same as what we ate beforehand without some discomfort in the short term. The whole point of a fast or a cleanse is to reset and readjust our relationship with the food we consume. So this time we take to focus inward away from the flow of spirit is an opportunity to think about what we do and don't want to let back in later. Not every source of information nurtures the authentic person we want to be.

Part III: Spiritual Detox

"I can trust myself with my freedom."

My family never had a lot of money, and as a kid that wasn't something I understood as deeply as I maybe could have. I didn't ever have the kind of allowance that gave me a real chance to explore the dynamics of money. All I knew was there were lots of things I wanted but couldn't afford. I never really knew how much money my parents made or how much the bills were, so I had no context for understanding why wanting a dollar to buy a soda from a vending machine was too much to ask. It seemed like such a small expenditure in the grand scheme of things.

When I went to college, I suddenly found myself with my own money, living away from home, no bills to speak of, and nobody to tell me how to make my own financial decisions. It was almost unlimited freedom compared to how I had grown up. I could buy all the soda I wanted.

I gained 40 pounds my freshman year.

I'd never had to say no to salespeople before, and now I could spend my money on dumb stuff if I wanted to. I'd never experienced buyer's remorse. I didn't know how to handle credit. I bought so many CDs from Columbia House that I had to take them all out of their cases and store them in binders, so that it wasn't obvious when I went home how many I had. In fact, there were so many I built a wall of decorative folding screens using the empty cases.

It took a very long time and a lot of negative experiences (including a bankruptcy at the age of 24) for my financial sense to get any better. To this day, I sometimes struggle to completely trust myself to be responsible with money, no matter how long it's been since I last paid a bill late or overdrew my account. I'm far too familiar with how thrilling it is to have complete freedom and to use that freedom to overindulge and make bad decisions.

Sudden freedom after a lifetime of restriction can be exciting, but it can also be scary and overwhelming.

While we're detoxing our spiritual lives and building our personal sense of truth, we're essentially stepping into a brave new world where the entirety of spirit is open to us. Even given that there's a ton of knowledge and understanding humans don't have access to about the universe, that's still a hell of a lot of freedom. And it's vitally important that we be deliberate in how we choose to interact with this vast pool of spirit in order to support our authentic selves and to expand it but not to give ourselves over to just any influence.

If there's one thing I learned from my relationship with money as a young adult, it's that, in the absence of an integrated soul and a strong sense of self, our shadow selves will take the wheel and set our direction. That feeling of denial from childhood made me value and therefore chase anything that made me feel unrestricted and able to indulge. So the more confident and secure we are in our authentic identity and core values, the easier it is to navigate the ideas and opinions around us without being pulled into questionable or damaging ones. If college me had been more driven by a sense of purpose, if I'd had some stronger, more deeply seated motivation to save money or put it towards things to benefit and grow my authentic self, I probably would have ended up with more than a useless pile of '80s music compilations and a closet of clothes that didn't fit to show for all the debt I incurred.

Our values are kind of like training wheels when it comes to learning to exercise our own authority and agency in our spiritual lives. They give us a way to trust ourselves to navigate our way through the vast expanse of ideas and information based on what we need rather than on what others think we need.

This time of spiritual detox gives us a chance to consider what types of spirit we actually want to bring back into our authentic spiritual life and what sources of spirit we trust. Most of us have been taught to trust in the legitimacy that comes from external validation, but when it comes to our authentic spirituality, external validation is meaningless if it's not filtered through our deep self values. And that's something that can really only be worked through in this state of separation from external spiritual influences. It gives us time to consider our past spiritual intake, who or what we've accepted as guides and sources, and how that has worked out for us.

Basically, this is time to consider our place in the flow of data. If we liken this to the spagyric processes, soaking dried plant matter in alcohol spirits is meant to draw out the essential oils so they can be filtered and isolated. It happens in a closed container, ideally where it's dark and warm, so as the liquids circulate and the soul is dissolved into spirit, nothing is lost to evaporation. The container gets shaken on a regular basis, too, to help keep things moving and dissolving.

The flow of ideas and information does the same for us. Being immersed in neutral ideas and information draws out aspects of our deep selves like our values, our motivations, our priorities, and our sense of purpose. The things we discover about ourselves during the detox period can then be more easily examined and brought into alignment with our authentic identity. And while we're in this spiritual detox, doing things like journaling and meditation can help shake up our thoughts and feelings and keep the process going.

Alchemists like to toss around words like "purification" when it comes to operations like this, but I think the idea of purity gets in the way here. We're not after purity in the sense of perfection. What we're really after is "refining." We're not removing bad things or impurities; we're just getting down to the essence of our own authentic spiritual self without outside influence because that's where our power resides. We're separating what we need from what we don't.

Authenticity means going after our own dreams and following our own values and motivations. It means learning to trust ourselves with spirit, much like I had to learn to trust myself with money. If the voices we've been listening to have been telling us what our goals and ambitions in life should be, it's time to get in touch with our own inner goals and deep ambitions instead and figure out why our deep self wants those things. If we're used to having our thoughts and ideas criticized and dismissed, it's time to explore those thoughts and ideas away from the prying eyes of judgmental people so we can determine for ourselves if they have merit based on our own values and intentions. If the voices in our life are constantly distracting us from our own experience and substituting theirs, it's time to submerge ourselves in our own authentic experience and find the personal truth in it.

This period of spiritual detox is meant to stop us from constantly consuming media, stories, and conversations that distract us, so we don't have to deal with the real issues in our life, our shadow work, our authentic passions. Seeking out spiritual diversions robs us of space for growth. It's like consuming "junk spirit" instead of "junk food." Not that any food is inherently good or bad – it all comes down to the why and how much – but the way we consume food can be harmful on an individual level. There is no one diet that's good for everyone on earth, and there's no one spiritual diet that works for everyone, either. But the more we learn about our own unique needs, the more we can trust ourselves to be responsible about our intake.

About a decade ago, I decided that I would train for and complete a marathon as a personal spiritual journey. I had never been a runner, I was overweight, and I hated running, but I did like walking long distances, and the whole point was to push myself to do something really significant as a challenge to myself. I'd done various diets over the years prior to that to lose weight, but one of the biggest lessons during my training was that it's an entirely different thing to eat to fuel change in our bodies.

It wasn't about good foods and bad foods. It wasn't about cutting these things out or only eating these things. It became all about timing and function. I had to be mindful of what I ate the night before a long training run and what was in the fridge ready for me when I was done because I'd need to replenish. I had to carry carbs and electrolytes with me on the trail and get some kind of protein after. Some of the choices were to support the physical effort, and some were to make sure I didn't have unexpected intestinal interruptions in the middle of a run. I stopped counting calories because I couldn't keep pushing my endurance if I wasn't consuming enough food. I basically had to learn about my body and how it processed what I put in it.

Doing a spiritual detox isn't like training for a marathon, but it is also an exercise in learning what our body really needs rather than just putting stuff in out of habit or expectation. The forms and sources of spirit we choose to consume in our life vary naturally depending on what we're doing at the time, the same way that we vary the types and amounts of food we eat depending on whether we're celebrating something, drowning our feelings, training physically for something, or trying to lose weight.

It's experiences like this that teach us more about what our authentic self needs in terms of spiritual intake, so we can make empowered spiritual decisions for ourselves.

When I do a detox or fast, the hardest

part happens a couple of days in when my brain starts with the cravings. I start thinking of foods I'd love to order for dinner. I get really distracted by commercials for restaurants. It's a temporary thing, but it's a part of the process that's not just an unpleasant thing to grit our teeth and muscle through. It's part of the detox. It's the brain part of the detox.

When we're doing this spiritual fast, not consuming sources of ideas, opinions, and distracting stories, we're going to have the same thing happen. What would this person say about the stuff that's happening? What am I missing on my favorite show? I should tell so-and-so about this epiphany I just had! And it's all just part of the detox. They're spiritual cravings.

This is also a process where it's important to keep things to ourselves because after doing significant shadow work we need to settle into our newly acquired sense of authenticity. Change has phases to it, and the one a lot of us forget is the stabilization phase, where things get solidified. So as important as it is to limit our intake of spirit, it's just as important to kind of keep the lid on the jar, so to speak.

One reason for that, of course, is that anything we put out into the world is an invitation to energetic dialogue. It's inviting other spiritual sources back in. So while we're in this process, we don't want to open the door and reveal it to everyone else. And if this is hard, there's a reason for that. There's a relationship between what we put out and what we want back. We want to trust ourselves to exercise full agency in our spirituality, so the last thing we need is to invite in are voices that would damage that confidence until it's established.

This is one of those lessons I learned early in life. Anytime we show a work in process to other people, we're going to get opinions and advice and all kinds of potentially unwanted input. I've always loved doing projects. Art projects, writing projects, research projects, personal challenges, all that kind of stuff. And I remember being eager to show people what I was doing because I was proud of it, and I wanted others to see. I wanted praise. I wanted to share the excitement with others.

That wasn't usually what I got, though. I got questions, advice, and people picking apart my choices and telling me how they would do it. So I developed an aversion to anyone seeing anything I do before it's done. I learned that nobody believed in me if they saw my processes, but if I showed the finished product it usually got praise. Hiding my unfinished work was the only way to give myself trust and freedom to achieve goals and finish tasks.

That's not to say there's nothing valuable to be gained from the critiques and opinions of others, but they aren't useful or valuable right here.

My point is that there's no way to put our own spiritual output or the manifestation of our spiritual activities out there without getting something back. Even if I had gotten the praise I wanted, that's spiritual input, too. So to learn to trust our own judgment, we have to give ourselves the space to make those choices, so we can watch ourselves choose well.

There's something beautiful and profound about conducting our inner work without sharing it with anyone, keeping that process to ourselves until it's done and we can emerge transformed, like breaking out of a cocoon. This time of fasting is like building the cocoon in which we're going to transform ourselves and come out more fully realized and authentic.

No detox process is pretty. Creation in progress isn't pretty. Transformation is especially not pretty. Even caterpillars turning into butterflies don't just go into their cocoon and grow wings. They dissolve into goop and rebuild themselves. It's not pretty until it's ready to emerge.

"I will not feel guilty for the things that bring me joy."

We have a hard time, as humans, really connecting with things that don't resonate with us on a personal level. The way we connect to spirituality is much the same as the way we connect to other parts of culture. We like what we like because of who we authentically are, and if we're going to embrace and embody our authentic selves, it means embracing our own quirky, unique sets of interests.

We've all been around someone who is overwhelmingly, enthusiastically into something that we just don't care for. We can almost tangibly feel their excitement from the way they talk about their interest, even though it literally means nothing to us. That's the difference between spiritual points of view. It's the difference between the way I see the universe and the way others see the universe.

My sister and I agree on a lot of stuff. We share a lot of fundamental core beliefs about the world. But our taste in movies is vastly different. In fact, it's not just my sister. A lot of people who I'm close to in my life, especially those who share fundamental beliefs and interests with me, assume logically that our taste in movies will be pretty similar. It almost never turns out that way. I can count on one hand the number of times someone has recommended a movie to me that I was glad I watched. My wife and I made my sister watch Mean Girls and they made us watch Love Actually, and we both had to just agree to disagree on what constituted a "funny movie." But differences in our movie preferences don't invalidate or diminish all the other things we agree about and connect over. We may be very much alike, but different things light us up on a personal level.

Step Six on our journey is to embrace your spiritual interests and passions, no matter now unusual or unconventional they may be.

There's no correlation between what resonates with us and what constitutes truth. What makes us feel strongly connected to a tradition, practice, or idea is the extent to which it sparks awe and wonder in our heart. If the things we place at the center of our spiritual life don't align and resonate with our authentic self, then our spirituality in general isn't going to feel fulfilling. Spirituality ties into the very root of us, the core of our lives. It's the line of communication and the link between us and the rest of the universe, and the key to establishing and maintaining that connection is to tap into those things that amaze and fascinate us, which hold our attention.

I'm one of those people who can watch science, archeology, and history shows all day long, while sitcoms and reality TV just don't tend to interest me. Knowing how stuff works turns my brain on. Experimenting, exploring, and researching is my jam. That's why stuff like alchemy really connects with me. Alchemy blends science and spirituality in one. I like tarot because it's a complex system, almost like the building blocks of the human experience that fit together to paint a picture and deliver a message like a code. I want to understand spirituality from an academic viewpoint because that's what I find inspiring and intriguing.

But clearly that's not the only way to approach those things. I've been told more than once that bringing science into spirituality kills the magic. Those people don't see the magic inherent in research and discovery the way I do, and neither of us are wrong.

So when we look at our differences, the times when we're talking to someone and we know there's some common ground there but their take is just so different from ours, it's really about what resonates with us and what resonates with them. It's about how everyone's authentic self is unique. We all find awe and beauty and magic in our own way. We know ourselves better when we embrace and celebrate those things that resonate with us and let go of the need to have that resonance validated.

For the first time in this process, the reasons why certain things fascinate and excite us aren't all that important. Knowing why doesn't make a ton of difference because we don't benefit at all from trying to change what we're drawn to. I'm not sure I've known anyone who had much luck trying to figure out where their tastes and preferences came from, and I definitely don't know anyone who has benefitted from the attempt. When it comes to figuring out our core values, recognizing the things we like, enjoy, and resonate with is important mainly because it helps spotlight the opposite. It lets us study and try to understand the things we continue to do and embrace despite not liking, enjoying, or resonating with them.

It's generally much harder to explain why something is awesome than it is to explain why something sucks.

So we don't need to worry about the why. We only need to worry about how we can lean into those aspects of self and incorporate them more deeply into our spirituality. If we want to keep digging into our shadows, we need to think about what has stopped us from embracing our passions and interests before now. But it's very likely that any reluctance to center our spirituality on those things that really light us up inside has already been explained in our shadow work.

Once we begin embracing our sense of spiritual agency and taking the reins of our spiritual life, it's up to us to shape what our spiritual existence looks and feels like. Not having been in charge this way before, most of us will struggle a bit trying to find the best way to manage our spiritual needs in an authentic way, and this understanding of personal resonance is the key. Find those things that are of the most spiritual interest and let those things point the way.

That's why my spiritual life is built on a foundation of research and writing. My efforts to dig into the origins of human spirituality have nothing to do with how many other people I think are interested in these topics or what expectations some other person has for my spiritual practice. It's all based simply on the fact that I love doing this stuff and have a driving curiosity about these topics.

Even if I could never publish or share any of it, I'd still do the research and writing for my own benefit.

And if we're going to fully step into our authentic identity and clear away those things that stand between our authentic self and the world, it's imperative to support our authenticity with a practice rooted in our passions. That does, of course, necessitate being in touch with our passions, so if in the past we've not felt comfortable engaging in or experimenting with the things we are drawn to, now's the time to change that. The safe spaces and comfort zones we've already established need to include places where we feel free to chase our interests and whims (if they weren't already included).

This is where we get to let our inner child out to play. Our inner child is the part of ourselves that can still look at the world from a less-jaded perspective and see the awe and wonder around us. The things we're deeply drawn to are often rooted in our deep past. That bit of our authentic deep self that has never had to shoulder a huge amount of

responsibility and still knows how to just relax and enjoy life can show us the way to our core interests.

And I actually think getting in touch with our inner child is a more literal process than a lot of us envision. Much of our personality from when we were kids is still locked deep down inside us because we didn't unlearn or unbecome that person as much as we just shoved it away and pretended it never existed. For many of us, our inner child has been part of our shadow self. We stopped indulging it because we were taught not to as we became adults. We were pressured to push it aside so we could "grow up." So elements of our younger self are still part of our deep self, our core identity. Letting that part take the lead and navigate us towards what it wants goes a long way to helping us embody all aspects of our authentic self.

Even today, I often realize there are parallels between things I was interested in or started to pursue as a kid and things I incorporate in my spiritual life now. I don't plan them out, but sometimes I realize that something I'm doing now feels a bit like déjà vu, and it's reassuring in the sense that I know it's a compulsion rooted very deeply in my identity.

For instance, part of what I realized during my inadvertent spiritual fast was that observing the changing seasons was incredibly important to my spiritual practice. I began incorporating small observances at first, little traditions like putting up decorations on the cross-quarter days (between the solstices and equinoxes). It didn't take long for the winter decorations to become a full-scale winter wonderland explosion in the house, and I realized that I had tapped into the same part of myself that always itched to change up the holiday decoration plan every year and make it special. My inner child has a lot to say when it comes to how each season expresses itself in my house, and now that I let it lead the way I have a fulfilling practice that keeps me connected to the turning of the wheel each year.

There's nothing particularly profound about any of it; it's just about what excites me and really resonates with my authentic self. If we can't indulge what resonates with us most, we'll never be fully able to embody our authenticity.

Step Seven
Creativity

"I gain more when I strive to express than when I strive to impress."

I sometimes describe the first portion of my life as one long series of "coming out to my parents" events. Literally, my formative years all the way through college and into adulthood were a process of embracing and growing into my authentic self, and that didn't mean just overcoming my own insecurities and baggage and becoming comfortable in my own identity. It meant reaching a point where the only way to fully embody my integrated, authentic self was to reveal it despite what I knew would be the reactions.

Some were little, inconsequential things, like not wanting to continue activities like choir or band even though I'm sure my parents would have preferred I do those than be a cheerleader. Some of it was pretty significant, like coming out about my sexuality or not believing in a deity.

And, of course, some of those revelations went over more smoothly than others.

But there's a common thread in all that history. Every single thing I revealed about myself happened by way of or because of the physical manifestation of my authenticity. And by that I mean usually my mom saw something that gave away whatever I'd been trying to keep hidden, like when she discovered I picked up smoking in college by finding a picture of me holding a lit cigarette. Or when she figured out I might not be straight when my girlfriend moved in with me in what I honestly thought could be plausibly passed off as a "just being a really helpful friend" kind of arrangement, despite the shared bed.

The point is that our authentic selves, including our shadow selves, manifest in our physical reality whether we like it or not. They find their way into our belongings, our actions, our behaviors, our appearance, and our relationships. If we're hiding things about ourselves, we're hiding the evidence in the "real world" as well. The deeper we bury our secrets, the more insidious and damaging the manifestation.

The more we fear what others will say about our authentic selves, the more we try to surround ourselves with things, obligations, and relationships that we hope will keep people from seeing and connecting with our deeper reality. All of that is a reflection of our authenticity, too. It reflects our authentic insecurities and our authentic fears.

The more our lives are full of masks and walls (metaphorically and sometimes literally), the less authentic our lives really are because we are restricted from fully embodying our authentic identity. We may not be pretending to be entirely different people, but we're not comfortable in our skin. We surround ourselves with things meant to conceal, protect, and draw attention away from the things we don't want others to see in our lives, and that stuff is a symptom of all the internal baggage we're lugging around with us. That baggage holds us back and ties us down.

I feel it necessary to point out again that the solution to this isn't minimalist living. If our authentic self isn't just itching to clear out the attic, yard sale our belongings, and move into tiny houses with the few things that bring us joy, there's no point in bothering with any of that just yet. It's not an inherently bad thing on a spiritual level to have stuff. Stuff is fine. It's just not very authentic to hide behind it. And by the same token, it's not bad to want less stuff, but it's pretty inauthentic to cram all the stuff we do have into hidden storage spaces so that people believe we have a tidy, minimalist life.

And that's both literal and metaphorical.

But I want to go back to the thing about revealing my authentic self to my parents over the years. I changed a lot as a person in college, learned a lot about myself, as people tend to do during those first years of freedom with the training wheels still on. The things I spent time doing, how I dressed, what I kept in my dorm room were all an expression of all the personal exploration and discovery I was doing at the time.

My parents were predictably not fans of all of it.

I distinctly remember when they finally noticed the small tattoo I got on my ankle for my 21st birthday. My mother was distressed, but it wasn't concern over whether I'd gone to a reputable and clean tattoo artist or the fact that it was permanent; it was only about what other people would think of me when they saw I had a tattoo. Would I have a hard time getting a job? What would the people at church say? There was lots of pearl-clutching.

The thing is, I honestly kind of liked the idea that some people might find it shocking. That's par for the course when we're twenty-one. I was learning to express the person I was becoming, and that included finding that part of myself that didn't want to go along with expectations anymore. My authentic self had a rebellious streak that had always been hidden away out of fear.

And my mom had a point, not about me struggling to get a job because I had swirly lines on my ankle (which was an absurd concern, even in the late 1990s), but about the opinions of others being relevant. They just weren't relevant in the way she imagined.

All the stuff we put on display in our lives is meant to paint a picture of who we are to other people. That's how we communicate our identity to them. It's part of human communication. As much as we like to claim otherwise, the way we dress, groom, and carry ourselves has everything to do with how we hope others will interpret our appearance and demeanor. And that isn't a bad thing in and of itself.

Everything we put out for others to see is either an authentic expression of self, an effort to get a specific reaction from someone else, or both.

I started wearing makeup on a regular basis as a

pre-teen in the late '80s when the eyeshadows were vivid, and we were all learning to match our color choices to our "season." My Celtic and Scandinavian roots have given me very pale skin, so as a "winter" complexion I wore a lot of very bold looks with dark eyeliner and bright red or fuchsia lipsticks. That meant when I didn't have makeup on, it was a pretty drastic difference. I literally wore makeup every day, so very few people had ever seen me without. The one time I was in a huge hurry to get to school and had to leave bare-faced, I spent an entire day being asked if I was ill, even by teachers.

I know they meant well, but it was a bit traumatizing.

It stuck with me into adulthood. I was convinced that I looked awful and sickly without makeup, so I never left home without my face on. I liked makeup just fine; it wasn't something I hated doing because I consider it a really fun artistic medium. But I had internalized the idea that I wasn't acceptable if I wasn't made up. I carried the fear that if I went out in public bare-faced, people would think something was wrong with me. And as much as I liked makeup, I resented having to get up early to do it every morning, especially when my daily routine started to get more and more complicated and demanding.

By my early 30s, I'd had enough. I was working two fulltime jobs, I was exhausted all the time, and I finally realized that I didn't give a crap if anyone thought I looked pale or tired. I was pale and tired! Of all the things I had to worry about, looking pretty and polished was at the very bottom of the list. So I just stopped. My daily makeup routine hadn't been about expressing myself since

I was a preteen; it had been about pleasing other people and making myself more acceptable.

I went out into the world bare-faced and nothing at all happened. Nobody asked if I was ill. Nobody said anything at all about the change. Life went on, and I felt more comfortable being myself in the world. I didn't waste any more precious morning minutes of sleep making sure that I covered up my hideous pale face so as not to disturb people whose opinions didn't matter anyway.

Authenticity doesn't necessarily require us to drag all our crap out onto the metaphorical lawn and figuratively strip ourselves naked for the whole neighborhood to gawk at, but it's good to start tossing out the things we surround and wrap ourselves with in order to fit and blend in. Once we are more closely in touch with our authentic selves, we owe it to those selves to stop self-enforcing the oppressive and repressive ideas that have been pushed on us our whole life.

In fact, the more integrated we are and the closer our relationship with our deep self, the more our authentic core identity is going to want to be fully expressed. The more we connect with our authenticity, the more uncomfortable conformity will feel. Authenticity makes us more aware of the limits placed on us and the unreasonable expectations of others. It illuminates the ways our environment fails to support us.

It's probably becoming obvious that the journey to authenticity isn't all fun and self-love. Conformity and inauthenticity can feel so comfortable and safe that authenticity can feel dangerous and difficult by comparison. This is the point where we begin to make decisions about how our authentic self is going to emerge into a world that may not be particularly welcoming. But the itch to fully bloom into our authentic self comes from the soul-deep understanding of how much there is to be gained on a spiritual level from a life lived as our true self.

"The assumptions of others do not define me unless I allow them to."

The reason authenticity is such a buzzword these days has everything to do with the extent to which we're all taught to hide and downplay things about ourselves. The complications that arise when we have to navigate the world as our authentic selves are some of the strongest driving forces in our lives, no matter how independent we think we are. I don't know of anyone who doesn't claim to not care what everyone else in the world thinks, to be totally unique, to reject the status quo, and avoid all kinds of conformity. But the reality is that we're all subject to this stuff, especially when it comes to our spiritual identities. We align with religions and traditions with the understanding that there's a culture and a set of expectations attached. It's a group identity, so there's only so much leeway within that identity to exert our own.

That's why this journey of self-discovery and building an authentic spiritual practice is so hard to do within the framework of an existing religion.

We've all taken on or been given spiritual labels over the years. I think for the vast majority of us, there's something important about having a label for what we are, to have something we can point to as our spiritual identity so that others can understand it. Discussions and comparisons of our beliefs and religious traditions are an important part of modern culture, so we have a common desire to put a structure and name on what we believe and how we live so we can compare and communicate it. And that means that our spiritual and religious background has involved taking on these larger cultural labels as part of our personal identity, conforming ourselves to the expectations that come with those labels.

It doesn't really matter if that conformity was something we willingly embraced in the interest of belonging or if we were coerced into that conformity; the end result is much the same. We've learned to mask parts of ourselves and hide them, either out of a desire to be accepted or fear of being rejected (which are related but not the same thing). We've learned to use labels to help us communicate aspects of ourselves to other people because they aren't just labels; there are expectations that go along with them.

My wife and I both love Nine Inch Nails. Alongside the *Year Zero* album, there was an alternate reality game that expanded on the narrative of the songs to depict a dystopian future ruled over by religious extremists. My wife got a window sticker for her car in the shape of a cross emerging from the barrel of a gun, which was the symbol of a fictitious militant Christian group in this dystopian world. To those who knew the origin of the symbol, it was a statement against religious extremism. But eventually my wife took the sticker off her car because more than once someone stopped her in a parking lot to compliment it in a way that made her think they were getting exactly the opposite message. She was appalled at the thought that someone would see it and think she was a "Christian gun nut."

We all care about what others think of us to the extent that we care about how accurately people perceive us. Even if we don't care if certain people like us, most of us do care if we're misunderstood and mischaracterized, and most of us don't really know how to define our identity outside of commonly understood labels, archetypes, and stereotypes. We've been taught to suppress and hide parts of ourselves that don't fit the way we're "supposed" to be, and then we're taught that the only way to express our identity to others is by cobbling together the right combination of labels so people see us and make the right assumptions.

Like I've said, I'm pagan. I don't mind calling myself a witch. I'm even a no-bra-wearing feminist. Knowing that, some may picture me in hippie clothing, hemp jewelry, maybe living in an old home full of macrame and plants with a huge yard and a garden. But that's not me. My house is full of pop culture collectibles, and I spend approximately zero time in my yard unless we're lighting the fire pit and drinking beer on a fall evening. Maybe nobody would peg me as a pagan seeing me on the street, and that's cool with me. That's authentic of me. I'm not purposely choosing not to embody witchy stereotypes in order to hide my identity. I don't wonder if I should be more obvious so I seem more like a "real" witch.

But those are the ways of thinking that a lifetime of traditional spirituality teaches us. We learn that certain aspects of our identities go with certain appearances or qualities. As humans, we love identifying patterns to help us understand the world, so we subconsciously pick up on the patterns that seem to tie identity to appearance or behavior so we have a way to order and organize our experience. We like the security of being able to assess and understand people just by looking at them, but then we internalize all those ideas and shape our own way of being to fit with those patterns.

There's nothing wrong with fitting the expected image that goes with any label we embrace. There are reasons that we expect people on certain spiritual paths to look or act or live a certain way. There are doctrines that explain an Amish person's clothing, a Sikh's turban, a Pentecostal woman's long skirts and hair, a Jain's vegetarian diet. Native and tribal traditions have their culturally important garb and grooming traditions. Even the "granola" stereotypical pagan image has roots in nature-loving environmentalist ideals.

All of that makes sense if we're part of a larger religious tradition that tells us how we ought to be and how we ought to live. But our authentic spirituality can't really be expressed this way, and in order to express our authentic self, we have to clear away a lot of the masks we've learned to wear along the way. Our authentic self manifests in our physical reality unless we work hard to suppress it, but in order for our authentic identity to fully emerge and express itself we have to clear the way. It doesn't work to construct an authentic expression of self by pasting on bits of stereotypes and images, because that's kind of like trying to create a costume of our self from bits of other costumes.

We have to let go of the ideas planted in our heads about the ways people will judge us for either conforming or not conforming to all these expectations and images. We have to define ourselves and our spirituality from within our deep self rather than looking to be defined by something external to us.

In fact, deeper than that, we have to let go of the idea that any of these expectations or images we're expected to conform to are even legitimate. They may be real patterns. They may even be actual rules put in place by paths we used to be on or traditions we used to follow, but outside of those traditions or away from those paths the expectations become completely irrelevant. The biggest fallacy we internalize from our spiritual indoctrination and history is that it matters what others think about us based on the external. We're taught to value the judgments of others so much that

NO OUTSIDE FOOD, DRINK, OR ENERGIES ALLOWED IN SANCTUARY

211

we shape ourselves to them. We're taught that perception defines us because what others see in us shapes how they treat us. And it's true that what they perceive about us is going to shape how they treat us, but that still doesn't define us. Nothing anyone else believes about us changes who we are.

"Home is where my soul is free."

Nobody has to be privy to our shadow work as it's going on. Like I said, it's best for the process if it's done in private. But what should be pretty obvious at this point is that we can't do our shadow and integration work, go through this process of spiritual detox on the inside, and expect to leave the external portion of our existence untouched. There are going to be changes that manifest themselves in our physical expression and environment whether we want them to or not. Nobody else may know why things are shifting in our appearance, expression, or environment, but they will likely see the changes happening.

The more we know about who we are and the more committed we are to nurturing our authentic selves, the more aware we're going to be of how our environment fails to support or even stands in the way of our authenticity. The more authentic we are, the more uncomfortable we will feel in places where we're expected to be inauthentic. It's only natural that we'll try to spend as little time as possible in those places and environments.

For me, my parents' house is one of those places. And yes, I've made the personal choice not to go there anymore. I'm not going to advocate that sort of choice for everyone, of course, but there's an awareness here that is important.

Honestly, I love a lot of the things that would take me to my parent's house on a regular basis. Holiday celebrations, for instance, are something I truly love. I'm not estranged from my entire family, so I don't want to avoid gathering with them entirely. I still celebrate Christmas in my own way, and in a way that totally doesn't preclude hanging out with the family and eating big holiday feasts. I love that stuff.

What I don't love are the restrictions that come with being in the environment of my parents' home. It is filled with their religious and political stuff, and it's understood that anyone in their home is subject to their standards of what's acceptable and what isn't. My authentic self is not welcome or supported in that physical place, so I choose not to go there.

Our lives tend to be filled with spaces and places where we're not free to be who we are, many of which we don't often have a choice not to frequent. And if we don't specifically make decisions that open up spaces where we do feel comfortable and free in our authenticity, they won't exist.

I lived by myself for the first few years of my life after college. I'd grown up in a family with a lot of siblings, though, so complete solitude and control over my living space were something new. It wasn't until I was a teen that I'd even stopped sharing a bedroom, and we always only had one bathroom in the house, so the privilege of privacy was something I always valued and sought out. I had to be creative in carving out space and time to do what I wanted without anyone else around to interfere. I never fell right asleep after going to bed, because that was one of the few times when I could trust that no one would be coming in to ask me to stop what I was doing to take care of a chore or answer a question. I did a lot of lying in the dark with my thoughts and my imagination, sometimes even reading, sketching, or writing if I could find enough light without drawing attention.

I've always craved solitude and privacy.

In college, I had roommates to share my space with up until my last year when I finally got an on-campus studio apartment on my own. After graduation, I moved to Chicago alone as well. My living space was finally mine alone, my sacred space and sanctuary of authenticity. I could be and do whatever I wanted in my apartment, decorate how I wanted, put anything on display without anyone else having anything to say about it, play my music and watch whatever I wanted.

Sharing a house with a roommate or even with my wife was a pretty hard sell after that. I didn't want to be forced to rein myself in again, to put limits on my authenticity to make room for someone else's. I had to learn how to make those compromises and to trust that sharing a space didn't mean that I had to stifle my authentic expression.

Part of the secret to having a safe sanctuary for our authentic self without being totally alone is being surrounded by people who welcome and support our authenticity. But an even bigger part is learning to assert our authenticity and carve out space for ourselves. That doesn't mean we have to be fully expressed and demand acceptance everywhere and with everyone. There are certainly places and situations where it's best to not be fully expressive of every authentic part of ourselves. But it's not healthy if that's true for the bulk of our day-to-day existence.

It's one thing to have a deep connection to our authentic self, but if our life is set up to stand in the way of our authenticity, we're going to be spiritually frustrated. And that's not to say that we can't live a truly fulfilling spiritual life unless we have complete control over our environment. But there's a difference between sneaking little opportunities for spiritual activities in between all the other things in our life and actually making it a priority.

We all need our own sacred spaces where we are able to be fully ourselves. They may not be private; sometimes they may even be wherever we can be around certain people or wherever we can do certain things regardless of the actual location. Sometimes those spaces are where we go to shut out the unwanted pressure and influence of the rest of the world. Sometimes those places are our sanctuaries where we can surround ourselves with the support and inspiration we need to fully embody our authenticity.

The idea of sacred things has always both fascinated and frustrated me. Sacredness means in part that something isn't to be damaged or violated or changed. It's valued and not to be lost. Sacred things are protected by the people who consider them sacred, which is important in the sense that declaring something sacred is basically the setting of a boundary.

Any time we set boundaries, other people may get upset and misunderstand. Sacredness is an idea that is misunderstood, resented, and twisted by a lot of people, mostly those who resent that they aren't allowed to do as they wish with whatever someone else has designated as sacred.

Honoring something as sacred also honors the entity that declares it to be sacred. That's why sacred objects, relics, and spaces are part of formal religion. Honoring those sacred things honors the higher power worshipped in that tradition. And it's why certain aspects of cultures, particularly cultures facing external threats to their continued existence, are held as sacred. Honoring the sacred status of objects and spaces and practices of a culture is also honoring and respecting that culture.

So creating our own sacred spaces, sacred objects, and sacred practices, and honoring those things is honoring us. It's not about setting these things aside as part of our spirituality. It's not about belief. It's about boundaries. It's saying, "This is important to me, and therefore I'm not allowing it to be changed or damaged or infringed upon because I refuse to deprioritize myself." Creating these sacred parts of our lives is demanding that respect from and for ourselves.

The place where I do my artistic work or my writing has usually been something of a sacred space to me. It's where I give my brain the space to bring forth ideas and make them into something new. We talked in the last chapter about what constitutes spiritual activities, and for me those are two of the most important. And that means that the materials I use for those things and the space I set aside for doing them (however temporary) are sacred things. And while there are lots of spaces in my house that I'd be willing to change or do away with if, for instance, my wife had a different thing she wanted to use them for, the art studio is not one of them. Having a space for artistic endeavors is necessary to my life. It's why in the last place we lived, the bigger bedroom was the studio/office and the small one was where we slept. It's why we dedicated a whole room to it in our new house and never let anyone, even the housekeeper, mess with it.

Sometimes the sacredness of a place doesn't have to be about its existence as much as our access to it. For some people, spaces in nature might be their most sacred cathedrals, and it's not important that no one else be able to go there but it's essential that they have time to spend and access to it when they need it. For others, maybe it's libraries or museums.

So creating a sacred space or making space for our sacred belongings and activities isn't at all about their connection to beliefs or religion or a higher power. This is about what's sacred to our personal spirituality, not sacred to the universe. It's what we place at the highest level of priority and value to our life and our evolution.

It's an act of drawing boundaries around our own authenticity. It's asserting our agency and not just finding our voice but using it to make space for our authentic self. It's making space for our authenticity to manifest in our environment rather than allowing external forces continue to stifle and silence us.

This is really an exercise in drawing our own

boundaries rather than accepting the boundaries others draw for us. Even if others aren't explicitly setting down lines we're not to cross, the less we assert ourselves the more we're fenced in by the boundaries others have set for themselves. It's like letting all your neighbors decide how big their yards get to be and then settling for what's left. It's a good way to end up with nothing.

Anyone who's ever had to hide a significant part of themselves knows how much difference it makes to have even one place where they can fully be their own self and feel safe about it. Even if we aren't able to express our authentic self elsewhere in our life, having one sacred safe space is crucial.

That's why the LGBTQ+ community has always had places to congregate, especially when and where it's been illegal, and it's why gay bars have always centered around drag, dancing, and finding partners. They're places where all the aspects of our authentic identities that were suppressed and criminalized by society could be fully embraced and even celebrated. Even if that safety was fragile and fleeting, having any at all is so necessary to existence that these spaces always sprang up despite the risks.

So if there are aspects of our authentic self that don't have any sacred outlets and safe spaces, it's time to remove the boundaries that keep us from finding, accessing, or creating them.

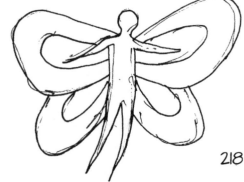

"I will not wait for anyone else to grant me space to spread my wings."

It's easy to feel like we don't have control over the environment we live in, especially when that environment is outright hostile to who we are. I'm a queer pagan feminist in the middle of the Bible belt. I'm intimately aware of how our larger environment can impede our ability to be truly authentic in the way we want to be.

But I also know that the key to some of this is making conscious decisions about the smaller environments in which we center our life. Our environment shapes us, but we also have the ability to shape our environment, and more important than that, we can actually choose how much time, energy, and intention we spend in the various spaces and environments that make up our day-to-day experience.

We all carve out sacred space for ourselves in one way or another just because our deep selves need it. That's what I was doing as a kid when I stayed awake past bedtime just to spend time with my own thoughts. We find ways to indulge and accommodate the things we want and value most, even if those ways are small and even if we feel guilty about it.

Alone time in a family with six kids is hard to find for the kids, but it's even harder for the parents. I didn't really understand that growing up, but I can see the struggle now that I'm an adult. As a kid I remember there always being a Reader's Digest on the back of the toilet. I remember my mom spending long periods of time in the bathroom reading. I picked up the habit myself, in fact, sometime in my teens. I still do it, only now it's a cell phone rather than a magazine. My wife finds it weird, but it was one of the few ways any of us could get real solitude at home. It was something of a sacred space because we all wanted more quiet and distance and privacy than the rest of our lives naturally allowed us. So we created it by grabbing the opportunity with both hands whenever we could find it.

That's what we do as living things. We turn ourselves towards the environments in which we can thrive like a plant will turn itself towards the sun. We are tuned in to the things our deep selves tell us we need, and we instinctively grab on to anything that feels like it fills that need. We seek out sacred space, sacred activity, and sacred objects to support who we are, even when we don't fully understand who we are and what we need. It's amazing how creative our subconscious mind can be when it comes to responding to those needs we feel deep down.

It's also amazing how guilty and shamed we can feel for acting on those instincts.

The more we've had to suppress and repress authentic parts of ourselves along our life path, the more our subconscious mind has had to do the work of seeking out spaces and contexts where we can embody our full authenticity, even for a moment. We usually learn to see them as guilty pleasures or bad habits. But we cling to them because the rest of our lives make us feel oppressed and held back from who we are.

Detoxing our physical and material existence of the

things that stand between us and our full authenticity is really a process of creating sacred space that then supports the process of crafting an authentic way of expressing ourselves. Our authenticity will manifest naturally in our way of being and in the way we occupy space in the world even if we don't give it the proper space, much like a weed growing through concrete. But weeds are only weeds because they're unwanted where they are. If we want to really support our deep self in this journey, we have to take purposeful action and make intentional choices to create the space our authenticity really needs so it can fully bloom.

This is the opposite of what we usually do in life. When our life doesn't feel safe and welcoming to who we are, most of us try to rid our spaces and ourselves of the things that make us feel vulnerable. We work harder to hide away things others might judge so that we feel more shielded and protected. We chop the weeds off at the roots whenever they start to grow up through the cracks. But this detox isn't about clearing away the ways we express what we're afraid to express; it's about clearing away the reasons we feel afraid to be ourselves and making spaces that are comfortable and welcoming. It's about clearing away the things we use to distract or hide ourselves from whatever we feel is not going to accept our authenticity. It's about clearing space in our life to claim as our own and to take control of that space. It's breaking up the sidewalk so the dandelions have plenty of space to grow.

Humans are creative beings. That's what the whole Cumulative Cultural Evolution thing comes down to. We are beings who have ideas and find new solutions. Creation isn't about reproducing something;

it's about making something we want from what we have. If we don't have something we need, we create it as best we can with the resources at hand. And that's exactly what is necessary to fully embody our authentic identity. If we don't have the environment we need to support who we are, we must create a new one from what we have.

My entire life has been centered on art and creativity. My parents figured out very early on that if they needed me out of their hair, all they had to do was give me a stack of paper and something to make marks with, and I'd be perfectly content to draw, scribble, and try to write even before I was in school. To keep me quiet in church services as a kid, mom didn't take me to the cry room; she gave me a notepad and a pencil. I'd sketch, write, and fold papers into shapes and not pay a single bit of attention to whatever my dad was saying from the pulpit. I took every art class I could manage from elementary school through college, and in my spare time I took up a long list of arts and crafts: embroidery, oil painting, calligraphy, sewing, knitting, papier mâché, jewelry design, collage, basket weaving... If I could get my hands on the supplies, I'd try out just about any craft I could think of.

So for anyone reading this who doesn't consider themselves creative, here's an extremely important artistic principle to realize: Creativity doesn't always mean adding more details or creating something entirely new. Processes like breaking things apart, carving bits away, or recycling something into something else are all creative, too. And I say this because when we think of creating an environment to support our authentic selves, a lot of us imagine new spaces, more stuff, and big changes. We think of actually producing something from component parts.

What creativity really comes down to is deliberate, direct action to shape something into an intended form. All the other details are irrelevant. What we want to do to support our fully authentic way of being is to take the life we have and take direct action to shape it into a life that makes space for us by removing the things that stand in the way.

It's also important to remember that this doesn't necessarily mean physical space. Sometimes what we need is energetic space, distance from the things that distract and discourage us. Sometimes we need time rather than physical space. Sometimes we need the confidence or authority to choose to spend time on our own things. Maybe we just need to tailor the spaces we do have into more functional ones. The main objective, no matter how it plays out, is to grant ourselves the permission to make ourselves a priority in our own lives.

Making sacred space for ourselves is also a creative endeavor because there isn't a template for what this looks like; we have to make it work for ourselves. It also means that nobody's opinions matter unless we allow them to. We can all look to each other for ideas and inspiration, but we have to create our own sacred spaces.

I always wanted a literal sacred space in my house. Back when my wife and I were doing clandestine rituals in the middle of the night and hiding our witchy things in a trunk, I dreamed of having a meditation and ritual room. When we bought a house, I thought about making one out of our screened-in porch or maybe in one of the spare bedrooms. In my ideal vision, it would have lovely curtains and crystals in the windows, space to meditate or do things like yoga, comfy chairs or beanbags for reading in, that sort of thing. Lots of candles. Maybe even tons of book shelves so it would be like meditating in a library.

But I live in a house with four cats. Four cuddly, beloved cats that I love like children, but they're the reason we can't have nice things. We don't have a spare bedroom because we needed a room for all the kitty stuff, including the litter boxes and the mess and smell that goes with them. They won't leave me alone for meditation, they think yoga poses are invitations to climb, and it's impossible to be in a room behind a closed door without them scratching to get in. The stuff I'd like to keep in a meditation space is often stuff they can't be trusted not to break, ruin, or poison themselves with. I can't even have live plants because one of our lovely fur babies can't resist eating them. It's extremely difficult to meditate without a dedicated space for it, but even more difficult to find a space in the house to turn into a meditation room that would be quiet and cat-free.

Except, I realized one day, the guest bathroom.

So I turned it into my meditation room. I put in shelves, curtains, a place for an altar. I got noise-cancelling headphones, so I could meditate no matter how loudly they scratched at the closed door. All my candles and incense and crystals and whatnot went in there. And it's great. Sure, our guests also use it as a bathroom, and some of my witchy friends and acquaintances find that to be an awful idea, but it works for me. It gives me the environment for doing things that are spiritually important to me, and I don't care that other people occasionally go into my sacred space and potentially touch my ritual things. It doesn't bother me that there's a toilet in my meditation space; I just put the lid down, pull the curtain to hide it, and ignore it. It doesn't matter if that solution would work for anyone else because it works for me.

But what I had to do to create that space was remove the obligation I felt to keep that room dedicated to guests. It's my house, so I can do what I want with my bathrooms, right? I had to push past the instinct to hide my spiritual life from people, because making my guest bath into a meditation and altar space meant putting my spiritual life physically out on display.

Carving out sacred space in our lives and making ourselves a priority is all about giving us the freedom and to be who we are and feel safe in the process. The physical manifestation of our authentic identity shows up in how we present ourselves, and having comfortable sacred spaces opens up more opportunity

and reason to begin creating our own authentic way of being, looking, and acting. Clearing the things that stand in the way of having those spaces in our life also clears away the barriers that stand in the way of us embodying our deep self identity.

When I converted to Catholicism, one of the things I did to commemorate the change was get a cross tattooed on my chest. It was a small thing, just over an inch tall, set right over my heart. It was lovely and well done, but a couple of decades later I had become more and more aware that having that symbol on my chest was at odds with my authentic spiritual self. It projected a message about me that I didn't want to project, that was inaccurate, and that could potentially impact what people thought about me or how they treated me. And to conceal it would have required me to not dress the way I wanted to much of the time. It needed to go. So I had it covered up.

I didn't regret getting the tattoo, and this isn't meant as a cautionary tale. It was authentic to me when I did it. It was important to me. Inking a cross over my heart was a deliberate spiritual expression of who I was, which at the time was at odds with what was expected of me. The tradition I grew up in doesn't regard Catholicism as a particularly valid form of Christianity, so it was a radical act of self-determination on a spiritual level for me to publicly embrace it. Tattoos, even religious ones, weren't acceptable to most of the people I knew in church growing up, either.

But our authentic self changes over time. Everyone's does. And that tattoo stood in the way of me fully embodying my authentic identity later in life, so redoing it was a significant part of my own spiritual detox and emergence.

Of course, not everyone has permanently marked themselves with a religious affiliation, but we do have things about how we look, act, and carry ourselves that say things about us that aren't true or accurate. Maybe we've had reasons for embracing those things and using them to shield ourselves from whatever judgment and disapproval we want to avoid, or maybe they used to be fully authentic to us and simply aren't anymore. Either way, we don't need them in our sacred spaces where they might hold us back from authentic expressions of self.

"I do not have to be taught how to be myself."

I know I have a tendency – a really deep-seated tendency – to overcomplicate things. I entertain really idealistic visions that always end in disappointment when I try to execute them. But as I've done more shadow work and gotten more in touch with my authentic self, I've realized that overcomplicating things is an effort to please and impress. I struggle to bring my crazy visions to life because I reject assistance and guidance.

Getting more in touch with my authentic self has enabled me to be more reasonable in what I take on. I've recognized a pattern of trying to cram in as many of my passion projects and interests as possible, no matter what other obligations I have at the time. My inauthenticities might have filled my planner with tasks I felt coerced to take on, but no matter how full my day was with those tasks, I'd do everything I could to squeeze in the things that were really important to me.

It's funny, though, how hard we work to deny and judge our natural lifestyle and state of being and to resist the changes that would make it possible.

This played into what I thought was my time management problem. Even knowing that part of my issue was the amount of stuff I tried to accomplish each day, I vehemently resisted efforts to get me to time block my day or to institute some kind of regular work schedule. I felt like my natural way of being was free and unstructured, flexible enough to do whatever I felt compelled to do from moment to moment.

Recently I realized that I was wasting a lot of time deliberating tasks and resisting doing the things I didn't want to do, and that no matter how good I might get at saying no to obligations I didn't want to take on, it wouldn't make much of a difference if I spent half my day trying to decide what to do next. So I finally gave in and blocked out my daily schedule. I made sure to set boundaries around when I would answer my phone for work things and when I would not.

And the result is that a lot more of my time gets spent on the things that are a high priority on a personal level. My authentic self has time to fully engage in a spiritual practice. It has nothing to do with what others expect me to do with my time.

Step Seven is to detox your life of anything which stands in the way of your ability to be yourself on a spiritual level.

We tend to cling to visions and concepts of what a fulfilling spiritual life and practice should look like, even if these ideas are unrealistic and come from questionable sources. If our vision for our spiritual life is daily meditations, leading weekly prayer groups, and spending every summer doing charity mission projects, then a reality check is probably in order. I used to envision some future reality where I'd be able to regularly meditate and do yoga in a dedicated spiritual space and engage in special morning and night rituals without fail.

But that's not authentically me, and that vision isn't rooted in who I am, who I ever have been, or what my reality is like right now.

Even if our vision for our spiritual reality is reasonable, it's super important to keep that vision in the present. Even if it's aspirational, it still should be reasonable, and spirituality isn't a goal for the future. We don't want to get in the habit of thinking of spirituality as something we will perfect and achieve somewhere down the line.

Spirituality isn't a goal in itself. We don't win a prize or get bonus blessings for meditating most or being the most super spiritual. We don't gain anything by waiting for "someday when I'm super spiritual." This is about authenticity, and authenticity is rooted in the present. Who we are and what our material limitations are right this moment are part of our authenticity. Our authentic self will live a naturally authentic life if we're not forcing it to live inauthentically.

We've just never lived authentically before because we've never given our authentic self that much power to determine things in our world.

229

This doesn't need to be a whole-lifestyle makeover. There are ways to work our spirituality into our mundane life. Our spiritual activities don't need to be different and separate from the rest of our life activities. Our cooking can become kitchen witchery, our book club time can focus on spiritual books, our vacations can be pilgrimages. It doesn't have to look like anyone else's spiritual life; it only has to make sense to us.

This is where our values and our personality manifest in our lifestyle. We behave the way we behave, and truly embodying our authentic nature means embracing those things we like without questioning why or sparing a thought for the opinions of anyone else.

I love crystals. My deeper spiritual beliefs say that there's no need to have a bunch of bric-a-brac to be able to do magic or to have an entirely functional and fulfilling spiritual practice. But just because I don't NEED them doesn't mean I shouldn't collect crystals, because I like them and they make me happy.

It might seem more logical to engage in this last phase of the spiritual detox by getting rid of things and tidying up the "stuff" we have that belongs to our spiritual life. But the "stuff" isn't the problem. The detox is

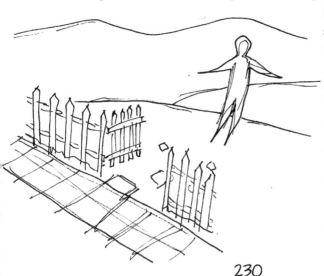

meant to get us to release those things that don't serve our pursuit of authenticity, and that is not helped by denying our authentic self the things it's drawn to. What we want to dump are the things holding us back from embracing our natural lifestyle, no matter what it looks like.

We've spent the detox clearing away the inauthentic elements of our spirituality and learning to fully step into our authenticity instead. But every detox comes to an end eventually. Sometimes when I do a food fast or a detox, I have a timeframe laid out, and even though I don't always get to the point where a real purge happens, it's still beneficial. I've also done fasts and detoxes where I just let it go on until I felt it had run its natural course. I knew when to start easing back into eating again when it wasn't a matter of cravings or wanting to eat again as much as just a feeling of the process having done what it was meant to.

In some ways it's a little like when I was vegetarian. After I did my marathon, I wanted to keep doing distance walking and running, and I knew a lot of runners swore by vegetarian and vegan diets as being better for their performance. So I tried it. I went vegetarian, somewhat slowly, and I felt great! I was vegetarian (sometimes pescatarian) for six years. It wasn't hard, I didn't miss meat, I loved how I felt without eating meat, and I didn't even mind the hassle of finding food to eat at restaurants and parties.

And then one day I realized that I was kind of over it. I wasn't running anymore – I'd moved on to different pursuits. I didn't feel as dramatically great as I had before. I didn't feel bad, but I wasn't sure it made a difference anymore. Plus I was getting lazy about it.

Cookies are vegetarian, but they don't make for a healthy vegetarian diet. The only thing keeping me in that culinary lifestyle was that when I started, it made me feel good. Once it didn't anymore, I recognized that it was probably time to stop. So I did.

The same thing happens in a detox, physical or spiritual. We know when the beneficial phase has run its course, and we feel like not only have we fully stepped into our authenticity but we're ready to grow into whatever comes next.

Part IV

The Power of Magic

Pause and Reflect
——— ——— ———

How much do you trust your own perception,
creativity, and logic?

Who do you look to as trusted teachers and
guides in life?

Where do you go to feel comfortable, safe, and
free to openly express yourself?

——— ——— ———

Step Eight
Evolution

"If we do not embrace change, we invite death."

When I got to the end of those months I spent doing my hardcore shadow work, after digging into all the dark corners I could find and crushing all the walls I'd built up inside to hide things away, I found myself standing in a pile of soul debris wondering what to do now. I think most of us know instinctively how to dig in and tear ourselves apart. It's emotionally painful and traumatic, but we know how to do it. Rebuilding ourselves afterwards doesn't come as easily. It's something we need help and guidance to do.

But making messes, literal or spiritual, is something we're naturally good at as humans, some of us more than others.

Not only am I a naturally messy person, my wife has never been tidy, either. It hasn't gotten better now that we're together. If we didn't pay a housekeeper to return our house to a baseline of "acceptable for guests" every week, we would rarely have company over. We're no strangers to the last-minute scramble to clean up a considerable amount of clutter and mess because a guest was expected to visit or because we had to move. When that's happened, there's always that moment where we find ourselves staring around at a room thinking, "Where on earth do we even start?"

All the shadow work we do is great and valuable and necessary, and it gets us in touch with who we are in the moment. Authenticity is about the present, so that's part of why it's so important to do. But the authentic self we find isn't the self we hope to become, and our authentic self at any given point in time includes elements that we aren't proud of, aren't happy with, or that hold us back. Those parts are still authentic. If we evolve away from those elements and we become a future version of ourselves that doesn't have them, that version of us will also be authentic and it will also still have things we want to change. We are always changing, but that doesn't make us an incomplete work in progress. That way of thinking implies that we are unfinished or missing something. We're always whole and authentic, no matter how much we do or don't like ourselves. No matter how much work we want to do on ourselves or how much we want to change in the future, the person we are right now is still just as complete and whole.

If we are ever at a point where we don't think there's anything about ourselves that we'd change, there's a 100% chance we're ignoring a pretty dark shadow. We are perpetually imperfect beings. Perfection simply doesn't exist and never will. So there's a good chance that as we're doing shadow work, we'll end up looking around at the state of our existence and inner self, seeing all the things we wish we could change and "clean up," and wondering where to even start.

Well, what happens next is evolution.

Evolution wasn't a popular topic in our house when I was a kid, so it wasn't until later in life that I really wrapped my brain firmly around what evolution means and how it works, both scientifically speaking and spiritually speaking. In fact, I remember hearing things as a kid that didn't make a ton of sense like, "Dinosaurs aren't real. They've just found unrelated bones from other animals and assembled them wrong." The benefit of growing up in all that, though, is that I've done an awful lot of participating in debates and discussions (from both viewpoints) about whether evolution is real, and as a result I'm familiar with the key misconceptions floating around.

For instance, it may surprise some to realize that there is no goal to evolution.

Evolution isn't shaped by intention. We aren't "meant" to evolve into anything in particular. Nothing is "meant" to change in specific ways. Evolution in nature is not a conscious force. It's a phenomenon. Nothing is "unevolved" or "incomplete." Evolution doesn't work like that.

The biggest thing I've realized on my own evolutionary journey is that evolution, even the spiritual kind, never looks like choosing an end goal and then doing what we can to grow into the version of ourselves that we have in our head. Evolution is about adaptation, not achievement. It's not "survival of the fittest" in the sense that we're all striving to be the best version of a human we can imagine so that we're more likely to succeed and survive.

What drives evolution isn't desire or intention; it's change in the reality around us. The world, the universe even, is constantly changing and shifting because it's alive. Living things do that. We're surrounded by people and organisms who are all growing and changing, and therefore everything we build and create changes as well. That change puts different demands on us as time passes, asks different things of us, and requires different skills, mindsets, and ways of being. Sometimes things change, and people who used to struggle suddenly find themselves well suited to thrive in the new reality. Sometimes things change, and those who used to have it easy suddenly find they're unprepared for the way things are. When reality changes and challenges us and we respond by adapting to the new challenge, that's more than growth; that's evolution.

When we do our shadow work and find parts of ourselves that are holding us back, elements of our identity that were forged in a different time and different situation and no longer serve us in a positive way, doing what we can to transform those pieces is what spiritual evolution is all about. It has nothing at all to do with transforming those things because they're bad or because we want to reach some future ideal. We work on what is challenging us and holding us back because we are living creatures meant to live and thrive in this life right now.

The fun thing about humanity is that we're the only species on earth who is aware of evolution and understands it enough to consciously participate in the process. We understand that our actions change our environment, which will in turn necessitate that we change to adapt. All other life on earth just deals with the cards it's dealt, but we get to stack our own deck because we understand the game.

Plus, with spiritual evolution, we don't have to wait for the next generations to see the results of our efforts. We become many different versions of ourselves spiritually as we go through life, so we can adapt as we live. In biological evolution, the traits and qualities that prove detrimental in a new environment get slowly bred out of the population, but spirituality is a uniquely human thing and we can move the adaptation process along much faster. We can look inward, evaluate our deep selves, and find the things in our base programming that are making us incompatible with the software and impeding our ability to function as well as we want to. This is a whole different process than envisioning who we hope to become and then trying to fit that mold. We don't know if that vision will be well suited for the world we'll find ourselves in.

Evolution is living to the fullest in the present by working on the things standing in our way. And that's the whole point of human spirituality. It's all about personal evolution. It's about being connected to this universe where nothing is static because it can't be. Life cannot be static or it ceases to be

239

life. The defining quality of all life is change.

———————————————

"I am not broken, so I do not need to be fixed."

———————————————

The overwhelming majority of religions in the world today are centered on various messages about what needs to happen to "fix" humans, either individually or as a species. Some traditions are less heavy-handed about these kinds of messages, but there's nearly always an ideal embedded somewhere in the teachings describing how things are "meant" to be, and we never live up to those standards. Most spiritual practices focus on the hoops we need to jump through to live up to those ideals as best we can.

No matter how flawed our spiritual understanding has told us we are, no matter what the end goal of the religion(s) we've been part of have been, I think we all ultimately turn to religion and spirituality to make us better people. In one way or another, we all want our spiritual practices and traditions to help us improve ourselves, to lift us up and show the way to some better future.

But what do we mean by improving or being better? Religion teaches us that there's an ideal state to strive for, that our goal is somewhere in the distance on the other side of a spiritual journey, possibly not even in this life or on this plane of existence. The standards we're taught to measure ourselves against often have very little to do with the life we're living right now. Our life at the moment is either something we're required to endure as part of the journey or it's of no consequence to this higher cosmic purpose we're supposed to chase.

No matter what series of religious paths have made up our spiritual life so far, we're almost guaranteed to feel like there's a better version of ourselves we're supposed to try to become, that we're not good enough now, and we need outside guidance to get us to that future ideal.

So yeah, as I've said again and again, all that messaging combined with the social messages of how we're not good enough or how we should be different results in emotional and spiritual baggage. Ultimately it all wounds our deep self and leaves scars even after we've done our shadow work. We can embrace our shadow self and bring it out into the light, but we still have healing to do after that.

Let's drag out the coming out metaphor again. Coming out doesn't miraculously make someone more comfortable with all the aspects of their gender identity or sexuality. Embodying our authentic selves and integrating our shadow aspects doesn't mean we automatically end up happy with who we are. We may get to a point where we stop judging and condemning ourselves, but that's not the end of the journey. Who we are isn't bad, but it may not be the best-suited self for the life we're trying to live. Religion tends to tell us to either be something inauthentic, so we struggle less with who we are, or to alter our lives to make them easier. But that's how we get to the shadowy, inauthentic state of being we've been working our way out of.

Our deep self, our soul, is the filter through which all energies come into our being, the base programming that shapes what comes out and manifests. The more integrated we are as people, the more consistent that flow of energy. But consistent doesn't mean it's all constructive, positive energy. We can be fully integrated, fully authentic people and still struggle to manifest the life we want because the authentic self we are isn't in a state to manifest the things we want. Authentic is not the same as whole and healed.

As we uncover and integrate aspects of our shadow selves, some of those aspects are part of us that we will choose to embrace as we move forward while others will be shadow aspects we don't want to continue carrying with us. But unlike regular baggage, the baggage we've been uncovering along this journey can't just be dropped off somewhere and left behind. There's work to be done because the baggage is part of our subconscious, part of our core programming, and there's no easy delete button in the human psyche. Religion may have taught us that some other power can take those things away, but in reality we have to do the work.

So all those things that our spiritual history taught us to hide and hate about ourselves have to be dealt with, and we don't just choose one day not to be those things anymore. There's a good chance that our spiritual past hasn't left us with very effective methods of healing and evolving or to really release those parts of our shadow that we don't want to embrace. In fact, the reason our religious histories have left us with wounds and scars is because they don't equip us to actually heal and evolve. They only equip us to ignore and suppress.

For the most part, we primarily learn to distance ourselves from those shadow aspects, to treat them as something external to ourselves. Lots of traditions treat the aspects of ourselves that aren't acceptable to us as something foreign, like we're tainted or contaminated. But treating those things as something we're supposed to fight against doesn't help us deal with them. In fact, the more we try and fight against our shadow aspects and fail to rid ourselves of them, the more guilty and inadequate we feel.

I was taught to pray things away, of course, which is not an effective approach to releasing a part of who we are.

Our shadow self is part of us. It's not a foreign entity to purge. And the things about us, shadow or integrated, which we resent or dislike are just aspects that hold us back and don't serve our higher purpose. It's like having a person on a team who doesn't do their part or pull their weight; we may not want to have to deal with them any longer, but until we actually let them go and replace them, they're still part of the team. So praying our shadow aspects away doesn't work because it's essentially wishing to be different rather than working at it.

We might have also been taught that change and healing come from the power of intention or positive energy. And while there's much power in intention and positivity, it doesn't change us inside the way we want it to. The biggest problem with most spiritual guidance when it comes to evolution is that we can't just toss aside something that's part of us. We can't just make part of ourselves go away; we have to undergo transformation.

Our deep self is a complex entity, and even if we could go in and excise an aspect that we wanted to let go of, it would leave a void and a bunch of broken connections. And no amount of positive thinking fills that void, nor can it accomplish that kind of incision in the first place. Any tradition, philosophy, or doctrine that teaches us to use positive thinking and energy to accomplish what is really a deeper transformation fails to recognize that what we're trying to release isn't just clinging to us on the outside. It's not just bad habits or stuff we've picked up and need to clean away. It's inherent to who we authentically are right now.

Healing is a form of transformation, and transformation doesn't change our fundamental identity. The butterfly is still the same creature as the caterpillar, no matter how drastically it seems to have changed. We're a different version of ourselves, but we're the same entity. And this is important because it's detrimental to healing to deny ourselves. We have to acknowledge that we are and have always been our shadow selves,

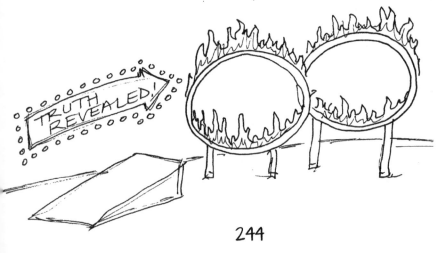

244

and we have to acknowledge that no amount of personal transformation or evolution will erase the versions of ourselves we have been. And that's why authenticity is so important. It's not that our past or future selves are irrelevant, but they aren't who we are now.

That's another thing we've probably learned from our religious past that holds us back now. Changing, growing, and maturing do put our past selves into perspective, making us very aware of the things we don't like about who we used to be. But we were those versions of ourselves, and no matter how much we want to distance ourselves from our old ways, we can't deny them. Doing that just creates more shadows. We learned things and became who we are because of who we have been, and erasing our history removes the context of our transformation. We don't have to like our old selves, but it is bad for our growth and evolution to pretend that we've only ever been versions of ourselves that we like and embrace.

It's not a good idea to get too attached to who we used to be, either. The greatest challenges and difficulties we face in life don't have anything to do with who we have been or who we want to be; it's all about who we are. It's all about our authentic self not being adapted to the moment. Our ideal future self isn't here now to manifest our intentions in the present, so that's all on our authentic self. And if we want to thrive, we have to heal and evolve ourselves as we are now to adapt to the environment we inhabit.

The spiritual tools we've picked up over the years are likely ineffective to actually transform and heal the shadow aspects of self that stand between us and a thriving, fulfilled existence. And that's not to say that those tools are useless. They just aren't good for this journey right now because religion and traditional spirituality aren't geared towards real healing and evolution. Our religious past has formed cultures around us that supported and nurtured us into their corresponding ideals. They were all environments meant to shape us into something specific to those paths, not specific to us as individuals. And the tools those traditions gave us were meant to help us open ourselves to that transformation, not necessarily to healing.

So if we want to evolve away from those shadow aspects we now know are undesirable baggage from our past, and if we want to heal the wounds left from all the ways we've been forced into molds we don't fit in, we have to leave behind all our old ideas about what healing and growth look like. It's not about another force coming in and taking our burdens in the same way that physical healing is not caused by transferring our illnesses or injuries to some other entity. Physical healing happens when we find ways to enhance and support our body's own abilities to regenerate and repair. It's also not about our ability to reject and discard parts of ourselves we don't like, just like trying to cut off a damaged part of our bodies only creates another wound to heal. Surgery requires special skill and a deep understanding of the body, so the surgery leaves us better able to heal than we were before.

Real healing and evolution of our deep selves means finding those same spiritual ways of enhancing the capabilities we already have and using our connection with our integrated self to do what prayer, positivity, and faith cannot.

"I am magic."

I titled this book Deep Self Magic for a reason, so let's talk about magic. Much like there are many ways to define and conceptualize spirit, there are lots of ways to understand magic, so I want to establish a broad understanding of what I understand magic to be and why it's important.

Those who have never intentionally practiced magic are likely to think of magic in the way it's been portrayed by the media: mystical and involving forces and beings more powerful than humanity, either all an illusion or very dangerous and special. But the thing about magic is that when we get into it, really start studying and practicing it, it's really just an applied form of spirituality – and yes, I mean that in the broad alchemical sense.

Magic is not just waving a wand and saying a spell, lighting a candle, and making something happen. Well, it CAN be that, in a certain sense, but it's really deeper than that.

First, at the most basic level, magic is the manifestation of intention. Humans more than any other life form on Earth are driven by desires far more complex than just survival, safety, or contentment. We want to know things for the sake of knowing, not just because those things might give us a survival advantage. We want to create things for reasons that go far beyond perpetuating our species. When it comes to our spirituality, we're back to that bit about humans compounding innovation, taking ideas, combining and playing with them, and building on them. So at its root, magic is about focusing on the ideas we want to bring to life, the things we want to acquire, the stuff we want to see happen. It's going beyond hoping and wishing, but actively intending to cause these things to manifest.

Of course, we bring our intentions into reality in mundane ways all the time. I intend to have ice cream, so I go out and buy ice cream. Voila! I realized my intention!

But we have lots of intentions and desires that aren't really simple to realize. We've been talking all this time about transforming ourselves, growing as people, tapping into energies, and out of that come intentions that aren't just a matter of will and direct action. Getting over a fear of rejection isn't an intention we can manifest as easily as going to buy ice cream. If we go about realizing our spiritual intentions through direct methods, they tend to involve long journeys (metaphorically and sometimes literally), impactful experiences, and patient dedication. And that's great, really. We should do those things. But that's not manifestation.

Manifestation is about leveraging spiritual means and energy towards an intention. It's not the same as tipping the first domino in a chain of events that logically ends in the result we want. We turn to manifestation most often when we don't see a logical chain of events that we can initiate to cause something to happen.

There is so much about the universe we don't understand, but all of that stuff that's still a mystery to us is linked with the stuff that isn't. The things we don't understand still impact our existence. And I think about magic and manifestation as what we turn to when our intended result happens via a chain of events that happens on the other side of the veil separating what we do know from what we don't. We push the domino on this side, eventually the chain reaction tips the last domino as we intended, but we can't see the whole central sequence because it happens off screen, so to speak.

Not knowing exactly what happens on the other side of that veil doesn't stop our actions and choices from causing ripples that we can't see, ripples that eventually come back our way and bring us results. We can even get really good at finding the right ways to get things to happen even though we have no idea why it works. It's kind of like the way many of us interact with technology. We push some buttons, we get what we want (or not), but we don't understand the devices or programming enough to understand what happens in between.

Essentially, that's the basis of manifestation and magic. We release concern for how things come to be but retain responsibility for our intentions and putting the energies in motion. The universe does what it does, our souls do what they do, they communicate through the energies flowing between them, and we learn to work with all of it to manifest what we desire.

Magic may be beyond our understanding, but it is not

beyond our capability. Actually, it's a natural aspect of human ability.

The thing is, all humans do magic. We all have various non-logical, indirect ways of trying to cause our desires to come to pass without our active participation in the process. We all have little lucky rituals, prayers, habitual behaviors, etc., which at some level, we do in hopes of bending reality in our favor. Sometimes it works because of things we can't observe and don't understand. Sometimes it works only because it's a synchronicity, a result we perceive to be true because we want it to be. It doesn't matter which is true. At its very basic level, it's all magic.

In developing and growing my own spiritual practice around magic, I've learned a few crucial basics of how it works and how best to work with it. The first is that it's not an external thing that we learn; it's inherent to each of us. We are magic and it comes from within, from our deep selves.

Even if we don't have a magical practice as in spellwork and witchcraft and the like, we still do magic. Humans are magical creatures by virtue of the nature of human consciousness. It's partly a factor of our being advanced enough that we understand the flow of time and the relationships between our existence and what's beyond it. We aren't just concerned with what could be better about our immediate situation; we can also see the reasons our momentary reality is the way it is and what might happen if we change it. We are able to take a vision and make changes to bring it to life, not just by directly altering things, but by making internal energetic changes, altering the energy we put out into the universe to manifest our intentions indirectly.

So, essentially, as we integrate our shadow aspects and get more in touch with our deep self, we're getting more in touch with the source of our individual magic. Authenticity is everything in magic because it's not some outside source of power we gain access to as if we were renting a car. The power comes from within us. Our deep self is the source of our deepest intentions, and that's important, too. Magic isn't ever going to work as well if we're still trying to manifest intentions that have been shaped and formed by what everyone else thinks we should want.

That's the next basic thing about magic: It comes from within us, and it's there for a reason. We have it so we can use it to benefit us. Humans evolved the ability to do magic along with the evolution of our higher consciousness, which means we have magic to help us survive and thrive. It's part of the skillset needed to exist in human society. We have gotten where we are as a species by the virtue of our magical power. It gives us an evolutionary advantage.

Magic is tied directly in with spirit. It's about our thoughts, emotions, and communication. We've come to be magical beings because magic helps us navigate relationships,

THE SOURCE OF MAGIC

challenges, conflicts, and cultures. It is a way of taking all the various kinds of spirit energy and putting them to work to help us through our life path. It gives us the power to shape our future. It allows us to transcend the limitations of direct action. It puts more tools in our toolbox for living our best life.

Despite the pop culture approach to magic where we think of it as a way to fix or manipulate the world by supernatural methods, the true power of magic and how it really functions is as a way to change and elevate ourselves.

"I will rise to the challenge."

Evolution doesn't work by intention. It's a process of constant adaptation to current circumstances. Evolutionary processes don't anticipate changes in the world around us. They can't reference historical change and predict what's next. This is a truly important thing to understand, because even though spiritual and personal evolution are very different processes than biological evolution, they follow a lot of the same general principles.

There are things about us that change because we want them to, and then there are things that only change through evolution. Biological evolution changes organisms on a genetic level. So if we're dealing with human evolution, there's a clear difference between changing our physical form through weight loss, surgery, hair color, piercing, or other direct methods and changing human bodies in general through evolutionary adaptation over many generations. The direct changes we make individually don't get passed on genetically to the next generation.

Spiritual evolution is a faster and more individual process, but the principle is the same. There is a difference between making conscious changes in our behavior or lifestyle and actually changing our deeper beliefs, values, and identities. The surface changes we make in our habits and choices don't automatically follow us to the next version of self as we evolve.

The various aspects of our deep self, all those beliefs, values, and elements of our worldview, are the spiritual equivalent of our DNA. They determine what manifests just as our DNA determines our physical characteristics. The difference is that we can far more easily make changes to our deep self aspects than our DNA. We get to guide and assist that process for ourselves.

But playing an active role in determining which aspects of self are detrimental and which are beneficial is a real challenge. With biological evolution, the selection process happens naturally in response to environmental pressures because the less-desirable traits remove individuals from the process of reproduction, and their genetic traits don't get carried from generation to generation. Detrimental traits get individual organisms eaten by predators, make them susceptible to disease, make them less attractive to mates, or in some way make them less likely to have healthy offspring.

Spiritual evolution, though, works by shedding and

retaining soul aspects as we become different versions and iterations of ourselves. Each new self we grow into is the spiritual equivalent of a new generation in the life of a species. Our detrimental aspects make it difficult to grow and develop, hold us back from our goals, and generally stand in the way of our moving from one version of self to the next just like detrimental genetic traits stand in the way of healthy reproduction. Our detrimental deep self aspects keep us spiritually stuck. So it's our responsibility, since our spiritual wellbeing is always entirely our responsibility, to stay connected to our deep self and aware of what aspects of self are not serving us – not just the ones we don't like, the ones that are our roadblocks.

Those are absolutely not the same thing.

It's so easy to distract ourselves with the things we don't like about ourselves or we feel self-conscious about, so that we don't have to face up to the aspects that are holding us back. It's easier to focus on things we wish we were, qualities or skills we wish we had, but no matter how much effort we put into bettering ourselves through learning and goal setting, the things we need to transform and release will still be there anchoring us to the current iteration of self.

The biggest leap forward in my own spiritual evolution came from running my art gallery. I struggled and struggled the first two and half years to figure out what I needed to do or learn to make it successful. I looked at other entrepreneurs for ideas and inspiration, trying to find the things I was missing. None of it moved the business forward, and none of what I sought to learn really made me feel like I'd grown or advanced either as a person or as an entrepreneur. Everything I learned made me feel like I needed to learn something else, and it was never enough. I constantly compared myself to others who were more successful, more knowledgeable, more connected.

When I got closer to the end of the lease on the building, I started to think about whether I really wanted to continue trying to make the business profitable. By this time I had gone through those months of shadow work and had started therapy, and I came to realize that all the ways I'd tried to improve myself hadn't failed; it was just that those new skills and bits of knowledge had zero to do with what was really causing the business to flounder. I had more knowledge about how to run a business, but that had never been the problem. What was holding me back were the things I'd been digging up in my shadow work, including the very shadow aspects that had made me want to open the business to begin with. It had been doomed to fail from the start because I had started the business for all the wrong reasons.

I opened the gallery because I was afraid to face rejection if I took my art to other galleries. I didn't want to deal with my feelings of being an outsider, of never being fully accepted in something like the art community, so I started my own gallery to give myself the opportunity that I didn't trust others to give. And even deeper than that, my belief that the only way to be liked, respected, and successful was to impress people and make a certain amount of money was the driving factor behind my desire to make a name for myself as an artist.

Once that came into focus and I was ready to face it,

I decided not to renew the lease. I closed the business and I gave myself time, space, and permission to work on myself. I recognized that even if the business had failed, that didn't mean I had failed, because the business wasn't my identity. My success as a person didn't hinge on my success in any given profession. I challenged myself to thrive in the life I had, the one where I didn't have a business of my own, didn't feel inspired to create for a while, worked a regular job and lived in my parents' rental house, with no idea what my next goals would be. I focused on making that life good, and that's when I finally grew and transformed spiritually in ways I hadn't been able to while the business was open and I was struggling.

The key to this is to really make that assessment from a place of grounded awareness rooted in the present moment. Our authentic self is who we really are in the moment, and that's the self we're evolving. It's not "fixing" our authentic self or transforming it into the person we'd rather be; it's looking at our existence in the moment and determining what our biggest lesson or challenge is and what aspect of self it traces back to. What is standing in the way of our moving into the next phase of our spiritual existence? Now that we're familiar with the process of shadow work, figuring that out should be easier than it's been in our past.

Evolution is about being the most effective, thriving version of ourselves that we can be in the moment. Life may challenge us and illuminate things about ourselves that we want to transform and release, but if it doesn't challenge us enough to actually facilitate that transformation, our natural instinct will be to seek out ways to make things easier. To actually evolve, we have to lean into those changes and challenges instead of running from them.

That's where magic comes in.

Not only is our integrated, authentic self the self we're evolving, it's the root of our magic. What we manifest comes from our souls, our deep selves, our values and motivations. The energies we take in are filtered through our souls and that shapes what comes out. So the more integrated and evolved we are, the more consistently powerful our magic will be.

But the coolest thing is that our magic is also the best tool for personal spiritual evolution.

Our own inner workings are among the parts of the universe we don't entirely understand. We can know what is found inside us at a deep self level; we can look at how we react, think, and behave to figure out some patterns; but none of us have completely cracked the code on how we work. Our subconscious minds are immensely powerful, largely mysterious, and mostly autonomic. We don't control them; they control us. Our subconscious makes most of our decisions, feeds us important information without telling us where it comes from, and shapes every aspect of our behavior. It is more of who we are than our conscious minds are.

The power of the subconscious mind gives us all kinds of cool powers. The advancement of human consciousness makes it so that we don't have to directly experience things to learn them. We can learn by imagining, by pretending, by having spiritual and emotional experiences rather than physical ones.

And our minds are powerful things. When we take

in an idea and really give it space and importance, construct spiritual experiences around it, and put it into action, it has deep ramifications on our behaviors and even how our bodies function. Believing that something has a health benefit is sometimes enough to make our bodies heal, as in the placebo effect.

So we can engineer things to impact our deep self, to guide and enable transformative processes, which then give us more insight and ability to keep transforming. It's like a feedback loop. We can use our logical minds in strategic ways to get down into our subconscious minds and do strategic reprogramming on ourselves.

And that's how we can push ourselves to evolve.

We can use magic in all its forms to create an inner, subconscious environment engineered to enable our transformation and growth. We can construct rituals as experiences that stand in for those we can't easily have in the "real world." We can put our authentic deep self through ritualized and visualized experiences specifically designed to help us release some aspects of self and grow other things in their place.

Remember all the things we've learned through our shadow work, integration, and emergence processes about how we came to be who we are. There are clues in there about the kinds of challenges we need to face in order to produce the kinds of transformation we're facing.

I know that I respond best to long-term challenging projects. When I want to work on myself, I usually set up some sort of regular practice around it because I know I'm very good at doing something one or two times but very bad at consistency. I like my life to be flexible and to have space for spontaneity, so to really challenge myself I have to uproot that. The biggest transformations I've undergone in my life have come after an extended period of struggle where I had no choice but to live in that state of frustration until I made the shift I needed to make. So when I want to push myself to release an aspect of self and encourage something else in its place, I create a practice that requires me to do the thing I'm encouraging.

That's why I ran the marathon. I knew that I needed to release the need to do things my way, so marathon training forced me to lean on systems and guidance from others to succeed.

When I recognized that I needed to release my desire to control and suppress my emotions, I embarked on a 90-day magical practice where every day I assessed and connected with my emotional energy and specifically used it in a magical working.

But that's the sort of thing that resonates with me. We're all wired differently and run on different core programs, so part of getting to know ourselves and mastering our magic is getting to know how best to hack our own subconscious through thought and action.

One important thing to keep in mind is that this process of evolution and transformation has to challenge us to strengthen the aspects of ourselves that we want to create and instill rather than attempting to force us to abandon the things we want to release. Using self-punishment and sheer willpower isn't an effective approach to transformation because it's not rooted in authenticity. This is not like setting a New Year's resolution; there's a reason those fail. It's not just replacing a bad habit with a good one. This is magic.

Magic means using ritual, symbolism, and energy to update our core programming. The results will manifest once we've made the changes in our deep self, so it can't be about a specific outcome. In fact, it's crucial that the magical workings we use have no connection at all to the motivating reasons for doing them. For instance, when I decided to do the marathon as a spiritual endeavor, the impetus was really about my pattern of avoiding the guidance or advice of others, mostly in career-related situations. If I wanted to achieve something, I would always choose to create my own way instead of doing it the accepted way. If there was a DIY option, I took it (and tweaked it, usually, because using it as it was taught felt too much like following orders). I knew that pattern hadn't gotten me anywhere and I knew where it came from, but knowing didn't change it. I needed a way to reprogram the core belief through my subconscious, not my conscious mind. And I don't run. Marathon training had absolutely zero logical connection to any other activity in my life that might be changed through this evolutionary process. If I tried to logic my way to change, my subconscious would push back and resist the way it always does when I act against my authentic way of being.

Remember that we are not dealing with inauthenticities to let go of; we are dealing with authentic parts of ourselves that no longer serve us.

"My life has made me strong."

Spiritual evolution doesn't just change the things that hold us back; it also reveals our strengths. Those aspects of self that do serve us well don't exist by chance, and it doesn't benefit us to always focus on what needs to change. If we want to thrive, we have to also nurture the aspects of self that serve us well.

It's easier to focus on things we want to change than it is to recognize the rest, just like it's easier to define why we don't like something than it is to define why we do like something else. That lends itself well to the process of evolution and growth because humans are inherently problem solvers. The things we don't need to change don't cause problems, so we don't have to solve them. That makes them much less important to the most active parts of our brains.

But while we're being intentional and nurturing our magical abilities, it's time to take stock of our strengths.

Step Eight is to do an inventory of your skills, talents, abilities, and other positive qualities and take time to celebrate and fully exercise them.

Our life experiences have pushed us to develop our skills and to hone the ones we already possessed. As we evolve, we'll continue to build on these things, but the strengths and abilities we have at this point in time are the aspects of self that have allowed us to get this far in life. Unfortunately, our natural human tendency to focus more on our shortcomings and challenges than our strengths means that there's a good chance we give more mental energy to the difficult experiences we've gone through in the past than the skills and lessons we learned in the process of overcoming them.

Think about the fears we've overcome. Not only is it a huge spiritual achievement and valuable evolutionary adaptation to be able to conquer a fear, the process of working through the fears we have allows us to step into our next iteration on our evolutionary journey. Any fear we've overcome in our past led to a leap forward in our growth as a person.

During my summer in France, we went to Disneyland Paris. I had never ridden a roller coaster before because I was afraid I would be the one to get sick and cause the ride to be shut down. But everyone else in the group wanted to go on Space Mountain. I could have just gone off on my own to do something else, but I also had a strong aversion to being the one singled out over things, to drawing attention to myself in any way that might lead to ridicule. So as I stood there in line with everyone for the ride, those two fears warred with each other. Do I get on the roller coaster and risk throwing up and embarrassing myself, or do I get out of line and chicken out and get teased about it for who knows how long? I knew deep down that neither fear was really very reasonable, and I watched as very young kids got off the ride looking like they just had the best time in the world, so why did I think things were going to be so awful?

But all that thinking about it, even thinking about

how unreasonable I was being, didn't really make any change in my behavior, and it definitely didn't result in any kind of deep belief change. What did change my behavior was applying a new belief – that I wasn't really any different from other people, and so if the vast majority of people could ride the ride and enjoy it and not freak out, then I could too. It was a a new way of coping, namely that I would pay attention to the people around me and follow what seemed to be the most reasonable average expectation. In other words, I decided I wasn't especially fragile or likely to react differently from most people, so if most people around me were getting on the ride and getting off with smiles on their faces, I should trust them and follow their lead.

Then I took action. I tested my new belief. I got on the roller coaster. And the lesson I took away from that had nothing to do with roller coasters; it was about my ability to overcome those thoughts that hold me back. I know now that when I have these thoughts, I can overcome them. They're just thoughts and beliefs, and they can be changed. If I don't like them, I can do the work, take the action, find the courage, and transform myself.

I might not have ever been held back in my spiritual journey by a fear of vomiting on a roller coaster, but I've had plenty of other fears. One of my true strengths now is knowing how to overcome an irrational fear and stop it from holding me back.

But overcoming fears isn't the only way we gain and hone our strengths. A lot of what constitutes our core values and deep motivations stems from personal experience, not just something someone told us was true. Something about the way we've experienced life, our very unique combination of life experiences, shapes what we learn, how we learn it, and who we trust to teach us. Every belief we've ever encountered has been shaped by our general experience of the world and reality. It changes how we define things.

Our unique life experience is a strength, and one we can't underestimate the value of. The particular combination of experiences and lessons we each go through in life shapes us into different people with very different beliefs and approaches to reality. A weird thing happens when we immerse ourselves in an experience for a significant length of time. From that point forward, we always have that point of view latent in our mind.

For instance, since I grew up in an Evangelical culture, there's always this voice in the back of my mind that is aware of how that culture would view things. As I'm watching a show like Supernatural, which takes Biblical ideas and treats them in an irreverent

and even sacrilegious way, sometimes I still find myself thinking that my parents and the people I knew in church would probably start planning protests if they knew about it. I don't think that's a reasonable

264

response, but I still know what the world looks like from their particular point of view.

The more we've experienced varied perspectives on life, the more easily we can empathize with others and view infinite possibilities when we're trying to manifest our intentions. Those are significant spiritual strengths that shouldn't be underestimated.

However much time and energy we spend releasing and reshaping the aspects of ourselves that we know don't serve us or help us thrive, we need to spend the same time and energy practicing gratitude and self-appreciation and recognizing our strengths and skills. Gratitude is another one of those popular spiritual topics when it comes to manifestation, but I think it's important to make a bit of a shift in how we approach it as a practice. We're told that if we don't practice gratitude, we'll go into manifestation with a sense of desperation or entitlement. And that may be true. But the bigger issue is that we aren't going to use strengths we don't recognize. We're not going to mindfully exercise the abilities we've learned to ignore about ourselves.

So be grateful for the experiences that gave us our strengths. Be thankful for the abilities that already exist in our authentic deep self and will help us evolve into our next iteration. None of us lack spiritual gifts; we just lack appreciation for them.

Step Nine

Empowerment

"I am the head of my own tradition. My doctrine is my own."

Our spirituality is always in service to our deep self. So if we're committed to personal evolution, our spiritual lives have to come into play to get us there. Of course, it's one thing to take responsibility for our own choices and our own reactions in the process of embracing our authenticity. It's another thing altogether to take responsibility for making the kind of changes necessary for us to truly adapt and evolve.

Spiritual evolution is a process of empowerment. We talked already about agency, which is accepting power over ourselves. Empowerment extends that power to the world around us. We can accept ourselves for who we are all day long, but that doesn't lead to evolution. For that, we have to believe that we're capable of seeking and causing change.

And the biggest piece of empowerment and feeling capable isn't the idea that we don't have the ability to do something; it's that we also have the right or freedom to do it.

I gained a lot of skills during the decade I spent in retail management. On the whole, it was what we might call an empowering experience. I managed teams of up to a dozen employees. I learned not just to hire and fire people, but to train and motivate people. I helped employees climb the ladder into management. I developed sales skills and learned to build and refine processes to solve problems. I discovered a lot of talents and skills I didn't know I had. More than all that, though, I finally learned to see myself as an effective leader and teacher, which had always been a serious source of impostor syndrome.

But anyone who's ever worked retail for a big company also knows that there are tight controls on literally everything. We weren't even allowed to sit down at work, so there were definitely limits on how original I could be with my methods as a manager. As capable as I learned I was, I also learned some hard lessons about what other people were willing to let me achieve.

There's a big difference between thinking we can't do something and thinking that we won't be allowed to do something. It's the difference between having low self-esteem and just lacking trust in the fairness of the systems we're in. Both are forms of disempowerment, but very different ones. I was proud of what I was able to learn and accomplish, but I was terrified to make mistakes because I feared the probable consequences. I knew I wasn't trusted to stretch myself far enough to make mistakes or learn from failure. Failure and mistakes weren't going to be tolerated.

And that's how I learned to see the world and my place in it, which is a very disempowering lesson to learn.

When I left that job and struck out on my own, I ended up working in a very different environment. I started freelancing and was hired by an entrepreneur with a growing coaching business. Over and over again she assured me that she trusted me to take on projects and make decisions without her input, and while I didn't doubt my ability to do things and eventually succeed, I was afraid to take that encouragement at face value. What held me back from feeling fully empowered was the voice in the back of my head questioning how much independence and trust she was really willing to extend. I had learned that bosses don't tolerate mistakes and failure, and without her involvement and guidance, it was inevitable that something wouldn't go as planned or we'd have different visions for how to do things.

It's hard to shift from a lifetime of having limits placed on our abilities by other people to personally controlling those limits and rules. Actually, I've learned that I have a trauma response when I make mistakes because my fear of consequences runs that deep, but even without that, it's really an evolutionary process to adapt to a world without all the limits I've always lived within.

It's like releasing a domesticated animal to the wild. It doesn't automatically know how to thrive in the outside world. It has to learn the skills and reconnect with the instincts it needs to survive.

But that's literally what empowerment is. It's learning what lies on the other side of the limits we've lived with and taking hold of the power we never knew we had access to. We've been trained to exist within certain parameters, but nobody else is going to step in and make sure we have all the knowledge and understanding we need to succeed once those boundaries are erased. We have to seek that power ourselves. And it's not usually others who decide to remove those boundaries, either. We get to liberate ourselves. It's a process of learning how to use that power and figuring out what it means to decide for ourselves what to use it for.

Empowerment requires self trust and granting ourselves the permission to use the abilities we have. It also means gaining enough understanding and command over our life in a spiritual sense that we can trust ourselves to wield those powers regardless of what anyone else has to say about it.

THE BoSS OF YoU:

That's what evolution requires, too. We have to get comfortable with our ability to make changes in our world and to nurture our own transformation. Stuff like assuring ourselves that it's okay to go against the

270

expectations and preferences of others, that we can be trusted to make our own decisions, that our worldview doesn't have to be adopted by anyone else to be relevant, meaningful, and true for us as an individual. To really evolve spiritually, we have to embrace our right to be the spiritual authority in our own life. We have to believe that it is okay for us to decide what's important, what our purpose is, to set our own priorities, and shape our own practice.

Part of my own ongoing process of empowerment is learning that although I may not trust the systems to treat me fairly, I can still work to change the system. I can choose to not remain part of the system. All of those choices are empowerment, too.

We've talked a lot about restrictions and limitations from our past that have left us carrying spiritual baggage into the present, but it's important to remember that we did leave those traditions behind. Whoever holds the most power in our spiritual life is the one who shapes our personal evolution. If we want to be authentic in our evolution, that power has to rest in our own hands.

"I have escaped my old cage. I will now learn to spread my wings."

The single biggest obstacle to any of us stepping up and taking the reins fully in our own spiritual life is that religion has always been framed as something that is beyond us. We don't get to argue with God or

Truth, and if that's the way we've always been taught to treat spirituality, it's going to feel wrong to take leadership, even in our own life.

In formal spirituality and religion, it's pretty common for leadership positions or positions of honor to be restricted and exclusive, so that even many of those who want to step into them aren't able to. My formerly Catholic wife still talks about how upset she was as a kid to find out that boys could be altar boys but there were no altar girls. She took it up as a bit of a cause to push for, and although she can't really take any credit for the change in policy, they did eventually start allowing girls to become altar girls.

She loves telling this story because when the policy was changed, everyone came to her all excited to let her know she could finally become an altar girl like she'd always wanted, but she didn't. She didn't want to BE one; she just didn't like that she was being told she couldn't.

But that sort of thing is really common in religious traditions, and it serves to teach us that we don't have a place in spiritual leadership. We're all impacted differently by this depending on our particular spiritual history as well as our age, gender, etc. But even if we were never told that we couldn't participate in ways we wanted to, even if we did participate in a position of spiritual leadership in the past, all of those leadership experiences happen in the service of an even higher power.

Now, growing up as a preacher's kid, I can absolutely say that every priest or minister or whatever has the ability to interpret and twist the meaning of scriptures and sacred texts and therefore really create their own sub-doctrines, at least to a point. Nobody takes the pulpit and just feeds doctrine straight from the Church to the masses. So we may not really acknowledge it, but spiritual leaders do hold more power than we like to admit.

But by and large, unless we've been in a cult situation, spiritual leaders aren't sharing primarily from their own personal take on spirituality. Their purpose is always to lead the lay people in their journey along the path set out for them. It's a lot like being a middle manager in a corporation. In a corporate environment, our skills as a leader are important, but we don't get to decide where we're leading

everyone. Our skills are put to use in the interest of the people above us, like upper management and the CEO. And in religion, that entity above us is either a deity or the higher powers in the church.

When I was born, my dad was still aligned with a denomination that determined where he served and dictated the particular doctrines to be taught. It was very much like being a middle manager in a corporation, and for reasons that went back to the time before I was born, my parents' personal beliefs diverged more and more from that of the organization.

Come to find out later, if that split hadn't happened, I'd have been raised in a much cooler, much more liberal branch of Christianity, and I've wondered how much different my spiritual journey would have been if that had been the case.

Anyway, what did happen was that my parents chose to leave that church, because, in their view, the will of God and the will of the church were at odds and they were following the higher authority. They felt the church was being too liberal with its interpretation of scripture and that the boundaries and limitations should be much tighter than the church did.

Yes, I do see the irony in Dad choosing to defy the limitations of a church that told him not to preach according to his own beliefs, only to preach a version of doctrine that was more restrictive to everyone else.

Even in less-formal contexts like neopaganism, it's easy to see how we can be so conditioned to defer to some higher power that we choose to take on limitations to our leadership, even over ourselves. We answer to ancestors, pantheons, or historical tradition instead of allowing ourselves free use of our mind and voice. We expect there to be rules and standards and for something or someone else to show us the way, and so we'll find something to put in that space one way or another.

From observing many people (including myself) going through the process of trying to find a spiritual path that fits their authentic self, I've recognized a few patterns. The big one is that when we leave one religion or tradition, depending on the circumstances that made us leave, we either look to something very similar to or completely opposite from whatever we just left. Either way, what ends up happening is that we don't really question the roots and foundations of the path we just left; we continue to accept them even as we look for something different.

We're so conditioned to it that a lot of us don't feel right creating our own spiritual life, designating our own dogma for ourselves, and seizing our own spiritual power. It might feel a lot like trying to start our own cult, even though it isn't. It requires healing and evolving those parts of ourselves that we've been taught over time not to trust. And it means testing the boundaries we've learned to exist within.

Not all of us are authentically comfortable with taking risks and breaking rules. But just because we've been taught certain rules in the past doesn't mean that they're still legitimate for us. Our religious and spiritual past has put boundaries and limitations on us under the authority of powers and leaders that we don't necessarily believe in anymore. The act of stepping past and dismissing those expectations and limits isn't rebellion or defiance. It's stepping into our own liberation.

———————

"I will not waste my will and power waiting on a turn of luck."

———————

Magic, beyond being about spiritual empowerment, is about energy. The whole universe is animated by energy. Spirit is energy and so is life force. And really, all of those terms refer to the very same thing. Spirit is all the different forms of energy viewed as one big composite universal force.

It can seem a bit contradictory to think of magic as something personal and internal while energy and spirit are external and universal. It's definitely not the way we commonly think of magic. The usual image of magic is a skill we're taught or is given to us, where the power and energy of it as well as the understanding and ability to do it comes from something bigger than and beyond ourselves. We think of magic in terms of methodologies and results more than anything, turning to books and teachers to give us the right words and rituals and tell us exactly what we need to learn to master our magic.

But I like to compare magic to art. A lot of people think of and talk about art as if it's all about the product. When we talk about art, we most often mean the paintings, the films, the music, the poems, the books, the performances, the drawings. We tend to make it about the end results in the same way we reduce magic to the spells, potions, and healing treatments.

But really, when we treat magic as something completely focused on the products or end results, we commodify it. We don't want to make our magic about competition and how valuable our skills are compared to others. The point of magic isn't just to become good at magic, just like the point of art isn't to become good at art. Art isn't about the ability to create a painting, write a play, or design a dress. The point of art is self-expression, not production, and the same is true about magic. The point of magic is manifestation, not achievement.

It's also not about the medium itself. Paint isn't art; art is made with paint. A plucked string making a note isn't art; art is made with the sound of a plucked string. And that's what energy is to magic. Energy isn't magic; magic is worked using energy. Energy is the medium.

Magic is about using the ability to work with energy in order to manifest our intentions. The energies and forms of spirit we use to do magic are media to be worked with, sources of power but not ability. Knowing how to work with fabric or watercolors doesn't make us an artist, but it's very hard to bring our artistic vision to life without learning to work with our materials, our media. Knowing how to transform spirit energy to help manifest our intentions doesn't make us an effective magical practitioner, but it's pretty well impossible to master our magical ability without learning to work with energy.

What we're really talking about here is using spirit and our spiritual understanding as a tool and a medium rather than just treating spirit as part of our environment that we've learned to interact with.

In doing our shadow work, we learned about our relationship to spirit, how it shapes and affects us. During our detox, we learned to take responsibility for determining the flow of spirit into our lives so that the influence of others doesn't hold us back from being ourselves. But we can also be the ones to assert our own influence over ourselves, to design and create and control the flow of energy in our lives towards our own purposes.

Nearly everything we do in life involves some spiritual flow, some energy exchange. It's not just spiritual, evolutionary processes that get us involved in spiritual connections and the transformation of energy. Everything is spiritual in life.

If spirit is the "soup" of energies in which we exist, then spirituality is any and all interactions we have with those energies. It's how we take it in, what kind of energies we take in, what we do with those energies, what kind of energy we put out, what we transform it all into. We're constantly interacting with information, opinions, and ideas. Even our relationships are part of our spiritual lives. Our interests, studies, conversations, activities, and the way we spend our time and money – all of it is spiritual at some level no matter how we define spirituality.

It's spirit that shapes our growth and development in the first place. It's the energetic and spiritual environment in which we exist that forms us into who we are. Sure, we can choose whether to consume and make use of the spirit that flows our way in life, but we can also go seek out what we need and bring it to us. Surrounding ourselves with the right spirit energy is the key to not just creating the environment we want to create for ourselves, but also to building ourselves up.

There are a lot of challenges that call for us to adapt and evolve in order to really thrive, and it makes a huge difference whether we've got access to the kinds of spirit energy we need.

When I opened my art gallery, I found myself pretty much alone in facing the challenge. My wife and my family were very supportive, of course. They invested financially in the business and volunteered to help out in the shop when I couldn't afford to pay employees, but I didn't have anyone around who really understood the ins and outs of that kind of entrepreneurship or business. I didn't have anyone who understood the unique stresses of that kind of job, and I especially didn't know anyone who had expert guidance to offer to help me find a way forward.

This was also before I started doing my shadow work and connecting with my deep self, so a lot of my inauthentic patterns held me back from seeking out those experts and advisors. I felt very alone in my endeavor, completely responsible for figuring out how to get past the hurdles. For all my intention to succeed, I didn't go out in search of the energetic flow I needed to do so.

That business failed.

Fast-forward a couple of decades to my time in the business coaching industry. One thing I've talked about over and over again with clients and potential clients is about how isolating and lonely it can be as an entrepreneur. So many people are in exactly the place I was in when I ran the gallery: unsupported, trying to figure it out alone, having no one to lean on for meaningful support or guidance. One of the biggest benefits most of them find in joining coaching programs, mastermind groups, or networking communities is that it gives them those connections to others who are doing the same thing. It might seem like that's really all about the emotional support and being able to learn from others, which is definitely a benefit and is certainly a form of spiritual energy exchange, but it can be used in a self-serving, insulating way.

It's actually very easy and attractive to just immerse ourselves in flows of spiritual energy that are more of what we already have and are, reflecting our existing patterns and preferences back at us rather than filling the gaps and helping us grow. What I see successful entrepreneurs doing, which I never did, is actively seeking out connections specifically to bring them what they don't have and support them where they struggle, to establish new connections and relationships unlike those they already have.

Every relationship or connection in our life is an exchange of spiritual energy. Every single connection either brings us more energy or is something we pour energy into. And we can choose to accept or deny those connections, break the ones that are detrimental to us and strengthen those which are beneficial, but truly mastering the flow of energy in our life means crafting those relationships and seeking out the sources and recipients of our energy based on our intentions and values.

And the energy we put out is every bit as important as what we take in. We've spent a lot of this journey dealing with the energies we take in and how they affect us, but we don't just hold them inside. They are transformed by our deep self and sent back out into the universe. If we just let the spirit flow as it will from within us, that's an authentic expression, and it will manifest a physical existence that speaks to who we are. But we can exert control over how that expression happens, we can shape every step of the process so we take in the spirit we need to convert it into the energy necessary for whatever expression that we need to manifest our intentions. The energy we put out can work for us as much as it expresses who we are.

Business and entrepreneurship is a good example of this as well. One of the mistakes I made as an entrepreneur was to put all of my energy into things that felt emotionally safe, like creating artwork and merchandise. I put energy into crafting my website and building internal systems to help the business run smoother. I poured a ton of energy into that business in a lot of different forms. What I didn't do was pour a lot of energy into promoting the business, and I told myself that it was because I didn't have the connections or resources that

other business owners did. I couldn't afford to have a regular advertising budget. I didn't know people who could help me run large-scale promotional efforts. I had nobody in my network who had any expertise in PR.

But, of course, there were other ways to promote my shop, and after a lot of shadow work I realized that there were lots of fears holding me back. It wasn't my lack of connections; it was my fears limiting my sources of energetic output and investment to what was already in my environment. Had I been committed to mastering the spiritual flow of energy in my life, I would have sought to create new connections whom I could pour energy into who would have helped manifest the success I envisioned for my business. I could have really taken stock of the energetic resources at my disposal and figured out the best way to invest in them to get results. I didn't have extra money, but I had time, ideas, merchandise, and motivation. All of those things are energy, and there are infinite ways to put them to use if we don't accept the limitations of the connections that already exist for us.

Ultimately, mastering the flow of energy and becoming an effective magical practitioner means not just recognizing and embracing our own sense of agency. It's great and healthy to fully exercise our ability to choose for ourselves rather than to let others make choices for us. But this is one step further. It's not just choosing; it's creating our own choices by adding whole new options to the list.

Part IV: The Power of Magic

"My power is not in what I have, but from what I can do with what I have."

What stands in the way of us thriving in our lives at any given time aren't the challenges we don't know how to overcome; it's that we don't have the abilities we need to overcome them. As much as we can feel comfortable with the freedom to assert ourselves spiritually, that doesn't mean that we're going to know how to overcome what we face. No matter how empowered or skilled any of us are at anything, there will continue to be challenges, and we will continue to need to adapt and evolve in order to thrive.

Spiritual empowerment means taking hold of spiritual power. Spiritual power is energy, and energy is the medium we use to do magic. Therefore, magic is a form of spiritual empowerment. And all that spiritual energy and power can be used a couple of ways when it comes to our evolution. On the one hand, we can use magic as a way to facilitate the internal changes necessary to grow and develop. As we talked about in the previous chapter, magic is a great way to hack the subconscious and reprogram bits of our deep self.

On the other hand, sometimes evolution just means expanding our abilities and there's nothing to be released. And in that case, the magic itself can be the adaptation. Magic literally expands our abilities beyond the direct and logical. It may not enable us to rule over others and bend the world to our will, but it does allow us to exert energetic influence beyond the limits of what might seem possible.

The allure of magical practice for a lot of people is the idea that it can give us abilities that defy the limits of the everyday. If we look at magic as supernatural, learning magic becomes a way for us to transcend whatever restrictions we might feel keep us from living the life we want to live or being the person we want to be. It's only logical, especially given the way magic is talked about in media and even by practitioners, to be drawn to magic as a way of becoming more powerful in the world.

Coming into the world of magical practice, I assumed that I'd be learning to access a form of power outside myself and learning skills and methods that "regular" people didn't know about. Magic seemed like this fantastic, supernatural realm that we gained special access to so that we could work with energies that we'd never or rarely encountered before. My biggest expectation when I started dabbling in spellwork and messing around with crystals and casting circles in my living room was that I'd feel a supernatural presence or the flow of magical energy in a way that I'd never felt before. And while I did feel different energies from crystals or different sensations in my body as we did various activities, it wasn't really supernatural. It was subtle pressure or warmth or a zillion other perfectly normal reactions, just in a new context.

And the more I studied magic and really poked around at what I was doing and why, the more it became obvious that magic is really a form of applied psychology and applied sociology. And by that I don't mean that magic isn't real. Magic is incredibly real. It just isn't supernatural. It's totally natural and inherent to human existence. We make magic by applying the functions of our brains in ways that leverage the subconscious rather than the conscious. It's that simple.

The energies we use in magic are the same forms of energy we deal with every day. It's scientific stuff like heat, light, movement, and electricity. It's the same mental and physical energy we use for everything else.

My "gateway drug" into magical practice was feng shui. When I first started reading about it, I was fascinated by the idea of qi, that there was supernatural energy flowing around the Earth and through my home and that it impacted the rest of my life. But as I started actually working on my living space, analyzing things and putting remedies in place, it all seemed very mundane.

Actually, there were more than a few moments where I had to step away from the process for a while because I started to hear my mom's voice in my mind harping at me to clean up my room, and I got resentful. I mean, there's no way that my mom would have ever entertained the idea of feng shui being anything but evil, but if she saw a feng shui expert telling me to pick up my shoes and make sure all my belongings were in their assigned places and tidied up, she'd be nodding along. And I'm mature enough to admit to the amount of rebellious energy I still feel around that.

Somewhere in my learning about feng shui, though, I came across an expert who actually just came right out and said that chi wasn't something transcendent; it was just the combination of all the energies we already felt in our homes. The movement of air and the play of light, the energies of mood and emotion, the perception of a space in terms of size and openness or even safety, scents and sounds, all of it combined together is chi.

And I think it's important to sit with this for a bit because this doesn't always land well with people who have a different concept of what magic is. I mentioned before how often I've been told that science and magic don't mix, and that if we can explain how something works, it takes the magic out of it.

The thing is, though, that magic isn't really supernatural. We're naturally magical beings. To do magic we're leaning on skills we already possess by function of the way our brains and bodies already work, and we're dealing with energies in the world that have always been there and always will be. It's all natural, it's all already present, and therefore, even if parts of it have not been thoroughly explained, by definition it still isn't supernatural.

To me, that's an empowering thought. Magic comes from within us. We're already capable of magic, and the process of learning and mastering it is a process of personal empowerment. It means that we all have more innate personal power and more ability to impact the world around us than we usually credit ourselves with. We may not naturally know how to really leverage that ability, but it's there and it always has been. For some of us, that's a shift in how we think about empowerment and about magical power itself, because power can mean the actual energies and forces at hand or it can mean ability or even authority. Many of us go into magic looking for the former when what we get is the latter.

In a lot of ways, magical energy is like money. We look around and see things we could do if we had access to more money. I lived my whole life that way, being acutely aware of how much less money I had than other people and what they were able to do because of it. I wanted a life that I thought I could only get if I made more money. I wanted it so much that I shaped my decisions around making money, and it became the way I judged my progress in life.

But here's what I imagined:

I always felt like I didn't have a lot of friends or people who really wanted to be around me. I wanted a life where I felt included and accepted. Most of all, I wanted people to want to be in my presence rather than feeling obligated. Thinking of the people I knew who had that kind of life, I concluded that I needed to make a name for myself and build a life others wanted to share.

I envisioned having a nice home that I'd designed myself, throwing dinner parties for friends, and I figured I'd need to achieve some kind of success to attract that kind of friends. I chased the money and the success because I thought they were the key to the rest of it.

Somewhere along the line, after all my deep shadow work and then therapy and magical practice to integrate my shadow, I had a huge epiphany. The money and success were just forms of energy, and I was chasing them instead of chasing what I really wanted, which was friends and a home I could invite them to. That didn't require jumping through all the hoops necessary to try and hoard more money or achieve impressive things.

I was putting energy into getting more energy instead of using the energy already on hand to get what I really wanted.

Essentially, the short cut to the life I wanted was to first of all, make friends and, second, make space for those relationships in my life. And that's when I realized that the bigger problem was that I'd never practiced making friends. I hadn't put the effort into mastering that skill the way I'd put effort into becoming wealthy and successful. And no amount of wealth and success was going to make up for me not knowing how to make friends.

Magic is the same way. The energy is out there. It's in us, it's around us, and it's not some special thing we have to earn or win access to. One of my personal mottos these days is, "There's always more money," and it's true of energy, too. We may only have a small amount at any given time, but there's always more out there to be had. It's just a resource.

The real challenge isn't acquiring more money or

tapping into sources of magical energy. To haul out the computer analogy again, plugging in the computer so it has the electricity to function doesn't accomplish much. It's the work that gets done after that that makes the difference. The real challenge is two-fold: First, it's mastering how to use and transform the spiritual, magical energy surrounding us, and second, it's putting those mastered skills towards appropriate intentions.

No matter what others might have told us along the way, the secret sauce of a powerful magical practice isn't in the energy. It's not even in our spiritual gifts. We all have spiritual gifts of one kind or another, points of view, or skills and abilities that come easily to us in this endeavor. The real power is in the intention and the knowledge of how best to put the manifestation in motion. That's magic. The energy we use to do it is just energy. It's not special.

So as we're pursuing spiritual evolution and personal empowerment, it's important to remember that the power is in the practice. No amount of energy, power, or resources hoarded around us will overcome our challenges and facilitate our evolution. Only practice will. We have to use those resources and energies towards a purpose, and that means gaining skill and mastering abilities.

When we stop thinking about magic in terms of how much power it allows us to hold and start thinking of magic in terms of how much we can learn to do with our power, it shifts the way we practice and the way we grow as people. It's the difference between asking what we would do if we were super rich and instead asking what could we accomplish if we were managing a huge amount of money? They're two very different questions.

So what growth and adaptation can we accomplish given that we are, actually, managing the flow of a huge amount of spiritual energy in our lives? Learning magic is expanding what we are capable of, and as long as we focus on developing the skills and abilities we need to rise to the challenges we face, then we're facilitating our evolution.

"I can always find a path forward."

There is no such thing as failure in spirituality.

Sure, lots of things we attempt to do or pursue turn out different from what we envisioned, but that's not failure. Spirituality doesn't have a goal, and it doesn't have a scorecard to grade us with. For a lot of people that might be frustrating, but in reality it's liberating and positive.

I was the class valedictorian in high school. Grades had been my entire focus in life ever since junior high, so when I entered college I didn't really know how to deal with anything lower than an A. I had a vague appreciation for the fact that now that I'd made it to college I didn't have to pack my schedule full of extracurricular activities anymore to try and build an impressive résumé. But I still assumed that my grades needed to be very high.

At the beginning of my sophomore year, the very first studio assignment in the architecture program was also our first attempt to design a built space. I was incredibly proud of my design, the drawings I'd done, and the model I built. I presented it for critique in front of the class, and all the feedback was positive.

Afterwards, each student had a conference with the professors for a private critique and to receive their grade for the project. I went into the critique room and had a great discussion with the professors about my design. They had positive feedback and complimented my work.

And then gave me a C+.

I was devastated. I don't really remember leaving the critique room. But before long, as student after student came back from their private critique in or near tears, we began to realize that there was something significant going on.

In the end, the professors explained that they had graded on a curve, so if we got anything above a C it meant we were in the top half of the class and that was very good. Anything over a D meant we had done satisfactory work or better. They wanted us to get used to focusing more on what we learned from the design projects and the critiques rather than on the grades. Design is a very subjective thing to grade, so in a lot of ways the grades don't mean anything. The real learning is in the experiences.

Lots of students were downright angry, but I found it incredibly liberating. I'd spent years of my life chasing the highest grades by choosing the most valuable classes regardless of my interest in them, and in doing so ended up taking classes I didn't care about and skipping over experiences I would have loved to have. Realizing that the grades no longer mattered the way they did in high school freed me to pursue my interests and passions rather than pour all my energy into competition.

Step Nine is to practice seeing every step on your path as an opportunity to learn.

There is no end goal to spirituality, and there is no end goal to evolution. Our only job in our spiritual life is to pursue learning and growth and be our authentic self. There's nothing at all to be gained by trying to live up to a perfect ideal or by comparing ourselves to others who are on different spiritual paths than we are.

There's no way to fail in spirituality. Even if we slip back into inauthenticity now and then, that's not failure. It's just part of our journey.

When we remove ideal goals from our spirituality, what we're really doing is revealing our infinite

potential. Having a definition for what we're supposed to become through our spiritual endeavors places a finite limit on what and who we can be. Without it, our evolutionary processes occupy the core of our spiritual endeavors, and we become limited only by our willingness to take action.

Each step in our evolution happens when we adapt ourselves to the challenges we face. There is no limit to the ways life can challenge us. Nobody is infinitely capable and resilient. The universe will always ask more from us than we can deliver in our current state of authenticity. So there is no limit to the universe's potential for pushing us to adapt and change. That means there's no limit to what we can become as long as we keep adapting and growing.

As we evolve, we find new sides of ourselves and step into new levels of ability and vision. Our understanding of ourselves, the universe, and our place in existence expands with every jump forward in our own development. Every new ability we master opens us to new situations where those abilities aren't entirely sufficient for success. Growth and change never ends. And the first evolutionary adjustment many of us need to make to fully open ourselves to growth and change is to foster the evolutionary mindset.

Positive thought and positive energy are big topics these days. In a world obsessed with manifestation, there's a lot of focus on positivity on the grounds that if we are always positive, we'll always be setting ourselves up to manifest positivity.

I find that troublingly naive and unrealistic.

What most people mean by positivity is happiness, contentment, and lack of struggle. When many of us make an effort to embrace positivity, what we actually do is reject anything that feels like discomfort or effort. But that's not positivity; that's delusion. Challenges and struggles exist, and this twisted image of what positive vibes really are just keeps us from acknowledging our hurdles and pouring energy into elevating ourselves to meet the challenges as they arise. It's like demanding a straight-A life where we barely learn anything rather than embracing the opportunity to learn and grow and not worry about what others think we should have done.

The way most people practice positivity is a direct path to frustration and powerlessness. It isn't empowering. In fact, it blames us for hardships that might come our way as if we are only challenged when we haven't been positive enough. If we think that struggle and challenge means we've done something wrong, how will we ever evolve?

Positivity is absolutely valuable and something we should exercise, just not in the way we've been taught to understand it.

When I was a very little kid, someone gifted me a book called The Lady Who Saw the Good Side of Everything. It's actually turned out to be one of the most influential books I've ever read. It tells the story of a woman who has a whole string of unusual disasters happen to her. Yet no matter what comes her way, she finds the silver lining. Even when she and her cat are swept away from their home by floodwaters, she says that she's always wanted to travel around the world, and she faces the prospect of floating all the way to Asia as a welcome adventure.

That's the kind of positivity that actually nurtures us and facilitates our evolution. It's simply about being confident in our ability to rise to those challenges. The lady in the book didn't pretend that a flood hadn't just washed her whole existence away; she just decided to focus more on how she could get the most out of the situation than on the things that she could easily get angry and frustrated about.

Finding that capacity for positivity in ourselves is a huge evolutionary leap forward. It changes our whole approach to spirituality and to life, and it helps us take the lead role in driving our spiritual existence. It equips us to handle what comes our way in life no matter what it is.

Step Ten
Design

"The only mold I will shape myself to fit is the one I design myself."

Now that we're on the other side of the spiritual detox process (for now) and easing back into a functioning spirituality, we have to be mindful of how that process unfolds. If we only make room for the things that reinforce the authentic self that existed at the end of our detox, it makes it extremely difficult to shift to the next version of ourselves. We can aspire to and think about it all we want, but evolution doesn't happen without actually making changes. If we keep living the same life and doing the same things, surrounding ourselves with the same people and sources of spirit, we only get growth and we never get evolution.

My wife and I have talked for a long time about

wanting to do more international traveling. We want to explore the UK now that we've gotten our DNA results back and know just how much of our family trees trace back to Ireland and Scotland. We want to go to Japan and bring back a whole bunch of crazy souvenirs. She traveled to Germany in high school, and I spent all that time in France, so we want to go back to show each other the places we've seen. Someday I want to follow in my grandmother's footsteps and take a trip around the world. It's a great aspiration, right? We've done lots of talking about it and lots of dreaming about the places we could go and what we could do there.

Just a few months ago, we finally went and applied for passports.

All that talking about what we wanted to do, things we might do "someday," and we didn't even have the necessary things to make "someday" possible.

None of that travelling was ever going to happen until we took action to lay the groundwork. Of course, there have been times in our lives when there was just no room to even think about that kind of travel being possible with our jobs, income, and living situations being what they were. But no matter how much our lives changed over time, without us putting in specific efforts, our travel dreams would have literally never been possible.

No matter how much different our life may be just based on the shadow work and detox process we've gone through and how those changes manifested in our material reality, our life is still specifically shaped to support the self that created it. It's not meant to support the next steps in our evolution.

What good does it do to go through the whole painstaking process of learning about ourselves, doing the hard work of embracing our authenticity, committing ourselves to personal evolution, and then fill our lives with things that get in the way of or distract from those evolutionary processes? The things and people we surround ourselves with both reflect us and shape us, and even the most authentically supportive environment can eventually hold us back from our potential and dreams. And this is especially true if the focus of the environment we build is our achievements, our identity, our material desires. All of that comes from who we are at a moment in time, and the more of it we get and surround ourselves with, the more likely we are to stay that person.

The more honest work we do towards an authentic spirituality, the less we're going to be focused on what we can have or what we can change about the world around us, and the more we're going to be concerned about the changes we want for our inner selves. Our environment, our self-expression, and our possessions stop being achievements in themselves.

Evolution is not driven by intention; it's driven by external changes. We evolve because we have to change to continue to thrive, and those changes come from outside, not inside. We evolve by adapting to our environment when it challenges us, so if our environment doesn't challenge our ability to keep thriving, we won't evolve. If our environment remains exactly as our deep self has manifested, we're not going to feel any pressure to be different.

Sure, life is going to throw challenges and changes at us no matter what, but that doesn't necessarily cause us to evolve, because our first and most deeply human reaction to change and challenge is to avoid it, hide from it, and ignore it as much as we can. That's how we accumulate all that stuff that we shoved into the dark corners of ourselves. Any changes we had to make or pieces of ourselves we had to lean on to deal with challenges in the short term didn't feel like who we wanted to be, so we pushed them away into the dark where we didn't have to acknowledge them. We seek comfort and safety, even if it means denying parts of ourselves because that's what our instincts tell us to do. But instincts aren't about evolution.

If we have any interest in changing, in elevating ourselves, in personal evolution, we've got to lean into the specific challenges that are most likely to trigger those specific adaptations. It means we have to make the appropriate adjustments in our physical environment rather than waiting for natural processes to shift on their own. We have to design our environment rather than just manifest or create it.

Basically, evolution means seeking out, and when we have to, creating the particular environment that is going to pressure us into the changes we want to make in ourselves. That's the kind of environmental design it takes to foster evolutionary changes rather than just personal growth. We have to surround ourselves with different people, situations, and things to become a new version of ourselves.

"I am more powerful than I've been told I can be."

We've talked a lot about how the various lessons and experiences of our spiritual path have taught us to hide our authentic self, to hate parts of ourselves, or to pretend to be different for all sorts of reasons. But at the core of all of that, of all the things that religion and spirituality and life in general have taught us, is our basic understanding of what we're capable of.

It's one thing to look at ourselves and question whether we're being who we are, to dig through the layers of ways that we've been taught to judge ourselves. But it's entirely different to realize that our self concept has been limited by what we've been taught in our life. And, unfortunately, religion tends to do a bang-up job of that as well.

There are a few common themes in religious doctrines: Either humanity was created or shaped into an ideal form by a higher power and has since fallen into a lesser state, or humanity is inherently flawed and lesser and we have to work to raise ourselves up, or only special humans are ever going to attain some higher level of being. And no matter where our past religious paths have taken us through those various concepts, the ultimate message is that there's a limit to what we, as individuals, are capable of in a spiritual sense. We're imperfect, flawed, tainted, and unevolved, and therefore we have to work really hard to be more.

The thing is, we learn from experiences as much as we learn from what we're told. And our spiritual and religious experiences were probably largely not designed to make us feel individually powerful or enlightened. Traditional religion presents us with experiences designed to make us need and trust something bigger.

Some of my favorite and most profound spiritual experiences were in cathedrals and monasteries in France when I was in college. I was on my foreign study trip, outside the country for the first time in my life, and eager to explore the world. I was still a Protestant then, but when I think of Europe, I think of old Catholicism, so I made a point of going to a few services at Notre Dame de Paris instead of trying to find a church more like my own back home.

Plus, we went to a ton of cathedrals because it was an architecture study trip.

The thing about cathedrals and other grand old religious buildings is that they were specifically designed to instill a sense of awe. They're massive to the point of incomprehensible for the time in which they were constructed. The echoes of prayers and singing and the light coming through the stained glass aren't supposed to make a person feel individually powerful; they're supposed to make a person feel small in the face of the vastness of their deity's power. And they do that. Even just walking through a cathedral is an exercise in feeling small against the incredible complexity and beauty of this space our forebears managed to create from stone with relatively primitive tools.

After our time in France, we went to the UK, and we made a point of visiting Stonehenge. Honestly, I was surprised at the time by how much less imposing it seemed than my imagination had made it out to be, but still, even without getting to go up close to it and experiencing what the space was like inside, it was a profound experience. I took six whole rolls of 35 mm film (this was 1997, after all) of the monument, capturing it from every angle I could manage. There was, again, this sense of awe that this seemingly impossible thing had even been constructed at all.

But that's the irony here. Humans did those things. People with much more primitive technologies and less knowledge of science and math did this stuff that makes us feel so small and in awe. And these weren't special humans, just regular ones like us. The awe we feel in a cathedral isn't about the power of a deity; it's the power of the beauty that we've learned to create. The disbelief we feel at Stonehenge isn't about ancient devotion to spirits or gods; it's the ability to cooperatively execute something so difficult with such precision.

Humans are powerful beings. We're capable of quite a lot of surprising things, and yet spirituality and religion tend to teach us differently. Some of this is because religion is tied in with power structures, designed to reinforce the hierarchies of the place and time where the religion is conceived, and the peasants need to be kept in line, so to speak. Okay, a lot of it is because of that. And there's no place for that in our authentic spirituality.

This isn't just about human capability in general, though; it's about us as individuals. All sorts of experiences and the agendas of those around us have damaged our sense of power and capability. Spirituality has to do with thoughts and emotions and such forms of spirit, so things like our perceived intelligence or our control over our emotions, our mental health, even our social skills all have something to do with how capable we feel as individuals in a spiritual sense. It's not just the judgments we have about whether the level of ability we have to do various things is okay and acceptable; our actual assessment is wrong.

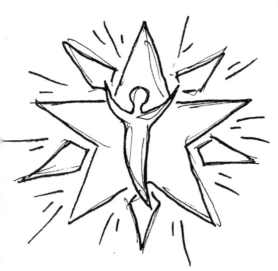

So the last step in letting go of the baggage we're all still carrying from our spiritual past is to really connect to our own inherent power. Not the power religion or spirituality give us, but the power we inherently have because we are human and the unique abilities we have as individuals.

Part IV: The Power of Magic

"If I can't change my world, I will change my world."

We aren't just vessels for storing energy; we consume and transform it into other types of energy and spirit as well as material forms. We know that our growth and emergence manifest in the physical and drive us to make different choices about what we surround ourselves with, but those choices are direct action. They might be emotionally or spiritually difficult as far as the choices themselves, but the action is simpler. If I need to set aside a space for my spiritual activities in my house, it only requires some new household rules, a few supplies, and whatever physical effort it takes to set it up. If I determine that I'm in a relationship that's harmful to my spiritual development, it's a matter of choosing to not participate anymore. It doesn't take special consideration to figure out how to make those things happen.

But we don't always have that kind of control over or ability to change the world around us directly. Direct action only goes so far.

All through my high school and college days, I was involved in philanthropy organizations. My parents weren't just religious; they were politically active. I was raised in a tradition that instilled the idea that I could and should work to change the world. That's one of the things I've carried with me through all my spiritual meanderings. So after 2016, I found myself called to do something, to participate more actively than I had in previous years. I wanted to do more than volunteer for a good cause. I wanted to lend my skills and knowledge to really push for change. I joined organizations, took leadership positions, organized to register votes and gather signatures, even threw my hat in the political ring.

It doesn't take very long in the activist community to start questioning how much difference even an organized group of people can make. That's why it's so much more rewarding to do local philanthropy rather than social activism. If we build a house for a homeless family or help feed the hungry, there's a result we can point to, and often, some expression of gratitude that affirms that we've done something good. When we work towards larger changes in the world, trying to get ballot measures passed or trying to educate the public, those tangible results and pats on the back are a lot harder to come by. We can't change minds as easily as we can swing hammers or serve meals.

Of course, not everything we want to change in the world involves social and political activism, but the reality is the same. Our capability to change things by our own will and direct action is limited. I can't make my neighbor's dog be quieter. I can't make people buy my books. I can't change my parents' minds about LGBTQ+ people. I can't even make my wife do the dishes.

That doesn't mean that we're powerless against all that, of course. I can take direct action to implement workarounds or to get closer to what I really want. I can improve the soundproofing, so I don't hear the neighbor's dog. I can learn to market my books more effectively, so that I reach the people who are already interested in spirituality and authenticity. I can choose not to be around my parents. I can very nicely suggest to my wife that we work on getting the house cleaned up, including the kitchen, so that we can have our friends over for game night.

But there's a limit to that as well. There's nothing I alone can directly do or say that's going to change all the things about the world around me that I want to change, even if I'm only looking at the things that impact my growth and evolution. Luckily, that's what magic is for. As powerful as magic is for changing us and shaping our energetic environment, it can also be used to manifest our material existence. We can bring it to bear on our physical resources and environment as well as on the people and groups we're part of.

Our communities are such an important part of our material existence because they are one of the biggest sources of spirit in our lives. They say we're the product of the five people closest to us, and that's precisely because the flow of spirit from them to us shapes how we change over time. I would argue that it's more than just five people, that all of the people who we listen to or whose opinions we care about factor into that equation. Still, we don't really get to hand-pick those people the way we might wish we could. We could all make lists, I'm sure, of people we spend more time around than we wish we had to and people we would love to spend more time with but can't. And by the same token, we can't force those people to change and act more like we wish they would. We can't manage, instruct, or train people who haven't consented to it.

What we can do is use our inherent magical abilities and our authentic spiritual energy to manifest the changes we want to see. The energy we put out into the world is going to attract and affect others who resonate with what's in our souls. The more aligned and integrated we are, the more influence we naturally have over the energetic dynamic around us. So working on ourselves is going to bring people into our life who amplify the energy we put out.

This whole concept of magic working via connections and casualties that we can't follow applies to our social networks as well. We don't know how our authentic spirit impacts others, who they connect with in turn, and what path those exchanges take in order to establish resonant relationships with people, but the more intentional we are about the community we wish to manifest, the more people we're going to attract into our circle who resonate with our intentions.

And the more powerfully we lean into that magic and the more energy we pour from the core of our authentic deep self into intentions for positive change, the more the spiritual network we've built around us will extend the impact.

The thing is that none of us have the power to transform the world by ourselves. Not the way we might want to. We can't possibly wield enough spiritual power to end all the things we think are wrong in the world and magnify what's right in it. And that's for a lot of reasons, including that we're all magical beings with vastly different ideas of what's good and bad. I think too many people do magic imagining that there's just an energetically open conduit between themselves and the things they want. The reality is that the energetic dynamics of the world make magic something like standing in the center of a crowd of people in a huge arena, trying to lead an activity when nobody recognizes us as a leader and without any way to amplify our voice. Finding a handful of people in our immediate vicinity who will work to help spread our message and seek others to help isn't nearly as hard as getting the attention of everyone at once. Once we create an alliance with the people around us and get them to spread out and recruit others, we can shift the focus of the larger crowd.

That's how external magic works. It's not fast, but one person can initiate a ripple of energy that can change in the world.

In our immediate life, our immediate environment, our power is much greater. Our intentions can be set to manifest more specific things in a shorter timeframe. We can intentionally attract and repel the things that do and don't support the things we value most. We can set these things in motion to attract not just the people who resonate with our energy, but the people who can shift our material reality.

As we grow and evolve, the things that stand in our way or anchor us to inauthenticity and old versions of self are often things like access to resources, lack of opportunities for change, material obligations and burdens, and even physical limitations on our abilities. Creativity and resourcefulness only take us so far to our intentions.

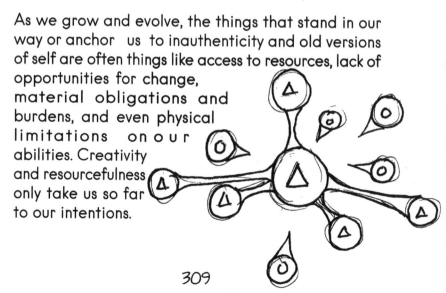

One of the very basic beliefs I was taught growing up was that success and achievement were a matter of hard work, skill, and perseverance. I was taught that I could accomplish anything I put my mind to just by working hard at it. Out in the "real world," I proceeded to watch people around me work very hard towards goals and fail to reach them, myself included. Even accounting for self-sabotage and other shadow aspects that we all battle with, there was a clear limit to how far hard work and persistence would take everyone.

When I finally looked back at the paths people took to their goals, a much different picture emerged. What matters isn't how hard we work; it's how many connections we make. Every success involves at least one other person who facilitated, assisted, or recognized that success. It doesn't mean we have to know someone at every turn who believes in us and will give us a hand up. Manifesting a community that resonates with our intention can also look like a community that provides access to the resources and opportunities we need to realize our intentions.

I talk a lot about how important it is to open ourselves to infinite possibilities when it comes to manifestation, and this is exactly why. Many people expect magic to work in such a way that we can ask for something, do the right work the right way, and get what we've asked for in the manner we imagined it. But that's not really how magic works, and I learned this by doing some experimental spellwork early on in my exploration.

I had just learned about sigil magic, and I decided that I would do a little trial run of sigil spells by setting the smallest, most inconsequential intentions

I could come up with. That way, if the methodology didn't work at all or worked in an unexpected way, it would be no big deal. Shortly before all this, I'd attended an event where a bra company had measured all the attendees for a free bra. Unfortunately, they had run out of my size when it came my turn, but the representative had taken down my address and promised to pick out one to send me after the event was over. It had been a few weeks and no bra had arrived in the mail, so one of my test spells was to manifest this free bra. And to throw in a fun aspect just to see if it would work, I specified that it be pink because I didn't usually buy colored bras. I didn't mention my spellwork to anyone and waited to see what would manifest. A short time after I did the spells, my wife went to visit her parents and her mom took her shopping. Unexpectedly, she decided that my wife probably could use some new bras, and without any input from me, my wife picked out a pink bra for me.

If I'd made a list beforehand of how I expected that spell to play out, my mother-in-law buying me a bra as a gift would not have ever appeared on that list. But ultimately, our intentions can only manifest via the existing connections in our lives. If I'd done that spell while living in isolation on a deserted island, it still would have been possible, but it pretty much would have had to wash up on shore by chance because there wouldn't be many other ways for it to happen. If we want to manifest things and changes in our material environment, we have to attract the spiritual connections that will facilitate that manifestation.

"What I want is not always what I need."

Our physical lives are a way to measure our own growth and transformation, not just to crack the code of our deep self. There's a certain amount of history encoded into what we have and how we live, personal history that traces who we've been and who we've become. As we change and grow over time, our lives expand and shift to accommodate us. To pull out yet another silly metaphor, this is a lot like snakes shedding their skins as they grow or a nautilus building new chambers on its shell for when it no longer fits comfortably in the previous one. Our physical lives have to morph to fit us or else our growth gets stunted. All this authenticity isn't really possible if we keep trying to squeeze ourselves into the same unchanging environment.

Now that we're facilitating our personal and spiritual evolution, we need to build up our material existence to accommodate who we are becoming even as it celebrates who we are and have been. That means we have to actively create space for our next self rather than just manifest our current self. And that also means being intentional and mindful about the choices we make.

Manifestation is a pretty popular topic these days, and there are about a zillion different ways to approach, define, and learn about it. But where I think a lot of our understanding of manifestation falls a bit short is that we make it about getting what we want, focusing on the end goal rather than the start of the process. We manifest our physical existence based on what's in our soul, but the important part isn't the stuff we manifest. The point of doing deep self shadow work isn't so that we can have the lifestyle we want. We do all this work so that the life we manifest supports who we are and who we want to be.

That's not to say that we can't or shouldn't actively work to shape our environment or our self-expression. Not everything can or should be done by magic. There's plenty of room in our existence for achieving and acquiring things through deliberate action, and that's especially useful when it comes to shaping our environment to facilitate and support our continued evolution and embodiment.

The biggest shift to make when it comes to our relationship with our physical existence is that the things and people we surround ourselves with are more than some end result we hope to achieve for our lives. Our lives and lifestyles aren't just something to attain; they are a tool that can either facilitate or hinder our personal evolution.

But that's not how most of us have learned to think of our material existence. When we think about shaping or manifesting the life we want, most of us have been conditioned to think in terms of our vision or goal for how we want things to be. It's the end point, the way we measure how well we've done or are doing in life. So when we look around at where we live, what we have, who we spend time with, we judge it in terms of whether it matches the ideal we have in our minds.

That tends to be how we talk about manifestation as well. Manifestation and magic are popular topics largely because they hold the promise of getting the material lives we want through spiritual means instead of just direct action. It's an attractive thought, but the vast majority of people who get into magic to manifest their dream life end up frustrated and disappointed.

We've already talked about how our material lives reflect our deep selves and how important it is for our physical existence to support our authenticity, but we've also talked about how our deep selves are shaped by the world we exist in. Our material life plays a very important role in our evolution and spiritual life. So if we are focused on making internal changes for the purpose of manifesting the lifestyle we want, we're all but guaranteed to disconnect from our authentic selves in the process. If we're judging our lives against an ideal vision in our heads of what we want them to look like, we end up focusing even our spiritual efforts and magical practices on manifesting some imagined life we think a future version of ourselves will fit into.

All those things about our authentic selves that manifest in our lives become flaws to fix rather than a vital part of our shadow work. And our disappointment with how our lives aren't yet the ideal we have in mind will be one of the primary forces shaping how we spiritually grow and develop.

It's actually spiritually damaging to focus our spiritual efforts on what we want to acquire and the indulgences we dream of having because it spiritually blinds us to everything else. That's not to say that having or acquiring things we desire is bad. There's nothing wrong with building the lifestyle we want to have or with having dreams and goals. But if our desires become the focus of our spiritual life, they will absolutely disrupt and derail any efforts to evolve and grow into and beyond our authentic self.

The best thing we can do for our authenticity is to shape our physical existence in such a way that it supports and nurtures who we are. To fully express and embody our authentic self, we have to have spaces in our lives where that authentic self is welcome, comfortable, and embraced. But if our interest is spiritual evolution, what we need from our material life goes another step further. It has to support the process of evolution, which looks like creating a physical environment around us that is intended specifically to encourage the adaptive changes we want to make and disincentivize things we want to release in the process. We want to build a life that doesn't just support who we are at the moment, but that is specifically tailored for who we need to be to thrive and flourish in the next phase of our spiritual development.

One of the craziest things I ever did in my life was move to Chicago after I graduated college. I had spent the last few months of my college career applying to various companies to secure my first "real" job, and as of graduation day I thought I was very close to being hired by a firm I was very excited to work for. But a week later, I got the bad news that they weren't going to hire anyone just yet, and unfortunately I had stopped pursuing other options because I'd been so sure that job was going to come through for me. So here I was, fresh out of college and facing a very uncertain future. My biggest challenge at the time was that I had to basically start my job search over again, sending out another round of applications and going to more interviews. I had focused on getting a job in Chicago because of the type of projects I hoped to work on, and I knew at that point that financially I could either afford to travel there one more time for interviews or to put down the first month's rent on an apartment and move there, but not both.

Of course, my goal at the time was very much rooted in this vision I had for what my ideal life looked like. But I did recognize deep down that my college career had been one of great personal growth. I was a different person coming out of college than I had been going in, and I knew that my next big leap forward necessitated asserting my independence and challenging myself to really jump into adulthood with both feet.

So I looked at my situation, did some quick math, and decided that the only smart thing to do was to move to Chicago and continue my job search from there. I didn't know anyone there, I had to begin fresh with the process of contacting firms and arranging for interviews, and I know for sure that was the most tense and argument-filled week I ever had with my mother until I began planning my wedding. But I knew that the only way for me to move forward in the way I felt life steering me was to make the move and, by doing so, make it imperative that I succeed at finding a job.

I wasn't as in tune with the spiritual dynamics of personal evolution at that time. I hadn't even made that initial transition away from my religion of origin yet. But instinctively I understood that the best thing I could do for my own growth and development as a person and as a young adult stepping into my own independence was to set up my life to support that growth and even take away all room to fail. Staying in Missouri would have meant working extra hard at trying to manifest the resources and opportunities that already existed in Chicago. Staying in Missouri would have made it much easier for me to change course, to get discouraged, and to settle for a life that might have made other people happy but would have slowed or interrupted my personal growth. My willingness to move nine hours away to an unfamiliar city where I was alone and without a support network was a manifestation of my increased confidence and self-sufficiency as well as an attempt to make it imperative that I grow and adapt.

It seemed like a huge risk at the time, but I knew that logically I was setting myself up with the greatest chance of success. I could apply for jobs and not have to worry about planning long distance travel to do interviews. I would already be moved in and settled by the time I got hired, so I wouldn't have to juggle the moving process with starting a new job. I would have access to local resources and listings that were hard to come by in Missouri. I would be pushed to build relationships that would support me in my endeavors rather than anchor me to my past self. The move made the best sense, even if it looked to outsiders like a huge risk.

I would never have looked at that decision as related at all to magic, but it's one of the best examples I can think of for how we can alter our physical existence to help manifest our evolutionary adaptations. It's a blueprint for how magic comes into play. I didn't just move far away from my family so I could build a life of my own. That's it in simple terms, sure. But what I really did was to design my reality to manifest the opportunities I was looking for and to push myself to make the necessary changes in me.

Manifestation isn't just a mental exercise. Sitting around thinking about our intentions will never bring them into reality. It doesn't matter how much time we spend envisioning who we want to become or the life we want to live, we have to take action to make it happen. Even without knowing about magic and manifestation, I did all the right things at the time to set the stage for the transformation I knew I needed in my life and in myself. I used my energetic resources to clear away as many limits as I could that would have held me back from stepping into this next iteration of self, most of which had to do with people like my mother pressuring me to stay in my past reality longer and do what seemed safe and easy. I cut away the things that bound me to my old self. I built the life that was most nurturing and supportive of who I needed to be to thrive.

If we look at our lives with an eye towards evolution, what we will see is not the differences between our

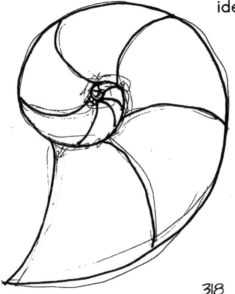

ideal lives and our real lives; we'll see the ways our lives do and do not contribute to the adaptations we need to make to spiritually thrive. And once we do, we can design and tailor our reality in order to support our authenticity and facilitate the adaptations we know we need to make.

I think about it kind of like casting a circle for a ritual or for doing spellwork. If we haven't practiced magic in this way, the purpose of casting a circle in which to do a ritual is to create a temporary sacred space to contain the energies of the working and exclude everything not related. The implements and tools for the ritual are gathered, the circle is cast and closed, whatever entities or powers the practitioner is working with are called down into the circle, and then when the ritual is done, those energies are released and the circle is opened and dissolved.

That's a lot like what I'm talking about doing in our lives. Our physical existence is the space in which we do the work of self-development. It's difficult to work in a space which is ill-equipped for the growth we're trying to nurture or filled with influences and forces that distract or detract from the transformation we're trying to undergo. If I know what's holding me back most in my life at the current moment are poor boundaries and the inability to say no, it's going to be incredibly difficult to make that shift if I continue to surround myself with people who are disrespectful of boundaries or if I don't put myself in a position where saying no gets me closer to my goals. We have to give ourselves the tools to succeed, place ourselves in an environment where our efforts are rewarded, and even take away the crutches we use to remain in our old status quo.

Be prepared, though, because this goes against our natural instincts. When faced with challenges in life, what we tend to focus on first is reducing that challenge. We don't instinctively analyze the challenge to figure out how to adapt ourselves to rise to the occasion. What we instinctively do is to try and reduce or eliminate the challenge itself, so we can stay in a past iteration where it feels comfortable already. But when it comes to our evolution, the challenges aren't the problem. In fact, the challenge doesn't even come from our environment. It isn't sent to us intentionally. Reality challenges us only when there is a mismatch between our abilities and habits and what it takes to do well in that reality. It isn't about us being targeted specifically.

When I was in third grade, my family moved from one side of the city to the other. Technically, my little brother and I should have started going to a different school when we moved because we'd moved into a different district, but since my mother still worked at the same job and still planned to drop us off at the same daycare we'd been going to for years, we got permission to stay in the same school we'd been attending. So for another two years, all of my school friends lived across town, and I never made any neighborhood friends. I wasn't very outgoing and I certainly wasn't much for playing outside, so unlike my brother, I didn't run into neighborhood kids on the playground.

In fifth grade, my parents decided it was too expensive to continue sending us to daycare and that my brother and I were certainly old enough to walk to and from school. So without warning we switched districts to go to the school a block from our house. It was a huge change for me. As a shy kid, I struggled to make friends even when I didn't feel out of place, and the difference in culture between my old school and the new one was staggering. I dressed differently, I didn't know most of the games they played on the playground, they listened to music I wasn't familiar with, and I was suddenly the only kid in class who was in advanced math or went to the gifted program once a week.

At the time, I blamed a lot of things and people for my struggle to thrive in that environment. The kids were mean, my parents hadn't given us any time to ease into the adjustment, and the teachers weren't helping me fit in. I looked at the situation as if it had been specifically tailored to be hard on me. But the reality is that nobody in that school or neighborhood was trying to create a culture where it would be difficult for a new person to fit in. My little brother had no problem adjusting. The problem was that I had never really learned how to make friends. I didn't know how to deal with being different or coping with changes in my life. That transition was a challenge because my authentic self at that moment didn't have what it took to thrive in the environment I found myself in.

Of course, ideally what could have happened was that I could have improved my social skills and learned to relate to the kids in my class, to do the work to begin bridging the gap myself. But I didn't, of course. Instead, I cultivated this idea that once I got to be an adult, none of this silly grade school drama would matter, so I just needed to focus on my schoolwork and achieve everything I could and not ever worry about everyone else. That wasn't personal evolution; it was just the easier way out. I was comfortable shutting myself into a little bubble of schoolwork and achievement. But that comfort didn't get me anywhere. I continued to struggle with those feelings of not fitting in and not being accepted for well over ten years until I finally realized that I was never going to feel accepted and included until I learned the friendship skills I should have learned as a kid.

So the bottom line is that if we want to evolve as people and to thrive where we are, we have to stop looking at our lives and lifestyles as the end goal of our endeavors and begin seeing them as a tool and reflection of the process of growth. We have to be aware of the things and people around us that anchor us to past iterations of self and be willing to detach from them when they hold us back from being who we are becoming. We can design our lives to support our growth, to encourage us to practice and hone the aspects of self that are key to our next evolutionary transformation rather than designing our lives to keep us protected and comfortable in the face of challenges.

"The sea of spirit ripples with waves of magic."

We've talked a lot about how our environments, the people, and things around us impact our own authenticity, growth, and evolution. It's been crucial to really understand how responsible we are for curating and creating the environment we need to support who we are and who we are becoming.

But life is not a journey we travel alone, and one of the biggest risks of cultivating our personal spirituality is that we can easily become so wrapped up in our own lives and working on our own deep self that we begin to see the people around us as part of our environment more than people on their own spiritual journeys.

Personal evolution has a purpose, and it's not just to feel good about ourselves and our lives. We evolve by adapting to the reality we live in, and that also means adapting to the demands reality places on us. It's easy to look at our lives and pick out the ways we're not thriving by our own definition, but it's harder to look around and pick out the ways we are not thriving in the role we play in the larger context.

All the spiritual connections to other people, places, things, and ideas in the universe go both ways. We may be the center of our own piece of existence, but that is a very tiny part of the grand picture. In reality, we are a piece of a vast web of spirit that literally ties everything in existence into one living entity.

When we look at ourselves in context, getting that long distance Overview Effect look at our role in the larger spiritual picture, it's easy to feel very small and inconsequential. It's like astronauts realizing that we are tiny beings on a tiny planet in an endless universe, and so what do our tiny differences even matter in the face of eternity? When we focus inside ourselves, though, it's easy to feel that our own spiritual and emotional state of being is the most important thing of all. Especially in a world that puts so much pressure on us to shape our being to fit the expectations of others, it's easy to get caught up in our own concerns to the exclusion of everything and everyone else.

Both points of view are important to be able to achieve. Our personal concerns, opinions, and experiences are not so significant that they have any bearing on universal truth. But it's also true that we are not alone or isolated in this reality. Things we do and choices we make have larger consequences.

For all that our environment impacts our own growth

and evolution, we are part of the environment for others, and we impact their growth and evolution. We belong to communities and cultures, and that means we are responsible for the impact we have on the world. When we make changes in ourselves and our environment, that sets other things in motion which come back to us like ripples in a pond. That's not something we can stop, nor should we want to. It's part of what sustains life, just like breathing. It's the natural flow of spirit.

Step Ten is to strengthen the positive spiritual connections in your life and practice mindful management of the flow of energy both into and out of your life.

There are a few crucial things to remember as we go along our journey.

First, everything we do impacts other people in the same way what other people do impacts us. We have been paying very close attention to the way the people around us shape and either benefit or impede our own authenticity and development, and once we've got that understanding of how people are sources of spirit and elements in our environment, it should be easier to look at how we function in that role, too. We can choose how closely we are connected to others, how much influence we allow them to have on us, and whether we even allow them to remain in our lives.

Other people get to make the same choices about us.

It's far more common for us to subvert our own will to please others than it is for us to impose our will on others and demand their conformity, but that does have a way of shifting after we get a taste of spiritual empowerment. When we take hold of our natural magical abilities and bring them to bear on our lives, it's often far too easy to forget about the larger perspective altogether and get caught up in our own power. It's the Spider Man principle: The more empowered we are, the more responsibility we hold.

The ripples that go out from our own choices and evolutionary adaptations come back to us, so if we choose an evolutionary path that pushes others away and ignores the impact our choices have outside our immediate life, those ripples are going to bring something very different back to us than they will if we choose an evolutionary path that is more mindful and aware. I'm not a big believer in ideas like karma or the Rule of Three, because the details of how they work aren't supported in observed reality, but the concept overall does hold up. What we put into the world shapes what comes back to us. Our choices make a difference for other people, and the choices they make further impact others, and so on.

I find it all very beautiful. It's the definition of life. If we all tried not to impact anything else for fear of what might come back to us, life would cease. Nothing would happen. Everything in the universe exists because of interactions between particles, objects, and entities. It's a constant dance of relationships forming and breaking, things being drawn to and repelled by other things.

There's no way to predict precisely how the choices we make will come back to us. That's why magic is so mystical and seems so hard to master. There isn't a straight logical progression to trace between what we do and the desired result. Mastering our magic requires some trial and error, careful observation, and openness to many acceptable outcomes.

But there are a few things we can predict for sure as we embrace our magical nature and nurture our evolution, the most important one being what happens if our go-to instinct is to disconnect and push away from anyone and anything that doesn't serve our intentions in the moment. If we push away anyone who isn't useful to us as we move from one iteration of self to the next, we end up isolating ourselves more and more. If we only focus on the influence others have on us and ignore the influence we have on others, we're likely to end up disconnected and spiritually alone.

The second thing we can predict is that if we contribute in a way that encourages and supports the authenticity, growth, and evolution of those around us, those spiritual ties and relationships get stronger and that will always be beneficial to us. No matter what path the ripples of influence and impact take on their journey through the universe, they arrive back to us via the things and people we're connected to in life. So the more we build relationships of mutual benefit, the more likely we are to be uplifted by the waves rather than overwhelmed by them.

One of the most important aspects of our spiritual life and development are the communities we are part of. It is vital to our growth to surround ourselves with an environment that nurtures our evolution, but that doesn't mean making ourselves comfortable and removing ourselves from any relationship that challenges us.

The biggest mistake I think we can make, whether in terms of magic and spirituality or just in our general life choices, is to dismiss any consequences our actions have on others on the grounds that their growth is their own responsibility.

The second biggest mistake I think we can make is to assume that our understanding of our own authenticity and evolution gives us the ability to decide what is best for others or expect them to make the same choices we would.

We have a responsibility to the cultures and communities we belong to. We aren't obligated to shape ourselves to the expectations of other people in terms of our identity and how we express ourselves, but we all have roles to play and contributions to make. All the connections that tie us to the larger human societal structures are relationships, and relationships are two-way connections. We cannot take without giving forever any more than we can give everyone what they want of us without suffering the emotional and spiritual consequences. If all we do is demand what we need and want from the people around us without ever making an effort to reciprocate when requested, eventually those connections get broken. Part of the process of designing our environment to support and facilitate our evolution is to actively nurture strong social relationships.

It helps our spiritual evolution to form strong spiritual connections with others who are also focused on their own evolution. We benefit from relationships with other people who are making adaptations and growing in similar ways to us. Forming ties with people who encourage us in our self-development efforts and who can help teach us the things we want to learn is important, as are ties with those for whom we can be that encouragement and guidance.

As we gather people around us who can support and further our personal spiritual journey, we're going to find that many of those people also challenge us and embody new or even contradictory points of view. Those relationships are important, too. The key skill here is to be mindful of the difference between a relationship that is challenging or even confronting, but that helps us grow, and one that pushes us towards inauthenticity and suppression of self.

Most of us make or break our pursuit of spiritual wellbeing in choosing and building our spiritual family. The people whose spirit we choose to surround ourselves with and the commitments we make to them on a spiritual level have more to do with our own growth, evolution, and even ability to be authentic than anything we do ourselves. So that choice is a matter of design. We've done all this work to settle into an authentic sense of self and spirit, and that authenticity allows us to make purposeful design choices to achieve a specific outcome for ourselves.

The crucial question to ask in designing our connection to community is, for each relationship we give time and effort to forming and nurturing, do we make each other spiritually stronger?

Part V

Spiritual Authenticity

Pause and Reflect
_____

When you think of a personal spiritual practice,
what does that look like?

Who in your life are the most like-minded and
like-spirited to you?

What aspects of your spiritual life are most
important to you as an individual?

_____

Step Eleven

Spiritual Practice

"There are many ways to travel along the same path."

Spirituality may be personal and individual, but there's a reason why humans are drawn to structure and ritual. After this whole process of digging into the individual, authentic aspects of personal spirituality, we might be left with just bits and pieces of what we used to know as our spiritual or religious lives.

There's no reason to push all that aside, and there are lots of reasons not to. There are real benefits to crafting a set of traditions and rituals our spiritual practice is preserved in. We never lack a spirituality, but we can absolutely lack a spiritual practice, a part of our existence specifically geared towards and focused on our spirituality. And we benefit from these regular practices in a lot of ways.

One of the hardest things for those of us not part

of an established tradition to do is to craft our own spiritual practice. Even within established traditions, those of us who observe that tradition alone struggle with fitting it into their lives. The most common questions from beginner pagans of all stripes are, "Where do I start?" and "Am I doing this wrong?"

That's one reason why community and culture have historically been so important to religion and spiritual practice. Nobody had to learn how to be whatever cultural spiritual identity they belonged to alone. They had a whole community around them with practices and rituals specifically created to pass on these traditions and teach the important values and responsibilities.

That's why religions and spiritual traditions look and are practiced the way they are. What we think spirituality should look like comes from times when these things had to be passed on culturally. Over time, as civilization and the structure of human society has shifted, and the focus of spiritual traditions has shifted away from being community-centered to being more personal and individual. These days, only the most orthodox and organized traditions insert themselves in any dogmatic way into the day-to-day lives of adherents. Our average Christian crafts their own way of weaving their beliefs into their lives, depending on how deep their investment in their religion as a culture really is. They don't all dress the same or even universally pray at the same times. Holiday celebrations vary from family to family and even church to church.

Even if we are part of a religion with daily traditions and observances, it's still up to each of us to figure out how that works into what we do. So the structured group worship and ritual isn't actually the biggest, most important part of a religious life. What we've been dealing with is spirituality, not religion.

But if we want religion-like elements in our life, that's something we can put in place for ourselves, and there are good reasons for doing so. If our spirituality holds space for and fits seamlessly with an established religion, and we want to use those traditions as a framework for our own spiritual practice, that's great. If not, then our spirituality will likely fit better with something that functions similar to religion. And it's entirely possible we don't need anything formal at all.

In any case, I think it's valuable to take a look at what a spiritual practice can look like and figure out what our authentic deep self needs. When I did my own spiritual detox, I found there were elements of spiritual practice that I missed on an emotional level and elements that I realized had been beneficial.

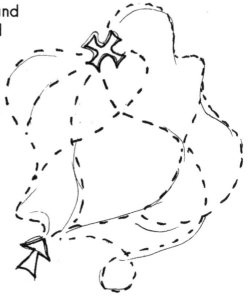

To some extent, we all put the core elements of spiritual practice in place in our lives in some form or another. Humans are social beings, and religion has the same roots in human interaction and development as other bits of culture. We all belong to various communities, we have places and things that are deeply significant and meaningful, and we find ways to describe, label, and codify our beliefs and values. Those things are part of religious traditions because we humans rely on those things for navigating our social and societal relationships.

When the first religions arose, culture and spirituality were basically the same thing. These days they're so separate that we can get what we need on a communal and cultural level completely apart from our spiritual pursuits if that's what our authentic deep self needs. But because it's about our deep self and the flow of spirit in the alchemical sense, all of it is still spiritual. Our spiritual lives don't have to look or feel religious.

Anything, really, can be the basis for a personal spiritual tradition.

For instance, my social activism filled a lot of roles that formal religion had filled in my life when I was younger. It gave me a community of people working for the same things, operating around the same moral and ethical codes and goals. There were even ritual elements to it, gatherings and important dates and such. For me, a protest march filled the same purpose as a church service had when I was a kid, complete with speakers at a podium talking about the ideals we shared.

So there's a good chance that, even if we don't mean to, we will fill whatever gaps and whatever needs we have for more traditional and formal spiritual elements in our life with things that resonate with us. A lot of the time, it will just be recognizing those things as part of our spirituality and purposefully working them into our practices and observances.

———

"We all need hands to hold and shoulders to cry on."

———

I think the best and most beneficial element of a traditional spiritual path or religion is that it ideally connects us with a framework of support for getting through difficulties. This is especially true for the difficulties and challenges that come our way just because of the way life plays out, but it should also be true for the challenges we put in our own way to help our evolution. No matter how capable and powerful we are as authentic and fully integrated beings, there are things that happen in life we're just not meant to handle alone. We may feel connected to a lot of people in the sense that they are spiritual kindred spirits or those who share our path of growth and evolution, but those people aren't necessarily the ones to whom we feel emotionally connected. When things happen in our lives, we don't just have thoughts and beliefs, we have feelings about t, and that requires the support of something more like a spiritual family than just a spiritual community.

Humans are social creatures. We benefit from belonging to a group of supportive peers. When we really dig into the history of human religion, it's all about social and societal dynamics. It's never been about truth; it's been about how well the groups we belong to actually function. One of the reasons we need traditional types of spirituality is because it helps us navigate human society. But, of course, not just any community of people is going to function well as a spiritual community when we're building it up around our individual authentic self.

I grew up in church, quite literally. We went to church every Sunday and Wednesday, just like all the other evangelical Christians. But being the preacher's family, we were among the first to arrive and the last to leave. Being part of the preacher's family in very small, independent churches meant we also helped clean the building, decorate for holidays, set up for potluck dinners, even go to the houses of congregation members for dinners. Church was a central part of our lifestyle as a family. But I didn't consider the congregation of the church my spiritual family. All that time in church and in church activities functioned as actual family time. My biological family was my spiritual family growing up.

As an adult, now, it's much the same with my pagan practice. I'm not part of a coven or practicing group (and have no desire to be), but I do organize a monthly local pagan meeting. It's a great community of people, and those gatherings have been a huge part of my spiritual path. But the people I truly consider my spiritual family are what I now call my "framily" – friends who are so close they function as family. We're all of different flavors of neopagan and

336

adjacent practices, and we don't truly share a common worldview. Our practices are similar enough that we have our own shared rituals, and we gather together for holidays like any other family.

But the important part of a spiritual community is the way it supports us on our emotional journey, the way it helps hold us accountable for our positive changes and growth, and the way it encourages our authenticity. We can choose to surround ourselves with those who inspire us, embrace us, and love us and not have to either settle for the spiritual groups we find ourselves in by default.

If we can build a community of people whose practices are enough like ours that we can participate in observances together, that's great. But it's not the most valuable part of having a spiritual family.

When I became Catholic, one of the things I liked most was the fact that I could go to Mass, sit in my pew, do all the stuff, and go home again without needing to talk to everyone the way I was expected to do in my family's church growing up. When it came to my spiritual observances and practices, those were it for me. And while I liked knowing I was part of a larger community, my connection to the practice itself was private and personal. That's the spirituality bit. It's about our inner work and our connection to the universe. Having a spiritual family fills an entirely different function in our lives. It's about creating a social environment that supports our wellbeing.

What that looks like is different for all of us, but certainly we need that energetic support and protection through the ups and downs of life. It's the mourning and celebrating together and working towards common goals that's most beneficial to us as we move forward along our path.

And that means that we need to let go of the idea that our spiritual family has to be made up of people who agree with our every thought, idea, and belief. That's probably the biggest mistake we make in trying to find a spiritual community. A group that is bound together only by a common mission or ideology is going to frequently disagree on the best path to fulfilling on their purpose and is likely to care more about ensuring that the others in the community meet standards of conformity than they are to care about the wellbeing and personal growth of anyone else. It's just a matter of reality. To get a community around us that cares about us, we have to build that community like a chosen family.

"If I want it for myself, I cannot withhold it from the world."

Traditionally speaking, spiritual traditions usually involve a set of standards and expectations for conduct and our way of being. And it makes sense for that to be the case because religions and formal spiritual traditions are societal tools that function to keep a community or culture together. They're meant to help teach people how to be good members of the group, what their responsibilities are to other people, and what behaviors or choices aren't acceptable.

The weirdest thing about being an atheist is being constantly confronted by people who suspect that without the threat of punishment by a deity, nothing is stopping people from running around murdering and stealing. We should all realize by now that there's no real link between religion and moral codes, but there's a very strong link between societal structure and moral codes. Most of us feel some responsibility to the people we're most tightly associated with, so even though our spirituality is deeply personal and individual, we can't shrug off all our connections to the people around us. We still need an internal code to live by.

Religion plays such a huge role in establishing cultural and societal rules of behavior that we pretty much define religions by their morals and myths. So if we're going to build up a more traditional practice around our authentic selves, it makes sense to start with that foundation of rules and expectations. What rules are important to our deep selves? What is the code that defines the way we see our role in the universe?

Of course, whatever code of rules we come up with for ourselves now are going to change over time. So this isn't something we're carving in stone.

I mean, we literally can if we want to. I do think codifying our personal ethics is a great ritual to do for ourselves.

But this isn't about defining some permanent ten commandments to live by for the rest of our lives. It's not about what we think is right and what we think is wrong. And it's DEFINITELY not about establishing any expectation for others. That need to convert and get others to behave as we want them to is one element of traditional spirituality that needs to be ditched forever.

It's important to establish our expectations for ourselves for how we treat other people. This is the part that doesn't necessarily come to mind when we're focused on our own evolution, but there's a reason why some version of the Golden Rule exists in just about every religion and spiritual tradition on Earth. It matters how we behave towards others, and that's really the point of rules.

We usually think of rules as something that is imposed upon us. Most of us like to think if people behaved the way they "should," then we wouldn't need rules at all. So when we think about rules, the most common assumption is that the most important rules are the ones meant to make other people follow the standards we think are important. Most often that means prohibiting others from doing things we don't think they should do, and since it's already what we want, then the rules aren't meant for us. Less often, it's about the ideals we want others to aspire to. But still, rules are assumed to be there to impose order on the chaotic.

But there are only two situations in which rules are effective and can be enforced: if there's a central authority figure with the power to impose rule or if there's a consensus between enough people with enough power between them to do the same. Parents make rules for kids. Voters create rules for their communities. Deities make rules for all of humanity, if we believe in that sort of thing.

We're just building our own personal spiritual traditions here, so neither one applies.

And what happens instead is that we get back what we put out. It's the basic principle of the flow of spirit. The relationships and energetic connections we enshrine in our personal ethical codes and commandments are really important. What we model in our actions is what we will get back.

It's a form of sympathetic magic.

A lot of rituals and magical workings are, essentially, symbolic actions done to evoke the larger intention. Spells are built on the idea that we act out or symbolize the thing we want the spell to do, and like will then attract like. That's the point of the Golden Rule. If we value family above all else, supporting everyone else's ability to have and support their family is the logical application of "do unto others." If we want people to support us, we have to support others. If we want people to be forgiving of us, we have to forgive others.

This isn't transactional. Magic is never transactional. It's not a matter of "I scratch your back so you scratch mine." It's energetic. It's about the energy exchange and the relationship represented.

If we want others to be more generous, we need to be more generous with our own resources. Or, to be more accurate, if we want others to be more generous, we have to recognize that others will also want us to be more generous and model the response we want to see. That's why it doesn't work for our own spiritual code to be solely about what others should and should not do. If we want others to follow our rules but we're not willing to follow the rules other people want us to follow, we won't get the response we want. We'll get exactly the defiance back that we put out. So if our concerns are focused on the actions of others, we're only going to be attracting the same focus on our actions from others.

So it's not about what we want from other people. If we make it about getting credit or recognition or even thanks for the good things we do, our need for that visibility attracts people who also want visibility. We end up surrounded by people who are happy to take what we're offering because it feels like recognition to them.

It has to be about what we want FOR the world, not from it.

And remember that part of magic is surrounding ourselves with the things and people who help nurture our evolution and who amplify our magical energy. So we want to surround ourselves with people who share at least our biggest and most important rules. They should especially be the ones who treat people (us included) how we think people should treat each other. They help remind us to live up to those standards ourselves. Modeling the behaviors and energies we want there to be more of in the world means attracting the people who also model those things.

Surrounding ourselves with hypocrites and inauthentic people encourages inauthenticity. Surrounding ourselves with people who don't recognize our boundaries or respect our intentions encourages us to do the same.

The thing about morals and ethics in traditional spirituality is that it's usually tied up in doctrine. Whether it's formal dogma or descriptive mythology, religions and traditions all have some kind of underlying worldview. I don't like calling this truth or belief, because the profession of belief isn't always very important to the path in general. But no matter what is expected of the members of a religious or spiritual group, the core of everything is a particular understanding of how the world works and what our place is in the universe. It's something that is shared as part of the spiritual culture, and it informs every other part of the tradition.

Traditional religion tends to be extremely restrictive and limiting when it comes to authenticity and evolution. We want to create a spiritual practice that remains authentic to us as we evolve, so the practice and the ideas behind it have to evolve as well, right down to the understanding of how the universe works. To truly be supportive of our authenticity, our spirituality has to encourage independent thought and free access to spirit.

So if we're going to build an authentic and still traditional form of spirituality for ourselves, whatever functions as doctrine can't really be static. Ultimately, it shouldn't be about truth at all.

Traditional belief systems tell us what's true and, by extension, tell us not to trust our own perception and experience. But since we're building this for ourselves, we are the higher authority in the

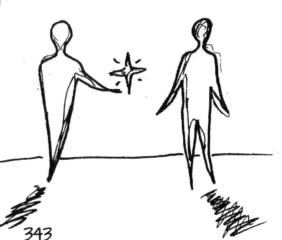

343

position of defining the worldview for our own spiritual path. There's no reason that a spiritual path has to be based around a core truth. To the contrary, given what we've been talking about regarding spirit, trying to settle on a truth to build our own tradition on is a bad idea for lots of reasons. It definitely doesn't support continued authenticity, growth, and evolution.

The whole dynamic around having a central doctrine in a religion is that acceptance of that doctrine is the ideal. That's the goal for the entire spiritual culture. But when it's just us, when the goal for our personal spirituality is the development and evolution of our own authentic being, the ideal isn't the acceptance of a truth. The ideal is evolution. So if we're going to pick something smaller to focus on as an ideal or a doctrine of sorts to build upon, instead of a set version of truth, the only thing that makes sense to look towards is a core priority or value.

The beauty of traditional spirituality is that it takes the foundational doctrines and uses them to inform everything else. The role of these central truths isn't just to be a thing we profess to believe, or at least it isn't meant to be. Religions also usually include certain expectations for what practice looks like, the rules, rituals, and observances. The foundational doctrines have a lot to do with this, so if we're the ones exploring the world and having varied experiences, it's our first-hand understanding of the world and the universe that shapes what the rest of the practice looks like.

Ultimately, it's a bit of a cyclical thing. Our experience changes our understanding of the universe, which changes the types of observances, rules, and rituals that make up the bulk of our practice; that, in turn, leads us to different experiences. It's a lot like the process of personal evolution, which also drives itself forward once we get the momentum going.

So instead of picking out a central truth about the universe, a central truth about what humanity needs to do to live up to a specific ideal, the idea for our own individual spirituality is to pick out a central truth about what is most beneficial to our continued evolution.

One way to do this is to center our personal spirituality on the pursuit of knowledge. The more we know, the closer to something resembling truth we get. Making learning our highest priority shifts the function of our spiritual path away from a static ideal and towards a pursuit that contributes to growth and evolution.

Another option is to place the highest priority on experiences that broaden our understanding of the world. Learning through research is good, but experiences are the most impactful way for humans to gain understanding. Instead of dedicating our spiritual efforts to conform to a predetermined outlook on the world, dedicate them to exploring and experiencing the world for ourselves.

But what is really most beneficial is to lean into the idea that experiences are how we learn and grow. It's important to recognize that it's the challenging and uncomfortable experiences that teach us the most about ourselves and reveal things we didn't know we needed to learn.

However we enshrine our evolution as our core priority, the pursuit of growth and transformation will cause us to regularly think about how our own ethical and moral code contributes or stands in the way of not just our own evolution, but everyone else's as well.

Deep Self Magic

"I cannot successfully lead even myself without the guidance of trusted counsel."

When building our individual authentic spiritual practice, even if we're shaping it in a way that echoes and reflects traditional religion, it's important to ensure it supports our individual authenticity and doesn't squeeze us into a mold meant to make us conform and fit within some other standard. But that doesn't mean that the center of our own practice should rely entirely on what's already inside us. Our deep self is not infallible, and it's never finished evolving. As long as the world changes around us, we have to keep adapting.

What most of us find attractive about the teachings of a religion or tradition is that it gives us truth rather than requiring us to find truth for ourselves. It tells us how to practice and how to achieve that culture's ideal, so we don't have to shoulder the burden of figuring it out for ourselves. This may be the single biggest obstacle to really creating our own private traditions. Even if we trust ourselves to figure out these things for ourselves, that takes time, effort, and exploration that not everyone has the patience or passion for.

There is a third alternative, though, besides letting someone else set our spiritual goals and itinerary or creating a spiritual philosophy and methodology from scratch. We can seek out the guidance of those who can teach us to get through whatever challenge we're facing in the moment or to adapt to whatever circumstances we're struggling with and lean on those guiding ideas and inspirations to help us evolve authentically.

Not every teacher has to become a spiritual guru we follow for the rest of our journey. We can worry about end goals by ourselves and simply seek out the expertise we don't have to help us get to the next step on the journey. We don't have to be infallible and neither do they. The goal is to adapt and change in whatever ways will allow us to thrive where we find ourselves in life. Inevitably, whatever we're dealing with, others have dealt with it too.

It's especially important not to get wrapped up in following the lead of someone else and letting them take the wheel. No one else can decide our direction for us and get us to a state of authenticity and continued evolution. We have to be very careful who, outside of ourselves, we place in authority positions within our own authentic practice, because as soon as we give someone else that central place of authority, we're essentially back in a position of being told who to be and how to think.

However, we can't be expected to know everything about how to grow, develop, and evolve. Spiritual evolution requires the intake of spirit from outside ourselves. We need to consume ideas and information and use what we consume to transform ourselves and our lives.

I think maybe the best metaphor for this is to think of ourself as an athlete. Let's say we're a runner, and we want to be truly competitive in races. We'll probably want a coach or guide to help us know how to prepare and to show us how to push through the setbacks and challenges we run into as we work towards our goals. But we don't expect that coach to teach us everything we need to know about fitness for the rest of our life. If we don't hire a coach, we'll at least want to consult resources to put together the best training plan on our own, seeking out the advice that's geared most specifically for the level of experience we have as a runner. We don't just ignore the vast amounts of training resources and amble along on our own, hoping that the things we choose to do in training will prepare us to win on race day.

In the place of doctrine and religious authority, we'll want to seek out sources of information, guidance, and teaching that support each step of the journey, but we want to keep those sources in the correct perspective and in the appropriate roles within our spiritual practice.

We don't need authority figures to follow or worship. We just need mentors and guides to join us on our path from time to time and share their knowledge.

And it's also important to remember that these sources of guidance are not sources of truth. Remember that authentic spirituality isn't about revealed truth; it's about personal evolution and personal truth. So what is most useful isn't philosophies that can stand in for doctrine; it's methodologies for adapting and transforming.

I think it's a natural human assumption that we can find one single example to follow, one expert opinion on how we can get to where we want to go. We're attracted to the prospect of expert leadership when we don't know where we're headed. But just like there's no one spiritual truth out there that we can all embrace and follow, no one expert has the key to everyone's evolution. We're all on different paths, so we have to pull from multiple sources of wisdom and guidance. It's our responsibility as leaders of our own spiritual practices to gather those guides around us and be mindful of the ways we change and adapt over time.

Part of the comfort we get from traditional spirituality is the sense that we're on a well-worn path where others like us walk. It's really important to take leadership in our own spiritual life, but that doesn't mean there's no room to look to others for expertise and guidance. We don't know everything. We can't know everything.

Humans often have too-high expectations for religious doctrine, expecting it to hold the answers for whatever happens in our lives and to help us navigate existence. It doesn't work well in formal spiritual paths, and it's even less likely for it to be true in our own individual practices. The things we discover through our spiritual development aren't going to reveal all the secrets we need to breeze through life without conflicts and complications. Ironic though it may seem, humans don't naturally know how to cope with the hardest of human emotions. We don't automatically know how to solve conflicts and get past challenges in our lives. We look outside ourselves for that guidance, usually to whoever is the authority in our lives that we respect and trust to tell us how things should be.

But spiritually speaking - and emotions are spirit

- if we're outside a formal tradition, we no longer have the same kind of respect for those authorities because they also come with beliefs and standards that stifle our authenticity. And once we've stepped outside of rules, boundaries, and a structure with a lot of restrictions like religion tends to have, it's pretty hard to cram ourselves back in. So it's probably going to be really hard, after we've done all this work, to free our authentic self, to be comfortable looking to formal religious traditions for advice and guidance.

When we're part of a larger tradition that helps us determine our direction and goals and then guides us on the path to get there, we still often have the responsibility and freedom to seek out those whose way of guiding and teaching and whose insight really resonates with and speaks to us. Bookstore shelves are full of religious and spiritual texts that aren't scripture, aren't official; they're just thoughts meant to guide others. This is an inherent part of most if not all religions because, to be frank, a lot of religious thought takes some heavy interpretation to be useful to modern humans living our everyday lives.

But really, it's not much different when it comes to our own spiritual lives. The human mind is still enough of a mystery that it takes more experience and insight than any of us have to truly understand how

SPIRITUAL HELP WANTED (INQUIRE WITHIN)

to navigate our own psyches. We benefit a lot from seeking the guidance of others as spiritual thought leaders even within our own authentic spirituality.

If we think about the way spiritual leadership tends to work in a formal tradition, a lot of it has to do less with teaching and more with helping people navigate the challenges of adhering to their faith in day-to-day life. We turn to our spiritual guides, whether that's a priest or minister or whether it's a respected author or thought leader, to help us with things like relationship problems, grief, moral quandaries, community disputes, and difficult emotions.

We don't go to our religious leaders to teach us the academics of our faith; we go for advice and life guidance. So it's important to have these same things as we're building our own spiritual life around us. This isn't the same as finding someone to teach us spiritual truth. We all need figures to turn to when we're at a loss and struggling.

Of course, the guidance we get from religious leaders is shaped by their beliefs. There's a reason people go to their priest or minister or rabbi for marital advice rather than going to a therapist for marriage counselling. We seek out the guidance of those whose expertise and way of thinking matches our own. There needs to be a shared set of values and priorities and a common worldview there.

One of the common challenges I hear from members of the neopagan community here in the Bible Belt is that it's very difficult to find psychologists who respect non-Christian ways of thinking. Some will treat a patient's practice of witchcraft as a problem to be solved rather than simply accept it as the patient's form of spiritual practice. And even if someone keeps their spiritual affiliation to themselves, lots of therapists will recommend prayer and church as part of the healing process because they simply don't question the idea that their faith and belief are absolute truth.

The point is, though, that even without a deity or church organization exerting control or authority over our spiritual practice, we still need to have those people we turn to for knowledgeable support and expert guidance. Separating that expertise and knowledge from the responsibility to provide spiritual teaching also makes it easier to find the right thought leaders to fill those roles for us. We can seek out specialist guidance from those whose advice resonates with our authentic understanding of the universe.

Most important, we can seek out the specific support we need and not have to shape ourselves to unsolicited input that would be imposed on us by formal religion.

And part of this dynamic involves learning from the expertise and guidance, not just following it. This is part of our evolution, getting what we need from those who know more than we do so that the next time we face similar struggles, we're able to handle them on our own. Eventually this can become something we're able to share with others.

"My education is never complete."

Our spiritual traditions should be healing and nurturing and help us evolve. Probably the biggest thing people look for in less-formal religious traditions is a path to some state of being that's higher than mundane life. Humans turn to spirituality to open our eyes to the bigger picture and to connect to the divine (however we define it). At the heart of human spirituality is the human desire to examine and investigate the world, and when we realized we were part of something much bigger, the universe. Even for someone like me who doesn't believe in the supernatural, there's plenty of unknown in the universe and that is where we stretch our imaginations.

It's really important to remember, though, that no matter how creatively we examine the expanses of reality and no matter how logical our philosophizing seems, none of the ideas we come up with as a species are going to constitute universal truth. We simply are not advanced enough for that. That doesn't mean that the patterns we find, the metaphors and parallels we dig up in the process aren't valuable or meaningful, but they aren't Truth.

The important element of all of these efforts to explain our purpose and describe our role in existence is that the search isn't just individual. We have always been compelled as a species to share these ideas with others who then build upon them and keep the ideas evolving. The metaphors, patterns, and theories that come out of this communal evolutionary thinking get woven into our mythologies, our philosophies, and our belief systems. They help bind us together and give us a focus. We use them to define entire cultures. The goal isn't conversion; it's alignment and connection.

And everything we seek as individuals, we seek as cultures. When we look to use our knowledge of humanity and the universe to guide spiritual evolution on a larger, cultural scale, we like to refer to that type of healing in terms like enlightenment. We try to define and seek examples of what it looks like to have healed, evolved, and adapted to the highest level that humanity can achieve.

Those examples vary widely. We're not all trying to achieve the same version of healing and enlightenment. We have yet to completely understand the universe and our place in it, and any one of us can only possess a small portion of that overall understanding. Together, though, we have a great deal more understanding and a greater potential to continue to advance understanding.

Of course, most traditions have some kind of formal or semiformal indoctrination or education system to teach us the lessons that tradition deems most important. Part of what we do in traditional spirituality is learn more about the tradition and how to live that tradition in life, what our purpose is, and how to be a proper adherent. We get to decide that for ourselves in our individual, authentic spirituality, so we get to structure the learning and exploration process for ourselves.

Learning is a key part of all spirituality, no matter how formal or informal the tradition. Learning, practice, and application of knowledge are the biggest ways we participate in the consumption, exchange, and transformation of energy. So our own spiritual tradition can include all sorts of opportunities to increase knowledge and understanding. As we pursue this type of learning and expansion of understanding, we're potentially seeking out those sources that might serve as our sacred texts. We get to choose them, so they can take all kinds of forms.

Probably the most obvious form of sacred text to emulate is mythology, and I think we can't really discount the power of storytelling in human existence. These days, the closest thing to modern mythology we have is fiction. Our movies, TV shows, and books paint a picture of the world as we understand it and put the social and ethical lessons we find most important into an easy-to-understand format. It may seem weird to think about the types of fiction we like as a form of education or indoctrination, but it's generally one of the most influential forms of modern media, and it undeniably serves to provoke dialogue about how society works and what is acceptable within our society. The characters we identify with help us understand ourselves, and the types of stories we connect to reflect our worldview.

I know it's strange to equate our favorite forms of fiction with ancient mythologies, but to some extent they're really the same thing. We can absolutely regard stories as fabricated fiction and still learn from them – that's the whole point of things like parables. And it's hard to look at fictional media, which clearly has a message of cultural relevance, and not see the parallel. Humans use storytelling to explore and converse about social issues, and we always have. And anyone who has spent time and energy on self-development understands the power of the stories we tell about ourselves.

But it's not just about learning about our deep self. Another form of sacred text speaks to a culture's history, and we all have our own histories that give context to who we are and who we are becoming. Learning more about where we come from, whether that means tracing our family history or our ethnic roots or even the growth of the groups and hobbies and professions we're part of, puts our existence in some context.

Nearly everyone I know at this point has taken a DNA test to learn about their genealogy. My sister took the test and shared the results with our family, and after being really into our Irish and Scottish roots growing up, we found out there's a significant connection to Scandinavia as well. And even though my spirituality only vaguely relates to anything truly Celtic, finding a genetic Viking connection has added to my understanding of myself. I'm able to put some aspects of my authentic self into a context where they take on a different relevance. For instance, I love the ocean and the beach but not the sun or the heat. I'd much rather be on a beach on a relatively cool, overcast autumn day or at dusk after the sun is down, which feels logical given my northern, seafaring roots but is just weird by most people's standards.

Of course, the ideas and information that help us move forward in our evolution are also a key part of our personal sacred texts. Those methodologies we've sought out to facilitate our adjustment and adaptation to the circumstances in our lives so we can thrive certainly deserve a place in our spiritual libraries.

The first book I ever bought about feng shui is still my favorite. I've picked up that book and used it as a reference in my practice more than I've ever used a mythological text. The most important books in my library, bookmarks on my computer, and podcasts on my playlist are the ones that have taught me valuable skills or become handy references for the spiritual activities that drive my practice forward. My shelves, real and virtual, are full of alchemy references, herbal medicine books, histories of world religions, science texts, and interesting stuff about psychology and sociology.

Even my dad, who I'm sure would say the Bible is the most important book in the world, actually turns to various references and studies more often than the Bible itself when he's preparing sermons and lessons. And I think even he would admit that the most impactful things he's learned over the years didn't come directly from scripture but from other scholars.

And last but not least, there's the stuff that just resonates with us. The things we want to learn because we're curious and fascinated. The stuff that trips our switches and gets us really engaged. If we like it and we're

interested in it, it's authentic.

The thing to remember here is how spirituality and evolution work in terms of humans having a compounding culture. The thoughts in our head can reveal a lot about us, but unless we continue to learn things from outside ourselves, from sources rooted in different experiences and different backgrounds, we will just continue to recycle our own thoughts. Creation means taking thoughts and ideas from others and weaving them with our own internal spiritual workings to get not just knowledge but inspiration and enlightenment.

When I first began working in the online coaching space, I was completely unfamiliar with how the coaching world worked, only knowing that there were people who made a living as life coaches, spiritual coaches, business coaches, and the like. But I'd never known anyone who was successful at it, and I had no idea what the industry looked like from the inside.

Admittedly, a lot of my friends thought the whole thing sounded weird and crazy, this whole industry full of people with few meaningful credentials all claiming expertise enough to warrant paying them for advice. But working in the industry, I quickly started seeing it as something different. There's actually great beauty in it, a global community of passionate people, largely women, who are taking their life experience and offering to share what they've learned with others who can use it. It's certainly not a perfect idea, but at its root it's all about building a career by sharing what we've learned and passing it along for the benefit of others.

So that's how our personal spiritual practices can

contribute to cultural evolution and the growth and development of the people around us. We can't drag each other kicking and screaming along the path to enlightenment or connection to the divine, we can't forcibly make anyone believe our beliefs, but we can absolutely share our experiences, lessons, and insights with each other. We can listen and learn from the experiences, lessons, and insights of others, and as a collective we can pool what we know to advance the larger pursuit of understanding.

We never get to define or judge anyone else's path to evolution or healing, and no one else can define or judge our path. The point of our personal evolution isn't to reach a predetermined level of achievement or attainment or to compare ourselves against others on similar paths. But the act of sharing our insights freely for the benefit of the larger human community is a beautiful mission and one that benefits us as well.

Another thing I've learned from this experience in the coaching world as well as the experience of blogging, podcasting, and writing this book is that sharing our passion and knowledge with others is a fast track to understanding of self. It prompts us to really examine what we know and refine our thinking about it. It makes us consider who might also benefit from our experience and how best to share that with those who want or could benefit from it.

We don't all have the passion for writing books or coaching our peers, but we can all look to the shared experiences of others to help inform our own understanding of the universe. Learning about our deep selves is certainly a personal endeavor, but no one human can understand the world without listening to and learning from others.

"I am powerful because I am different."

We don't need to belong to a religion. We don't all need to agree on what is true and what a spiritual tradition needs to look like. But we do all need to have some part of our lives focused on our spiritual growth, development, and evolution. It ties right into our mental health and the social health of our communities.

When we don't focus on that, and when we don't honor our own authentic selves, we end up in a world filled with people trying desperately to be someone else and trying to drag everyone else with them.

Step Eleven is to practice being present in the moment and mindful of your spiritual practice so you know when it's time to start with Step One again.

So much of what we've grown accustomed to when it comes to spirituality and spiritual practice has to do with trying to become someone we're not. As much as it is empowering and uplifting to connect with and support our authentic way of being, keeping up that connection and resisting that pull to conform and belong is an ongoing mission. Being mindful of who we are, what we need, and what we offer to others is a spiritual practice of its own. This journey isn't something we do once and never have to revisit again.

The world is always going to be full of spiritual seekers looking for truth and guidance through this experience of being human. On the one hand, we're this single form of life on a tiny planet in a single solar system in a seemingly endless stretch of universe with who knows what lurking beyond. It's humbling to realize how inconsequential we are in the context of all of reality. I think it's really a testament to the potential of humanity that we even entertain the idea that someday we could understand it all.

Even as individuals, we are driven to know and understand things that don't seem to have any bearing on our day-to-day existence. My desire to understand the roots of human spirituality comes from deep within myself, but it doesn't help me put food on the table or pay my bills. Humans could seemingly exist just fine without wondering what's beyond the confines of our corner of the universe or trying to trace history back to the dawn of time. But part of what defines human history is the unceasing push to know more, to investigate and problem solve, to find out where we come from and what our future holds.

It didn't take me long in researching the origins of humanity to see that, whatever seed the roots of human spirituality grew from, it wasn't the idea that there's a creator deity who needs to be worshipped. We started with a need to understand our reality and solve the problems that threatened our ability to survive.

Fast-forward to modern humans, and we're still doing the same thing, but with the benefit of many millennia of cumulative knowledge and insight.

We aren't all engaged in solving the mysteries of the universe, and it would be absurd if we were. But we are all engaged in solving the mysteries of our own selves and the dynamics of our own personal experiences. As an alchemist, I understand both of those pursuits to be the same thing. And we do this because it's part of our nature. Humans are driven to discover and explain everything and create new things from what we find, and that drive is necessary to our survival as a species. It is what paves the way for advances that have let us evolve and overcome even the biggest challenges to our existence.

This is what spirituality is at its most basic. Spirituality is what we do as humans to contextualize our existence and live as best we can.

Having this context for our existence in the face of the vastness of the universe, the endlessness of time, and the countless other individual humans who have come before us and will come after are what makes our understanding of authenticity possible. If we didn't have an idea of how impossible it is to be here as individuals at this point in time on this tiny planet spinning around a timeless universe, we wouldn't feel any need to understand what makes us unique. That's a human thing, too.

We need to embrace our authentic individuality precisely because we are inconsequential in the grand scheme. We are one of a kind out of an incomprehensibly vast number of individual human lives, and our human consciousness pushes us to try and make sense of that. We are unique individuals with unique lives, even in this passing moment in history, and that's what makes us significant. Our unique experience contributes to the collective understanding, and if we have a purpose as a life form, it's to keep pushing and building on that understanding.

That's what humans do.

And our individuality serves a vital purpose. Evolution doesn't happen without variation. If every new individual in a species is exactly like the others, the species doesn't adapt to change; it only responds. If a new threat comes along, it dies off because there isn't anything to make some individuals more or less vulnerable.

So there's a reason why we are each different and why it's important to embrace that difference and nurture it. We are not meant to all be the same. Humanity has continued to advance and evolve because we are all different.

Our authenticity is spiritually significant and sacred. We are spiritual, magical beings, and our power doesn't come from being just like everyone else; it comes from being who we are.

About the Author

Bridget resides in Missouri with her wife and (as per stereotype) their small family of beloved cats. Her hobbies include starting multiple craft projects which may or may not ever be finished, starting multiple home improvement projects which may or may not ever be finished, and the usual geeky pastimes like cosplay, D&D, and getting deeply invested in fictional worlds. Explore all her spiritual endeavors online at www.bridgetowens.com.

Other Works by the Author

The Feminist Tarot Deck features only female and femme figures on all cards, creating an inclusive and modern depiction of a world in which women can do and be all things. I searched for a deck which depicted the world without filtering it through a patriarchal lens of traditional gender roles in which women are relegated to figures of fertility, motherhood, and gentle femininity. One which didn't resort to depicting women only as goddesses and queens. One which didn't focus on famous or powerful women without reflecting the experiences of everyday women.

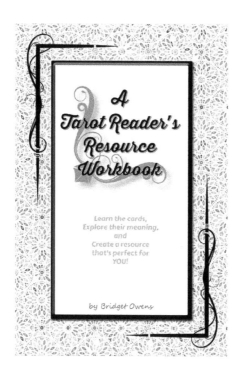

Tarot reading involves much more than memorizing card meanings. Mastering the art requires learning how to apply those meanings in context and how to explain the result clearly. A *Tarot Reader's Resource Workbook* prompts you to think about the meanings and interpretations in a way which makes sense to you, aiding the process of memorization and making the cards easier to remember and explain. You'll end up with a reference book of your own creation, customized to how YOU read.

Mantras and Affirmations Coloring Books are a series of adult coloring books with a purpose. Adults all over the world are rediscovering the joy of coloring and the calming, centering effect it can have. These books combine that calm with specific phrases chosen to focus the mind. Each page is a visually rendered phrase intended to motivate, encourage, and challenge you as you color. Each edition is tailored for a specific audience, including editions for activists and allies as well as all 12 zodiac signs

Spirituality is not a one-size-fits-all proposition. Join writer, alchemist, and pagan community organizer Bridget Owens for a deep dive into what spirituality is and how to build a deeply personal tradition. The Waxing Soul offers food for thought and guidance to find your own brand of mindful modern magic. Grow your soul, expand your spirit, and nourish your spiritual life in an exploration of religion, philosophy, psychology, culture, ritual, and our place in the universe.